Buffalo People

Buffalo People
Portraits of a Vanishing Nation

Mildred Valley Thornton

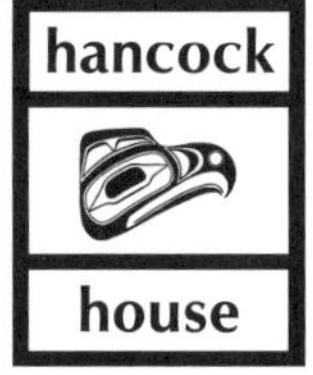

ISBN 0-88839-479-9

Copyright © 2000 Mildred Valley Thornton estate collection

Cataloging in Publication Data
Thornton, Mildred Valley, 1890-1967
  Buffalo people

  ISBN 0-88839-479-9

  1. Indians of North America—Prairie Provinces—Portraits. 2.
Indians of North America—Prairie Provinces—Biography. I. Title.
E78.P7T56 2000   971.2'00497'00922   C00-910520-4

We acknowledge the financial support of the Government of Canada through the Book Publishing Industry Development Program for our publishing activities.

Editing: John M.Thornton
Production and cover design: Ingrid Luters
Consultation: Anthony R. Westbridge, Westbridge Fine Art Ltd.

Published simultaneously in Canada and the United States by

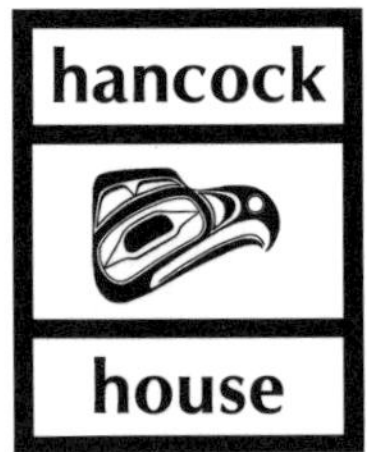

HANCOCK HOUSE PUBLISHERS LTD.
19313 Zero Avenue, Surrey, B.C. V4P 1M7

HANCOCK HOUSE PUBLISHERS
1431 Harrison Avenue, Blaine, WA 98230-5005

(604) 538-1114   Fax (604) 538-2262
(800) 938-1114   Fax (800) 983-2262
Web Site: www.hancockhouse.com   *email:* sales@hancockhouse.com

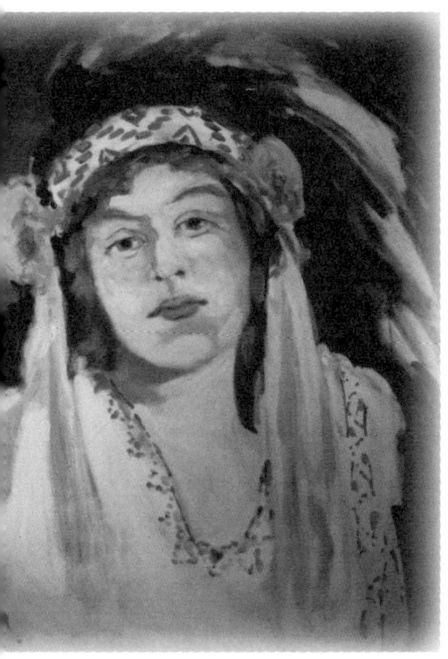

Mildred Valley Thornton, self-portrait

Contents

▸ *colour plate page 97*

Introduction

My mother, Mildred Valley Thornton, had an abiding passion which she pursued with almost missionary fervour throughout her life—the preservation of Canada's native culture. For over fifty years she dedicated herself to that purpose through the medium of her paintings, writings and lectures. During the course of her self-appointed career, my mother not only painted the portraits of many prominent and historical Native Canadians, most of whom are now long dead, but she assembled an accompanying catalogue of anecdotes, folklore and legends, mostly related in now long-forgotten native tongues, which today provide a unique chronicle of a vanished age.

As her collection grew, she came to believe that her work had assumed the aspect of a patriotic duty to her beloved Canada. Through her brush and pen she was providing a unique window on the first Canadians preserving a legacy that should be enshrined in Canadian history. However, though widely acclaimed by critics, academics, art and literary circles, she never obtained the official governmental recognition that she had devoted her life to achieving. This disappointment profoundly affected her in her later years.

She compiled her notes into narrative form and in 1966 approached Mitchell Press Ltd. of Vancouver. Her manuscript envisaged a number of chapters, each illustrated by one of her full colour portraits describing the circumstances of the sitting and the dialogue that ensued. The manuscript was divided into two categories: the Indians of the West Coast and the Indians of the Plains. The enthusiastic publisher suggested that the manuscript be divided into two books and thus was born the first of two projected volumes featuring the Indians of the Pacific Coast entitled *Indian Lives and Legends* (Mitchell Press Limited, 1966). The book was an immediate success and copies today are considered valuable collector's items. Alas, my mother died the following year before the second volume, describing the Indians of the Plains, could be assembled.

Recently, Anthony Westbridge, of Westbridge Fine Art Ltd. in Vancouver, expressed an interest in resurrecting the second manuscript and in consultation with him I have undertaken to edit the now more than fifty-year-old text to bring it into line for the modern reader.

Mildred Valley Thornton was very much a "woman of her times" embracing the perceptions, ideology and convictions of her era. In an age before residential schools, cultural genocide and religious paternalism were stigmatized, indeed they were largely accepted and unquestioned, she moved about the Indian settlements in her quest to preserve for posterity the images and legends of what she recognized as a fast-vanishing way of life.

To the politically correct perceptions of the twenty-first century reader much of her written terminology seems quaint and even condescending, perhaps even patronizing. Such terms as "The Noble Red Man" and "a fine specimen of manhood", which abound in the original manuscript, would not be palatable to the modern reader. This perception would have appalled my mother, for her admiration and respect of the Indian peoples was profound and deeply genuine. Indeed, in her writings she frequently comments on the conventions of "white society" compared to those of the Indians, invariably to the detriment of the former.

With the foregoing in mind, I have attempted to edit my mother's copy to the minimum, keeping as much as possible to her own words and only making alterations where necessary in order to clarify or modify the text in keeping with contemporary usage. In no case has the meaning of the text been altered.

JOHN M. THORNTON

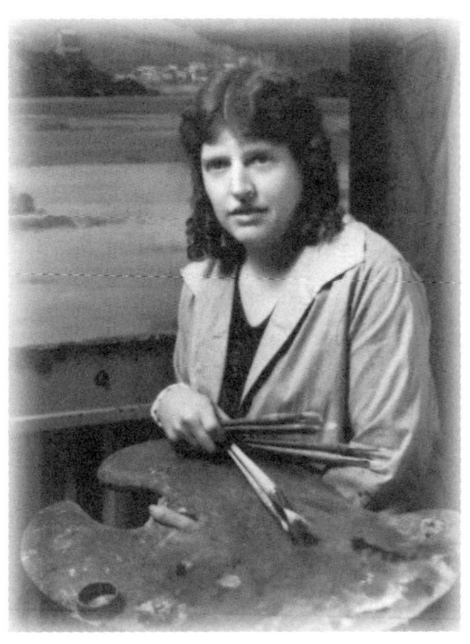

Mildred Valley Thornton, F.R.S.A., C.P.A.
(1890–1967)

Born of a large farming family in the small Ontario town of Dresden at the beginning of the last decade of the nineteenth century, the young Mildred Stinson soon demonstrated to her parents that she was not destined to remain on the farm. They recognized her artistic abilities and sent her to study at Olivet College in Michigan, from which she graduated in 1910. She continued her studies at the Ontario School of Art and the Art Institute of Chicago before the lure of Canada's burgeoning prairie beckoned her west.

Arriving in Regina, Saskatchewan, with little more than a valise and her paintbox, she immediately fell under the spell of the vast, limitless plains and, even more avidly, developed a lasting fascination for the then nomadic Indian tribes who inhabited that immense solitude. It was then and there that she commenced her life's work to preserve on canvas and in the written word the countenances and culture of what she perceived to be a threatened and fascinating society.

In 1915 she married John Henry Thornton, some five years her senior, who had immigrated from Sheffield, England and operated a thriving business in the growing prairie town. The partnership was a long and happy one and, though John Henry was a man of few words and infinite patience, he became what would be known today as a devoted "support system" to his young wife's endeavours.

This was perhaps best exemplified by a brief paragraph on the fly-page of her book *Indian Lives and Legends* (1967) which stated: "This book is dedicated to the memory of my husband, John H. Thornton, whose patience, encouragement and co-operation made this whole project possible." By then her husband had been dead for nearly ten years.

A decade after her marriage she gave birth to twin boys in Toronto and they were largely brought up by their father owing to their mother's frequent absences from home. Mildred would embark on extended sketching trips for weeks at a time, living with the Indians in their camps and tepees, painting their portraits and recording their legends. Her energy and single-minded focus was tenacious. Suspicious at first, the Indians gradually came to accept and trust her and she became privy to many ceremonies and rituals that few non-Indians have been privileged to witness. Upon occasion she took her sons with her much to their excitement and fascination. For long periods the only "whites" whom she would encounter would be the RCMP constable, the Indian agent and the missionary clergy.

Though her primary interest was to paint the Indians she was also an accomplished landscape artist, in both oil and watercolour, and her works became much in demand. Her style was frequently described as "majestic, powerful and bold." Vivid colour, particularly in her watercolours, became an earmark of her work. She was tremendously prolific and was often compared to her near-contemporary, Emily Carr, much to her annoyance, and frequently identified with the Group of Seven.

It was her Indian portraiture, however, that became her life's obsession. She came to refer to the ever-growing number of paintings as "The Collection" and, as such, they became quite inviolable. She refused all offers to sell the paintings individually. An abiding patriot, it was her ambition to hand this priceless legacy of Canada's native history intact to the Government of Canada, the only custodian that she would accept. As the Collection became more famous she refused generous offers from the UK, USA and Germany. The Collection was a unique assemblage, depicting Canada's aboriginal peoples and its constituent parts, and they were often the only graphic record of events in existence.

Her husband's business became a victim of the 1929 depression and the almost destitute family moved to Vancouver in 1934 where John Henry, by dint of hard work, began the difficult road back to financial solvency. For Mildred it was a wonderful new world to which she could transfer her talents and at once she fell in love with British Columbia and the Coastal Indians. British Columbia's mighty mountains, coastal inlets and, above all, its native peoples provoked her to even greater efforts. Many of the truly colourful chiefs and Indian personalities were still prominent in their tribes and she hastened to capture them in oils before it was too late. She painted from life, usually at a single sitting, and always paid her subjects from her meagre purse. She soon became accepted and trusted by the coastal Indians and was able to add many more paintings to her Collection depicting their tribal ceremonies, totem poles and coastal encampments. The Collection became numbered in the hundreds.

As her fame spread she became much in demand as a lecturer. Her lively talks were illustrated by colour slides of her paintings. She also found time to write poetry and chaired the Vancouver Poetry Society. In addition, she was appointed art critic for the *Vancouver Sun*, a position that she held for sixteen years. She became internationally recognized as an interpreter of Indian life and culture, but it was, above all else, the welfare of the Indians that motivated her throughout her life. She became a staunch advocate for the rights and welfare of the Indian peoples.

In 1954 a fellowship of the Royal Society of Arts was bestowed upon her and, adding to this distinction, she became the president of the Canadian Women's Press Club.

Her husband died in 1958 and it was many months before she took up the palette again. In 1959 she moved to England to live with one of her sons. In London she achieved instant recognition and a major exhibit of her paintings was staged by the Royal Commonwealth Institute. Unfortunately, a strange malady, akin to leukemia, which would eventually lead to her death, prevented her from attending the prestigious showing.

She returned to Vancouver in 1961 and continued to paint, enduring ever-failing health, until her death in 1967, aged seventy-seven, her life's ambition unrealized. Her great Collection remained in security vaults, unwanted by the Government of Canada, which despite all her offers, had declined to accept it on behalf of the people of Canada. She died an embittered soul, having added a codicil to her will that all her paintings be burned to ashes after her death. Fortunately, the codicil was not legally witnessed and the Collection was saved, though destined to be disposed of piecemeal.

During her life Mildred Valley Thornton achieved many honours and distinctions, but the ones that gave her the most satisfaction were her honorary Indian titles. The Kwakiutl, one of the fiercest of the West Coast tribes in early days, made her a princess of the Clan Eagle, giving her the prize name "Ah-ou-Mookht," which means "the one who wears a blanket because she is of noble birth." The Crees called her "Owas-ka-esk-ean," meaning "putting your most ability for us Indians." There were several others.

Her paintings can be found in the National Gallery in Ottawa, the McMichael Collection in Kleinburg, Ontario, the Glenbow Foundation in Calgary, the Vancouver Art Gallery and in the British Columbia Legislative Buildings, as well as in many private collections.

JOHN M. THORNTON

Preface

Early adventurers have described the Plains Indian as "the finest type of physical manhood the world has ever seen." This rather flamboyant description could have been due to the principle of the "survival of the fittest," for surely none but the hardiest of human beings could have lived and flourished facing the harsh realities of mere existence in the environment in which they lived in those far-off days.

Life must have been incredibly hard before they came into possession of horses. With the acquisition of horses the Indian's entire lifestyle changed drastically. It was still demanding and dangerous but now, exhilarating too. Horses became a symbol of wealth and power. A man bought his wife with horses.

Though thievery was not tolerated in any tribe, horse stealing between tribes became an honourable profession, and the man who could creep into an enemy camp under cover of night and get away with some of their best horses was considered a great hero.

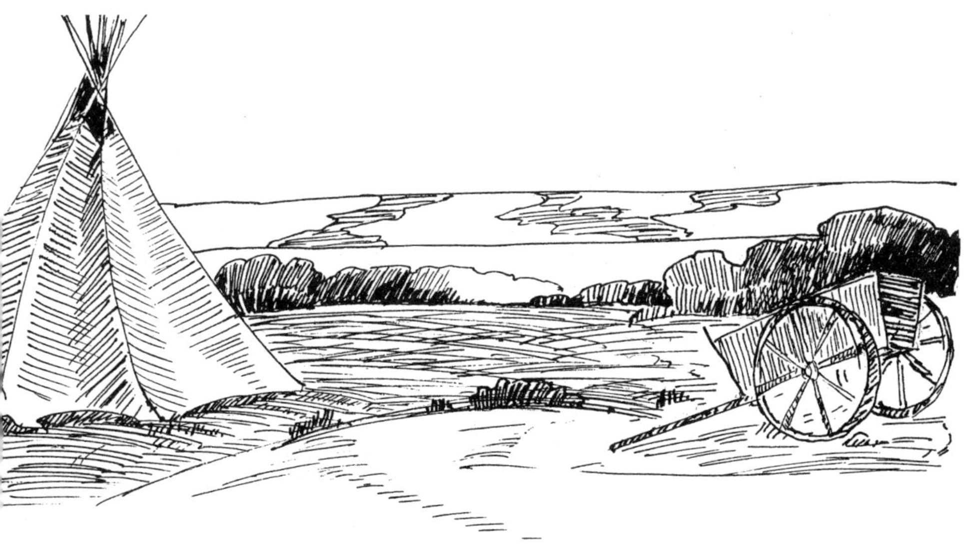

Because the Indians lived so close to nature and to the spirit world they were exceedingly psychic, and, in their own way, deeply religious. At important councils the pipe of peace was first presented to the Great Spirit. At feasts the choicest morsel of food was cast into the fire with the prayer, "Great Spirit, partake with us." There were among them prophets and seers of enormous wisdom who performed many mighty and mysterious deeds. These wise men spent much time in meditation but seldom revealed their thoughts except to those chosen and trained to succeed them. Indians had great respect for the dead, but did not flinch from death. A man composed his own death song and sang it fearlessly as he embarked on his last and greatest adventure.

They revered nature and all of God's creation. "No man owns the land. It was put there by the Great Spirit for the use of all his children and through all the years it would give life to men," said the great Blackfoot Chief Crowfoot. What a terrific concept!

How humble and ashamed do we stand before the exalted vision of this unlettered Indian chief! Crowfoot was as fine a man as ever walked the Great Plains. Later, when the buffalo had disappeared, it was mainly with Crowfoot, after long months and patient consultation and negotiation, that the Blackfoot Treaty was finally worked out. Other chiefs attended also, but they all looked to the inspired Crowfoot for final decisions.

The Indian society was a true democracy where all shared alike. No one went hungry if there was food available. I saw so much to respect and admire in the Indian character and soon realized the enormous contribution they could make, culturally and spiritually, to the Canada which is our common heritage. As my

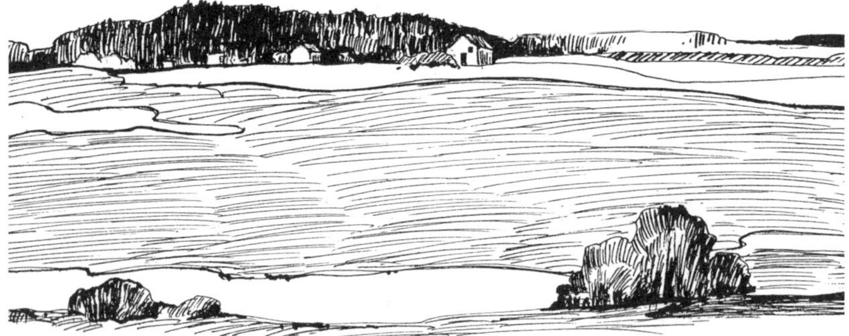

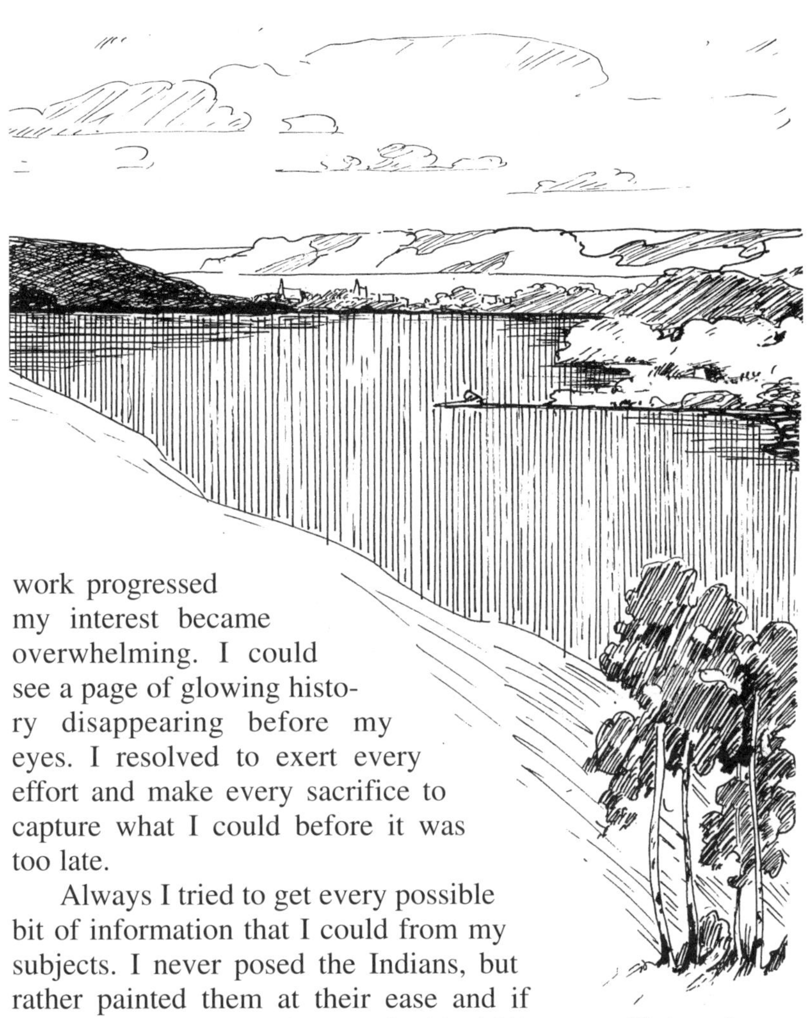

work progressed
my interest became
overwhelming. I could
see a page of glowing history disappearing before my
eyes. I resolved to exert every
effort and make every sacrifice to
capture what I could before it was
too late.

Always I tried to get every possible
bit of information that I could from my
subjects. I never posed the Indians, but
rather painted them at their ease and if
they moved, that was just my bad luck! It was sufficient for me
just to be there, accepted as a friend and to be permitted to do my
work. It was my very good fortune to meet many fine older people who had vivid memories of the early days, of buffalo hunts,
the Sun Dance and other tribal rituals which had been such a vital
part of their lives, but which sadly have little meaning to their
descendants today.

Mildred Valley Thornton (1966)

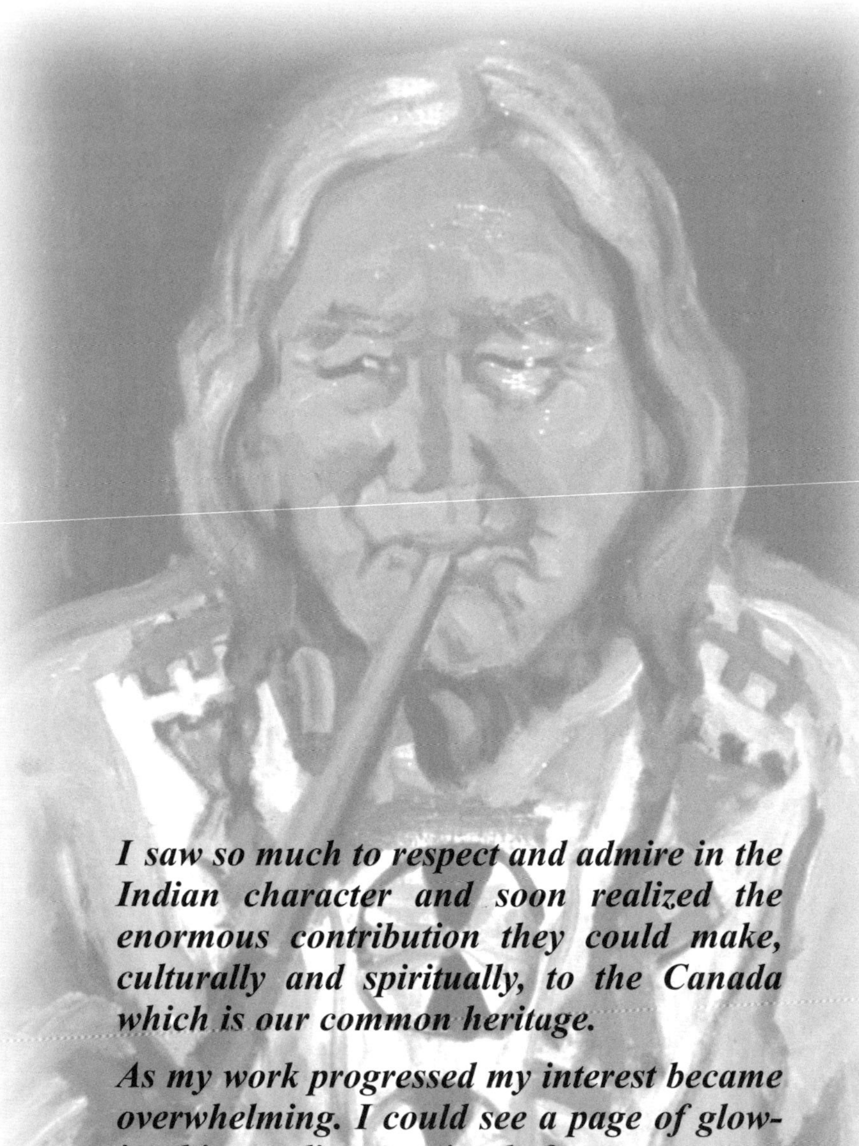

I saw so much to respect and admire in the Indian character and soon realized the enormous contribution they could make, culturally and spiritually, to the Canada which is our common heritage.

As my work progressed my interest became overwhelming. I could see a page of glowing history disappearing before my eyes.

I resolved to exert every effort and make every sacrifice to capture what I could before it was too late.

The Cree Indians

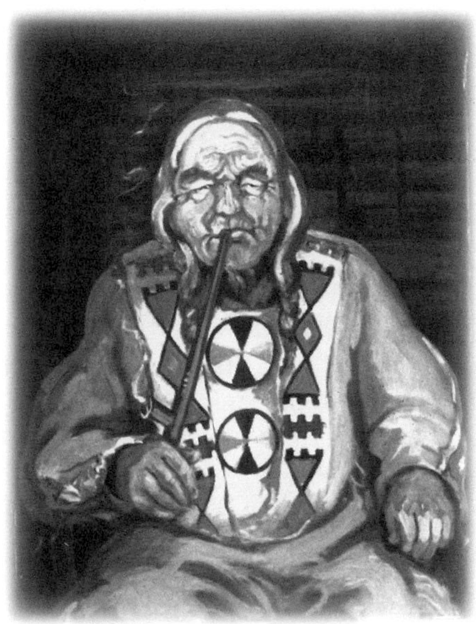

Manitouwassis
"Child of God"

An old, old Cree was Manitouwassis, which means "Child of God." Very old indeed was he when I painted him, at least a hundred years that the government had record of, and goodness only knows how many more besides!

He had been a mighty man in his prime and had played his part in the colourful years when he and his brothers, of many tribes and languages, held undisputed dominion over the measureless prairie. That was until the coming of the white man with his firearms, his railway, his commerce and his complicated political structure, all of which brought catastrophic change to the Indians.

Many times he had participated in the wild exultation of the buffalo hunt when the mighty beasts moved in tumultuous masses across the Great Plains. He had watched them approaching like a living dark cloud on the horizon and had felt the earth tremble beneath their thundering feet.

Time and again he had witnessed the epic climax of the hunt and had brooded with sorrow and foreboding over the gradual elimination of that which meant shelter, food and clothing to his people.

Those were the days when Indians had their own moral code and their unwritten laws. The order and precision with which a buffalo hunt was conducted was symbolic of the Indian's intuitive regard for fair play and the rights of others. There were strict rules governing the roundup of the buffalo and severe penalties were meted out to those who dared violate them. No person might break away, lag behind, or go ahead of the hunting party without permission. If any of the rules were broken, even in ignorance, the offender was severely punished.

Everything was left open about the encampments and stealing was almost unknown. The Indians shared and shared alike. If anyone was so foolish to pilfer that which could be freely had for the asking, he was quickly apprehended and placed in the centre of the camp where the others danced around him taunting with loud cries of "Thief!" and other humiliations. Needless to say, there was seldom a repetition of a misdemeanour.

But that was all long ago. Other memories crowded into the aging brain of Manitouwassis, memories which brought visions of the days when he had brought his harvest of furs to the old Hudson's Bay trading post at Fort Qu'Appelle. It is now one of the historic landmarks in Saskatchewan. If it could speak, this old building could tell many a tale of anxiety and valour, for it had been General Middleton's headquarters during the Riel Rebellion.

It looked strangely quiet and reminiscent of a past age when I sketched it many years ago. Loosened boards and crumbling plaster spoke mutely of the havoc that the years had wrought. Archibald MacDonald had been factor there, and the building stands in a corner of the grounds that had once surrounded his home. The Saskatchewan Historical Society had undertaken to preserve it and due to their efforts it had undergone a face-lifting process which will, no doubt, add to its longevity.

Here was Manitouwassis with his equally aged wife, dreaming of a throbbing past. For years they had been on relief and I found the two of them sitting on the bare board floor of their tiny one-room dwelling, just as they had sat in their tepee fifty, sixty, seventy and eighty years before. Between them, without the formality of dishes, were hunks, not slices, of bread and the remains of some sort of wild fowl, over which swarmed flies in a thick, black buzzing crust. Two cots, a stove and a single chair comprised their furniture.

They could not speak a word of English but, by enlisting the aid of a young neighbour, I made them understand what I wanted to do. A ladder led to a loft above the room, up which the old woman climbed slowly and laboriously, to return after a long interval with a huge dunnage bag, from the cavernous depths of which she extracted an astonishing pile of beadwork. We managed to get Manitouwassis dressed and seated on the one and only chair, contentedly smoking his long, ancient peace pipe.

I then faced the dilemma as to how I should work. I had no easel with me so I could not work standing up. In lieu of an easel I would have to use the hinged lid of my paint box. Sitting on the floor was definitely out and there was no other chair, either for me or my paint box. Seeing my predicament a neighbour brought in a chair and quickly disappeared. I put my paintbox on it and had no choice but to sit on one of the cots. I confess I eyed the cots with profound suspicion for they were incredibly ragged and dirty. If I were to sit on one, what might I carry away as a souvenir of the occasion? Suddenly I made up my mind to take the chance. I was not going to be cheated by so small an obstacle and what did it matter anyway?

Manitouwassis paid absolutely no attention to me. I was nothing more to him than another fly, though not quite so troublesome, and he did not care how long I "flew around." His ancient wife sat on the floor, immersed in a deep, impenetrable silence. There was no sound but the uninterrupted buzzing of the restless multitude of flies. Once or twice a dark face came and peered in through the grimy window and then, as quickly, vanished. It was a strange brooding atmosphere.

When I finished the painting I showed it to the old folks. A few unintelligible grunts was all I received, of praise, or condemnation, I knew not which. I paid the old man, shook hands with them both and departed, glad to be out in the sunshine and to inhale the clean, sweet air which came rushing down the valley to meet me, or that's how it seemed!

All this transpired many years ago and I presume that Manitouwassis and his old wife have long since departed to the Happy Hunting Grounds, where buffalo roam in infinite numbers and countless winding trails lure their celestial feet—a domain where the Great Spirit bountifully provides for all their needs.

Only the painting and the memories remain for me as records of one of my most interesting experiences and as a link with the romantic past.

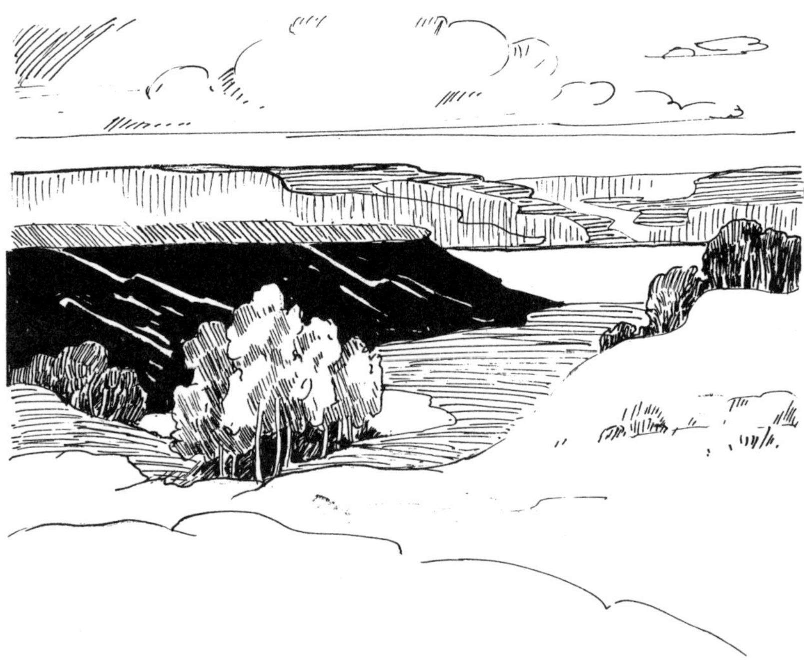

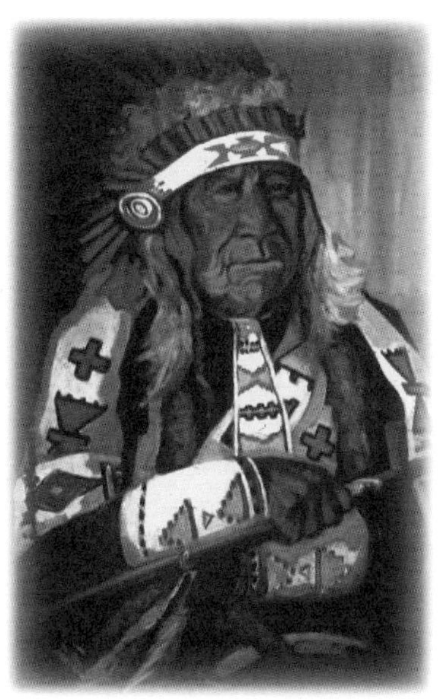

Buffalo Bow

It was my privilege, years ago, to visit a very large Cree encampment. Many beautifully designed and coloured tepees were pitched in a great circle and in the centre were the tents of the chiefs and head men. Also in the centre were a number of fires over which the women cooked meat and prepared other food. It was a sort of community affair and there was much banter and good-natured talk going on. Some distance away their patient horses, which had brought them together, were contentedly munching their fodder.

My first subject was one of the chiefs and when it became known what I was doing the Indians were much interested in my work. One old fellow, in particular, followed me about like a little dog, desiring to get in on something which promised to provide him with a little ready cash. Neither walking or running, he had a jogging trot that never varied its speed. Buffalo Bow was a very old medicine man and a most interesting character and I was glad to have him sit for me because the medicine man, with all his romance and symbolism, was one of a fast-disappearing breed among Indians of all tribes.

I discovered that Buffalo Bow was 105 years of age and that he had witnessed catastrophic changes in the Canadian West. Born into the hardships and perils of nomadic life on the plains, he could remember the arrival of white men into his ancestral territory. In a vague way he knew about the signing of the Indian treaties with the Canadian Government. He had been present at the last big buffalo hunt on the site of the city of Regina when the fledgling community got its original name, Ooo-Skuna-Sta-Ka-Ka, which means "Pile-O-Bones" because buffalo bones were stacked in huge piles after that historic event.

Buffalo Bow could speak no English nor could I speak Cree, but somehow we understood each other perfectly and got along famously. He knew I wanted him to dress up in his "Sunday best" so he disappeared into his tepee and when he eventually emerged he was a brave figure indeed. He wore a black costume (the only black costume I had noticed so far) and it was heavily beaded. The gay colours of the beadwork contrasting the black background made a very striking picture. To tell the truth, he was a most impressive sight until he turned around. From the rear he presented a ludicrous appearance, for squarely across the seat of his trousers was sewn a huge piece of crimson cloth, a foot or more in diameter, which showed up against the black cloth of his vestments like the headlight of a train, or perhaps I should more properly say, the tail light. At any rate, there it was, and Buffalo Bow was undoubtedly proud of it and probably thought it quite a smart refinement. Because of the handicap of language I was restrained from questioning him about the adornment but I am still curious as to whether there was a hole in his trousers and the crimson swatch was really a patch or whether he had affixed it merely because he liked the colour and considered it to add to his general sartorial appearance. In any case it had distinction and he had utilized the only available unoccupied space to attach it.

Buffalo Bow was a most satisfactory sitter. He was as pleased as a child when I suggested to him the way I wanted him to sit and fluffed out the feathers on his gorgeous headdress. I painted him holding a lovely hand-carved peace pipe and that also added to his happiness.

I cannot imagine anything more immobile than an Indian when he wishes to sit still, unless it's the Sphinx or the pyramids! Indians can remain perfectly quiet for an indefinite period without so much as a flicker of an eyelash and seemingly enjoy it. What would be agonizing constraint to a white man is just peaceful repose to an Indian.

Some months after I painted this portrait, Mr. Stewart, who had been with the Department of Indian Affairs for over thirty years, was visiting my studio and he stopped to linger over the rugged features of Buffalo Bow. He recognized the old fellow immediately and told me a very interesting story concerning him.

It seemed that in the early days Buffalo Bow had been quite a handsome and likeable fellow. In the course of time he fell in love and brought a pretty little wife to his home. It was a real love match and the two were ideally happy. A year or two passed and one day he went on a hunting trip, as was his custom at certain seasons. Luck did not attend him, however, and he returned home, footsore, tired and discouraged. As he entered his tepee his wife greeted him in her usual bright manner but he answered her abruptly with no responsive smile on his face. This was a situation she had never encountered before and something for which the young woman was totally unprepared. Stunned and grieved, she laid aside her tasks and, without a word, walked out of the tepee. Buffalo Bow busied himself about the place but when his wife did not return he surmised that she had gone to her cousin's tepee a short distance away, and so ate his supper alone. Later some friends came in to talk and smoke, and so the evening wore away. When his company left he went to the cousin's tepee to bring his wife home but she was not there nor had the cousin seen her all day. Thoroughly alarmed, Buffalo Bow walked back by another path and there, but a short distance from her own home, he found the lifeless body of his wife hanging from a tree. Her sensitive spirit could not endure the first unkind word he had ever spoken to her and she had sought forgetfulness in the solitude of death.

The Indians have their own way of doing things, even of hanging themselves. A white man might make elaborate preparations or jump from a high elevation. An Indian just fastens one end of a rope round his neck and the other end to a tree branch which he can conveniently reach from the ground. Following the line of least resistance, he finishes the job by merely lifting up his feet and taking a sitting posture.

In the years that have passed since I painted old Buffalo Bow I have visited a great many Indian encampments but I never crossed his path again which is not surprising considering his age. Never have I beheld another costume embroidered on black such as he wore and never have I encountered again a pair of trousers so brilliantly adorned as his. My only regret now is that I did not have the foresight to paint a second picture—rear view.

While I was painting Buffalo Bow I had my eyes on a tall, dark, fine looking man about forty years of age. I asked if I could paint him when I got through with Buffalo Bow. He was not awfully keen about committing himself but finally consented and followed me into the building where I was permitted to work, taking along his buckskin shirt, his beautiful headdress and a long peace pipe which, specifically, I asked him to bring.

I had painted Buffalo Bow holding his ceremonial pipe and now wished to paint an Indian with the contemplative look they have when smoking. As it happened, the painting of Buffalo Bow was standing on the floor in full view. My new model donned his buckskin tunic and his fine headdress and settled down in a comfortable position for the ordeal—minus the pipe.

"I want to paint you smoking your pipe," I said. He soberly answered, "Me no smoke pipe."

"Oh, yes," I said, "that is the way I especially want to paint you." But he stubbornly and gruffly said, "Me no smoke pipe" nor could I persuade him to change his mind.

Very much annoyed, and not a little uneasy, I walked over and opened the door of the room, thinking that if he scalped me others would at least hear me scream. Then I said, "All right, you not smoke pipe, then I not paint picture. You go home." He was a big fellow, fully six feet tall, so I sounded much braver than I really felt. Without a word he pulled off his beautiful headdress and costume, preparing to leave. My curiosity, getting the better of me, compelled me to ask, "Why won't you smoke your pipe?" With overwhelming dignity and not a little scorn, he pointed one long forefinger at the portrait of 105-year-old Buffalo Bow and said, "Old man smoke pipe, me no old man." Vanity, a sense of proportion, self-respect, or whatever you wish to call it, these attributes know not the artificial barriers of race or creed. People are pretty much the same the world over.

In lieu of painting a man smoking a pipe I persuaded a little five-year-old boy to sit a few moments for me. He was a dear little fellow with four tight little braids of hair neatly tied with red ribbons. Almost anyone would have taken him for a girl but I had seen him dressed in a little Indian costume, dancing at a pow-wow a few nights before. He was a miniature copy of the stately chiefs and his little body sagged and swayed in exactly the same rhythm as his elders to the steady beat of the tom-tom at the ceremonial dance. The crowds had been much amused to watch him dancing between the legs of the tall chiefs, keeping time with the best of them.

All Indian children are very shy in the presence of white people. This sweet little lad was no exception and though he obeyed me readily and explicitly, he spoke never a word. I would liked to have given him a loving embrace but dared not do so in the face of such dignified solemnity. The painting, however, was a source of much interest and pride to his elders when they came to view the finished product.

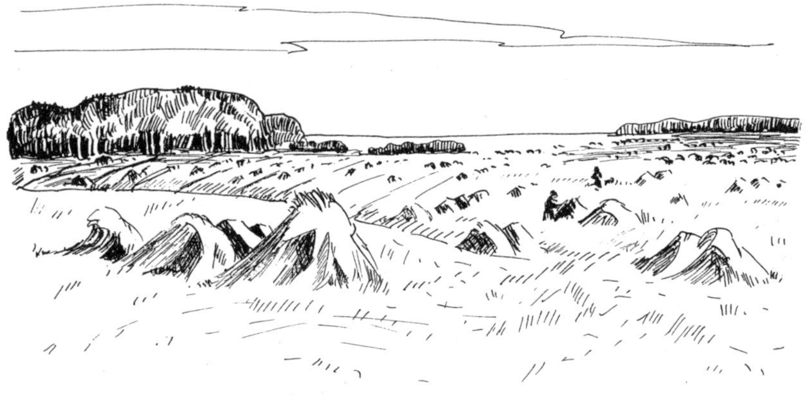

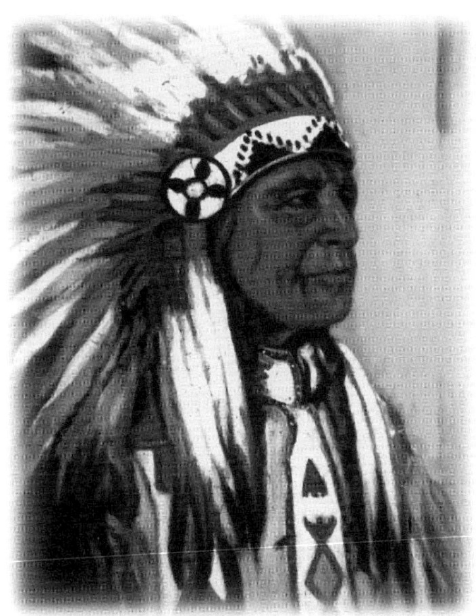

Chief Red Dog

R ed Dog, chief of the Crees, was an arresting character and one of the finest persons I ever met. He commanded respect of all who knew him by his splendid qualities of heart and mind. Dignity, intelligence and rectitude were written on his calm face and evident in his chivalrous bearing.

I have never forgotten Red Dog's eyes, so deep and brown and liquid. They were like shady pools of still water and seemed to be forever brooding as though they gazed in sober reflection over the long history of his people and into the future before them. Of medium height and rather slight build, there was a quiet dignity about the man which bespoke his proud lineage. His father was the famous Star Blanket who had kept his band out of involvement at the time of the Riel Rebellion and thereby doubtlessly prevented much bloodshed.

When that regrettable disturbance was over and peace once again prevailed over the broad prairie, the wise men of Ottawa, eager to recognize the wisdom and restraint of Crowfoot, Star

▶ *colour plate page 101*   26

Blanket and a number of other chiefs who had kept out of the conflict, took them on a trip to Ottawa and other eastern cities, where they were feted and lavishly entertained. It was a gesture of gratitude and good faith and, no doubt, impressed the wise old chiefs as a sincere and practical demonstration of the value of co-operation with the white men.

Star Blanket had seven sons and when he died Red Dog succeeded him as chief.

When I painted him Red Dog's tepee was in the centre of a large encampment. He shared it with his two daughters who had cared for him with the utmost devotion since the death of his wife some six months earlier. I was much impressed by the tender consideration they bestowed upon him.

Red Dog's costume was the most beautiful I have ever seen. His headdress with its magnificent eagle feathers and ermine skins reached to the ground. It was said such feathers had become increasingly difficult to procure and that sometimes the Indians paid as much as a dollar, or more, each for them. Add to that the fine workmanship and great quantities of beads and buckskin that made up an Indian's costume and one can readily understand why such articles were costly. The foundation of Red Dog's suit was deerskin. Almost every part of it was heavily embroidered with beads of many colours and it must have been exceedingly heavy to carry about.

The mounted policeman in charge of the camp told me that this costume aroused much interest among visitors, and he had overheard a wealthy American offer Red Dog two hundred dollars in cash for his outfit, but Red Dog would not think of parting with it for so paltry a sum.

He was quite willing to sit for me when I broached the matter and at first I painted a small sketch of him outdoors. Then I became so interested in the man himself that I wanted to do a large canvas. He followed me into the armouries at Regina where I had been given permission to use one of the rooms as a studio.

It so happened that this was the day on which Lord and Lady Bessborough were scheduled to visit the Regina Fair to officially declare it open. Absorbed in my work, I had quite forgotten about the impending formalities until the band outside struck up

"God Save the King." Red Dog had been sitting very patiently and quietly but at the sound of the music his great brown eyes kindled with sudden interest. The band drew nearer and then entered the armouries. The room where I was working opened off a balcony which ran around a large assembly hall below. I laid aside my brushes and stepped out to see what was going on and beckoned Red Dog to follow. Coming directly towards us, below, was the vice-regal party and behind them the city fathers and other dignitaries. I felt very inconspicuous where we stood and it never occurred to me that we might be noticed, but Red Dog's resplendent costume must have looked like a beacon, for it immediately caught the eye of the governor general. He stopped suddenly, turned and spoke to Lady Bessborough, and the procession was held up while he stood gazing with a smile at the gallery above. Conscious of my dirty, paint-besmeared smock, I slipped back into the studio and left Red Dog to take his bow.

Presently he followed me back into my temporary studio, full of elation and curiosity. "King, uh?" he grunted.

"Yes," I answered, "Big Chief, Ottawa."

"Big Chief, Ottawa," he repeated after me with immense satisfaction in his voice.

Then realizing that this unexpected incident really meant something to Red Dog, I said, "You saw him."

"You bet," was his fervent reply. He spoke very little English but what he did know was emphatic.

Often in the future, no doubt, he would recount to his tribesmen the story of the day he had been the focus of a great royal occasion.

Years after this episode I saw Red Dog again for the last time. He was sitting lonely and forlorn outside his tepee, and at first I did not recognize him. The lovely eyes which had held me with their melting beauty were swollen and inflamed, and were terribly sore. He had become a victim of the dreaded trachoma, a disease of the eyes, which had become a scourge to the Indians. I was genuinely grieved to see my old friend in so sad a plight and was relieved to learn some time later that he eventually recovered from the malady.

It is many years now since Red Dog departed for the "land" to which all Indians go when they lay down their worldly burdens. According to custom he was buried in his beautiful costume, minus the headdress, and thereby hangs a tale. When General Motors of Canada opened their huge plant in Regina Mr. R. S. McLaughlin, president of the firm, came from Ottawa for the official opening. It was considered a very important event for both the city and the province and the city fathers wished to present as attractive an appearance as possible. The Indians were invited to lend their quota of colour and romance to the great occasion.

Red Dog and his warriors, with their tepees and tom-toms, trekked in from the File Hills Reserve, forming no small part of the gay scene that met the eyes of the distinguished visitor.

As a proper climax to a significant enterprise, Mr. McLaughlin was made an honorary chief of the Crees, with Red Dog performing the ancient and honourable ceremony. The name they chose to give McLaughlin was "Kitche-Kah-Soo-Kin-Eskago," meaning Chief Strong-Arm. Not only did they make Mr. McLaughlin an honorary chief, but they also made one of his granddaughters an Indian princess, giving her a complete Indian costume. Such eminence is not lightly conferred and Mr. McLaughlin fully appreciated the implications of the gracious gesture and never forgot the distinction that the "red men" had bestowed upon him. Year after year thereafter, a box containing generous treats and other gifts, arrived at Christmas time on the reserve in faraway Saskatchewan to gladden the hearts of Red Dog and his band.

There was someone else who did not forget. When the old chief died it was found that he had willed his headdress, his most precious possession, the symbol of his chieftainship and the pride of his heart, to the white brother in the East. He had never allowed an act of true courtesy to lapse from his memory.

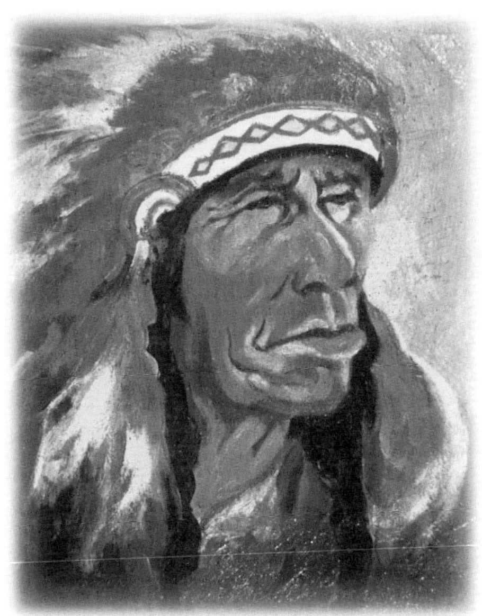

John Sugar

John Sugar, Piegan, Mrs. Rock Thunder and No Name

As I walked past the tepees in an Indian encampment in Saskatchewan one day I saw the most beautiful Indian woman that I had ever laid eyes on. She was so lovely that I thought she could have posed for a statue of a Greek goddess. She was not slim, nor was she stout. Her features had a calm, classical mould and her colouring was warm, pure and luminous. She looked like the mystical Indian princess of my dreams. I could have worshipped such beauty and would have given anything to paint her.

I asked if I might do so, but she merely smiled and gave no other sign that she either heard or understood what I said. When I repeated my request a second and third time she quietly arose with much grace and disappeared inside her tepee.

I waited around hopefully, thinking that perhaps she might be dressing for the occasion but, after a long period of fruitless expectation, I had the effrontery to go to the flap of the tepee and inquire for her. I was not prepared for what followed. An Indian man came toward me, pouring out a volley of verbiage. I could not understand a word he said, but one can recognize curses in any language, so I took to my heels with what composure I could muster.

I can still visualize that beautiful face and still regret that she would not allow me to paint her portrait, for in all my travels I have never seen another woman of any race with such quality of feature. However, in thirty years of painting Indians, that was only the second time that I had ever been refused.

Some years later, when I was driving down the Qu'Appelle Valley with the Indian agent, he pulled up to a little unpainted house and said, "I think there is a man here you might like to paint. I'll go and talk to him."

He went to the door and, after a friendly conversation with the occupant, said, "Yes, you can paint him but I think you had better work outside."

It didn't matter in the least to me where or how I worked, so I sat on the woodpile, my subject settled for the back steps, and, lo, we had a studio.

John Sugar was an interesting person. His enormous protruding lower lip was an unusual facial feature and gave him a dour, rather cunning look, but I had learned to ignore outer appearances and found him to be most co-operative. I soon finished a small painting, paid him for his trouble and we were on our way again when the agent divulged the reason why he thought it best that I should paint outside. It was because one of the family who occupied the house had just recovered from small pox, so he thought I ought not to go in. Needless to say, I was not sorry that I had taken his advice.

I painted a Cree named Piegan when he came into the agent's office one day, on the spot, of course. He wore a headdress of badger hair and had a crimson kerchief tied about his throat. He seemed terribly bored with the whole proceeding and almost went to sleep on me. Indeed, he was a most indifferent person and the only Indian I ever painted who seemed disappointed with the money that I paid him. Perhaps he had heard some wild stories about the fabulous sum some artists got for their work and

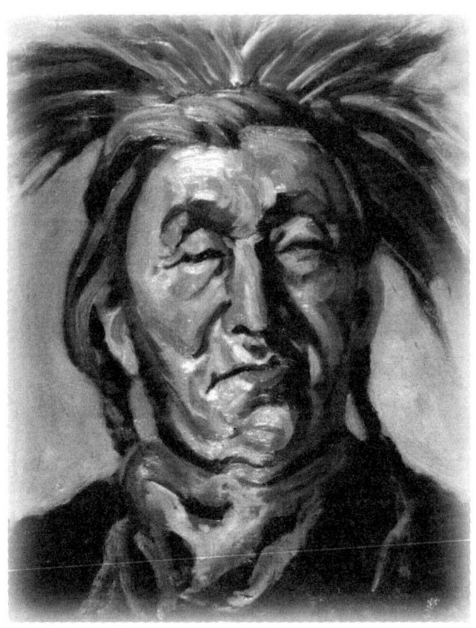

Piegan　　　▶ *page 134*

expected to be rewarded accordingly. As for me, I was sorry I did not belong to that category of artist and hence unable to gratify his expectations.

I never forget visiting another Cree camp in Saskatchewan many years ago. As I wandered about, I noticed a Cree woman sitting beside her tepee, wrapped in a blanket and peacefully smoking a pipe. She could speak no English, neither could I understand Cree, but she was such a fascinating subject that I showed her my paintbox and brushes and some money to indicate my wishes. Understanding immediately, she merely nodded her head while I dropped down on the ground and began to paint.

She never took her eyes off me but just sat with a half-amused, inscrutable look which reminded me of the Mona Lisa, while I worked furiously to catch what I could before she might change her position and, perhaps, run away. Summoning every ounce of energy that I possessed, I finished the portrait in less than an hour and she had not moved, even an eyelash.

Later I found that her name was Mrs. Rock Thunder. Her husband had been the last Indian on the plains to have two legal wives. Both had survived him and this woman was registered in the treaty book as Mrs. Rock Thunder, widow No. 1, which probably accounted for her satisfied smile.

The same day an unusual looking Cree man caught my attention. He wore a black kerchief over his head and tied under his chin, with two little black braids hanging over his shoulders and a felt hat with a beaded band. When I inquired about him I learned that he was a grandson of the famous Chief Piapot who had camped on the Canadian Pacific Railway right-of-way many years ago, determined not to allow the railway to go through his territory.

As they confronted the railway men Piapot's band had been in an ugly mood and it appeared to be an extremely serious situation. Two Mounted Policemen faced dozens of angry armed natives. The story of how they solved the situation without bloodshed is just one of the many chapters in the glorious record of the Royal Canadian Northwest Mounted Police.

Since I had painted and paid Mrs. Rock Thunder, the Cree man decided the money looked good to him so he gave me an hour of his precious time. When I asked his name, he said, "No Name." I thought that the poor fellow never had a name, but further investigation revealed that really was his name—"No Name."

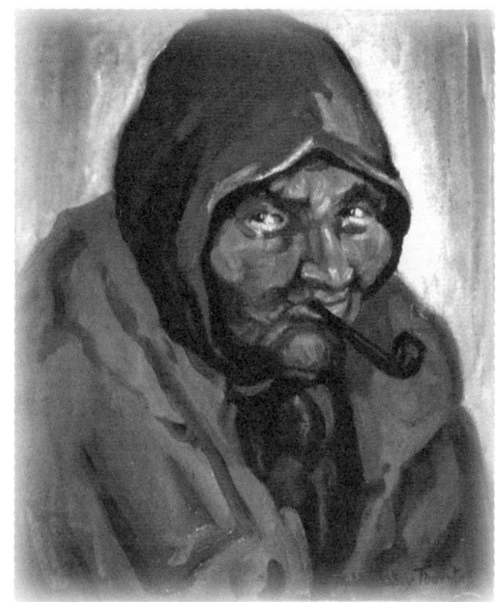

Mrs. Rock Thunder ▸ *page 105*

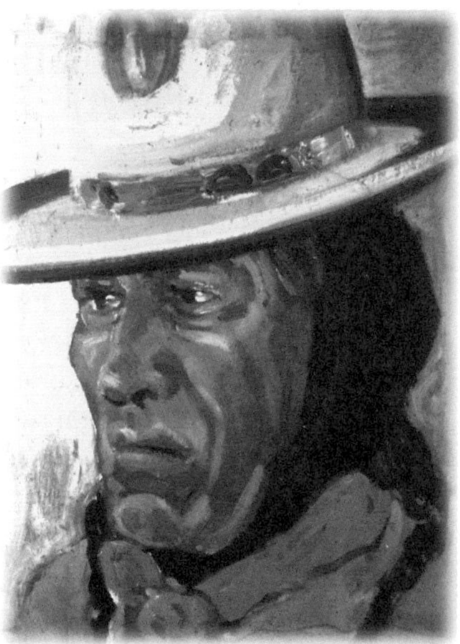

No Name ▸ *page 106*

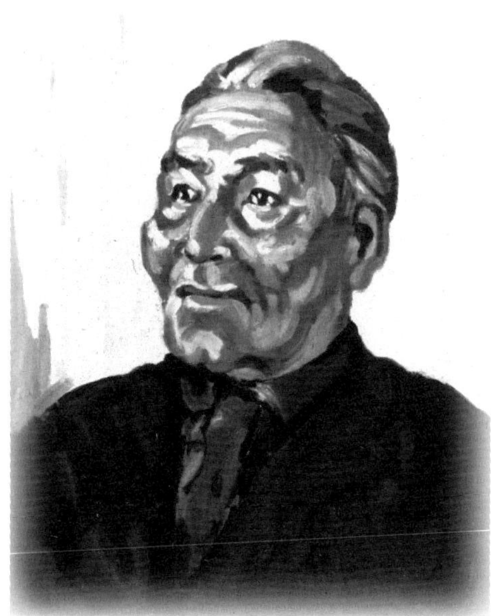

Mistatatim
"Horsechild"

Mistatatim had been on my mind for years. Nobody knew how much I wanted to paint this last surviving son of Big Bear of Riel Rebellion fame. I was within a hundred miles of him once, hoping to make a quick trip from Saskatoon to where he lived on the Little Pine Reserve, but a lukewarm response from the Indian agent over the long-distance telephone had cooled my resolve.

"You just can't do it that way," he said. "It's a long drive out in the country to his home and I would have to make arrangements with the farming instructor to take you there. You would need several days at least, maybe a week."

It didn't sound very hopeful and because I was rushed for time, I relinquished the idea for the moment but it was always lying dormant in my mind. A couple of years later I was within a day's journey of Mistatatim again, but I was tied to the unyielding demands of a lecture tour itinerary, so once more my yearnings went unsatisfied. "Never mind," I comforted myself, "I'll get him yet."

Meanwhile I heard disturbing rumours of Mistatatim's failing health. If I didn't get a move on I might miss him altogether. He was an old man and time waits for no artist or writer either for that matter. Thoughts of Mistatatim were forever creeping into my mind, urging me to let other things go, to make the trip regardless.

Then, at long last, having moved to the West Coast, I made my plans to go to Battleford to secure the much coveted portrait. I arranged a painting trip up the coast of British Columbia with the Indian agent on the government vessel to visit many remote reserves. After that expedition was accomplished, I would travel to Prince Rupert and from there go directly to Battleford and Mistatatim.

How smugly we make our little plans and with what magnificent disdain does nature brush them aside! While I revelled in the majesty of the coastal scenery, unexpected floods struck the province. Torrents of white water roared down from the mighty mountains, swelling the rivers, wiping out roads, obliterating railway tracks. Men stood helplessly by and watched nature explode.

I took the first steamer back to Vancouver from Prince Rupert and waited. Waited once more to get a chance to paint old Mistatatim. Three weeks later I was on the first train that departed after the floods. The train left four hours ahead of schedule and arrived four hours late in Edmonton. Newly graded sections and hastily reconstructed bridges had to be navigated with care. Many miles of track were still deep under water as we moved slowly along. Roofs of houses and barns poked above the water and one could only guess what lay below.

Finally I arrived at Battleford and inquired about the old Indian. I was told that a big celebration was taking place on a reserve about a hundred miles to the north, and that it was just possible that Mistatatim might be there. Once more my heart took a tumble. Was I going to miss him again? Perish the thought! I would go to the reserve anyway and hope for the best! Somehow I would get that portrait and I hoped I should not have to wait too long to get started.

Battleford! Spacious, quiet and lovely is the setting of this historic town. Here was the first seat of government in the Northwest Territories and some of the original buildings are still standing. Here the Mounted Police had their headquarters at the time of the Riel Rebellion and their old quarters have lately (circa 1946) been converted into a museum of great interest.

Not far away is Frog Lake and Cutknife where bloody chapters were written into the history of the area in the days when the hills gave back the echoes of Indian war cries and the earth shuddered beneath the pounding hoofs of millions of buffalo.

It is all very quiet today. You will be shown the old guard room with its tiny cells and heavy iron doors and you will be told that this is where Wandering Spirit and seven other Indians were held before they paid with their lives for the folly and brutality at Frog Lake.

Just over the hill, close to the river's edge, their bones lie buried. The tall grass and tangled Saskatoon bushes have covered the tragic site so that the casual visitor would never know the sorrows of the soil.

Forty miles away was Little Pines Reserve where Mistatatim was living out his days in peace and serenity and there I hoped to find him.

Mr. Campbell Innes, curator of the historical museum at Battleford, drove me to the reserve one lovely summer day. Mistatatim's little white-washed house gleamed brightly in the brilliant sunlight. We could see it plainly from a long way off. Would he be home, I wondered, or would there be that uncompromising padlock on the door? Time would tell.

As we approached we could see that all the windows were boarded over, but when we drew up beside the house and honked the horn, a handsome young Indian man came out to greet us. We explained our mission and he disappeared into the house. We sat in the car and waited. Presently the young man came out again. Yes, Mistatatim was home, yes, he would let me paint him when he was ready. Would we just wait?

So we waited. We waited while the young man got a hammer and axe and pried off all the boards from the windows. He explained that they had been put there for protection during the winter. This was late June so they had been in no hurry to take them down, evidently preferring the dark rooms to the exertion of removing the boards.

We kept on waiting while the job was done, about an hour's time, and then we were invited in. I could see instantly the cause for the delay. The old man's wife had done her spring cleaning while we sat in the car! The little home had been swept and dusted from end to end. Fresh covers were on the beds, doilies on the little table, everything spick and span.

Mistatatim looked as if he had just been returned from the laundry. He was wearing a new, bright blue shirt and his Sunday suit. His hair had been brushed as slick as a whistle and he had the freshly scrubbed look of a little boy all ready for Sunday school. He seemed immensely pleased with himself and no wonder!

I had expected to see a wrinkled old man with grey hair in braids and an old handkerchief about his neck. This eager subject, with guileless satisfaction on his face, had little in common with the old war chief who had been his father. It was quite evident that Mistatatim had not had his portrait painted before. This was a special occasion and he was anxious to look his best! As I painted he spoke of the past. He told of when he was a boy of twelve at the time of the Rebellion. He remembered when they took Big Bear to Regina for trial and Mistatatim went with him. The white men and their ways were all very strange and unaccountable to him them, but he just wanted to be near his father so they let him stay in the jail where he earned his keep by washing dishes for the prisoners.

There was a lot more that Mistatatim remembered much more than he cared to tell and, besides, it was all so long ago. He was content now with his weekly ration of food from the agency and his winter's supply of fuel. He asked little else from life.

He smiled happily when I finished the painting and wanted his wife to see it, but she, poor dear, had taken to her heels and vanished out the back door the minute we had entered the front one. We hardly caught a glimpse of her. One of the men, who had gathered outside the house, carried the wet canvas around to the back of the house to satisfy her curiosity, but he could not

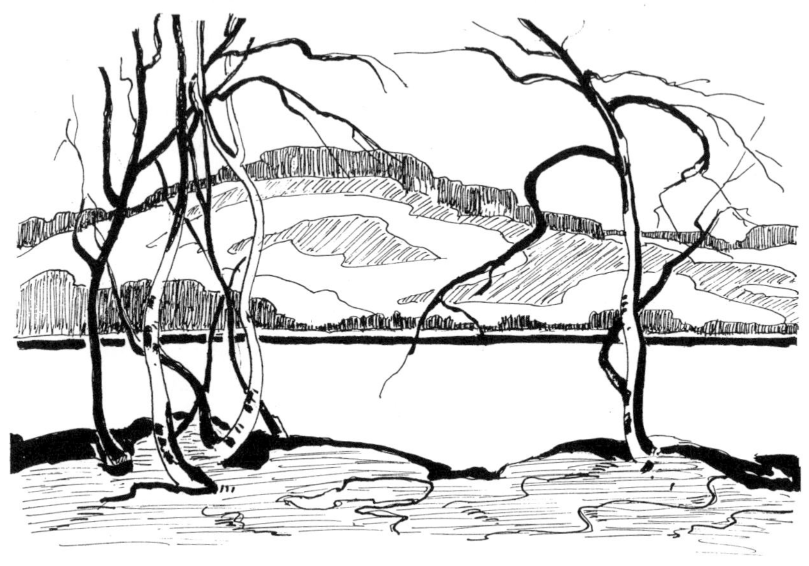

persuade her to come in to meet us. As we drove away, however, I caught sight of one black eye peeking cautiously around the door, watching us in a wide arc as we circled the yard and drove away.

Before we departed, however, I reflected upon what Mistatatim had told me during the painting session. After his father, Big Bear, was released from the Regina jail because of failing health, he had returned to his old reserve and there he had died many years ago. He was buried in the little Indian cemetery by the river, a few miles away, so Mistatatim said. We decided to look for the grave and took the old man along with us to show us where it was. The forlorn, neglected, over-grown but sacred plots are very lonely and pathetic. A few small mounds, a few broken slabs were all there was to mark the spot.

Back and forth old Mistatatim stumbled through the dry grass looking for his father's grave, searching vainly for a sign which he felt was surely there, yet never finding it. Dismayed and puzzled, he stood motionless, gazing at the blue hills in the distance, as though half expecting to see his father come riding over the plains. For a long, long time he stood, looking and dreaming, and we dared not intrude. What was the old man thinking, what did he recall, what did he see in the future? We would have given much to know.

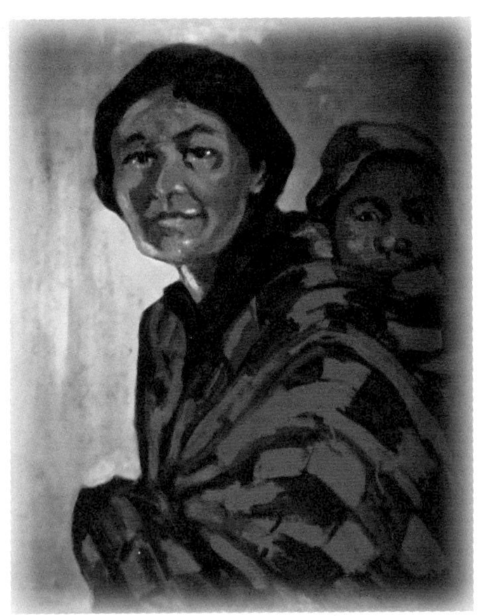

Cree Mother and Child

Looking back over my experiences painting Indians, it seems that I have worked under almost every conceivable difficulty and in some of the most preposterous places, but for sheer unadulterated misery, I think that the time I painted the young Cree mother and child capped them all.

It was a cold, very windy day in the fall and I stood gazing wistfully out of the window of the farming instructor's home at Piapot, Saskatchewan, wishing that Providence would provide suitable material for my eager brush. Providence must have caught my thoughts and immediately decided to do something about it, because it was no time at all until I spotted the red-clad figure of a woman going down the road with a papoose on her back. She had passed the house before I noticed her and was some distance on her way. Here was the subject that Providence had provided! A roughly ploughed field separated me from my quarry, but what are ploughed fields for, if not to leap over?

Cold, wind, ploughed field and all, I suddenly made up my mind that I wanted to paint that woman and her offspring. Hastily

I threw on some wraps, seized my paintbox and went skipping over the rough ground but not for long, for ploughed fields simply do not lend themselves to the sportive glee of skipping. Anyway, I finally got to the other side of the obstacle with my anatomy intact, with the lady still walking a good piece ahead of me. Once or twice I had tried to halt her by calling, but the wind was not co-operative and insolently cast my voice in exactly the opposite direction. Now, I am not a good sprinter. Nature just did not provide me with the proper architecture for that useful ability. Yet, when necessity demands, I am able to accelerate. Besides, I was travelling light, even with my supplies, compared to the burden of the young Indian mother, and though she swung along in a steady rhythmic stride, I soon caught up with her.

She was really a very sweet looking woman, and quickly consented to my request to paint her. I looked around for some sort of haven. In a field nearby stood an old unused barn with its doors nailed shut. It did not amount to much but it was the only sanctuary reasonably near which offered any protection whatsoever from the bitter wind so we made for the lee side of it, where I paused to catch up on my breathing before beginning to work.

Then I was confronted with a new problem. The mother was willing to pose but the baby was not. He opened his mouth as wide as he could and roared in protest. Whatever swear words babies use in the Cree language, I think he exhausted them all on me that afternoon. When he paused for breath I would make a wild endeavour to paint his flat little nose and his beady brown eyes. Then he would let out another blood-curdling yell. The echoing war whoops of many fierce and long-dead generations of ferocious ancestral warriors were loosened in unbridled fury upon my innocent but tenacious head. Over and over I tried piecing my picture together, getting in a stroke here and another there, painting

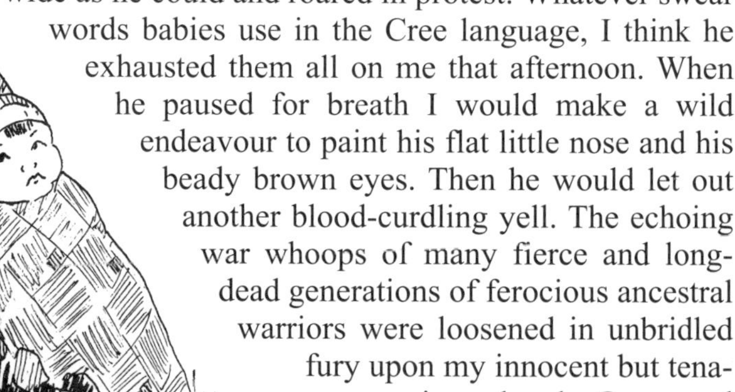

the mother when I could not paint the baby, but since he wriggled and flopped every time he yelled, his mother was not exactly a stationary target either.

If, by any act of mercy, the baby happened to be still at the same moment as his mother, the wind seemed to take a malicious delight in sneaking around the corner of the building in sharp little gusts, laying long wisps of grass and dust upon my wet canvas and palette with heartless disregard for my painting or my feelings. Suddenly, my hat blew off and started off on an expedition of its own over the vast prairie. As I jumped to catch it, I upset my precious painting, "butter-side down" in the soft dirt. Ruefully I picked it up. What debris I could not blow off I brushed and picked off and, undismayed, settled down again, determined to finish or die in the attempt.

It is simply amazing the amount of punishment that one can take over something that one really wants to do. If it had been a disagreeable task I should have given up in disgust early on in the venture. To tell the truth, I did not think I was creating anything worth salvaging, and when, at last, the three of us were stretched out in utter exhaustion, I would gladly have given the painting to any good Samaritan who would transport me to a place of peace and comfort. Weakly I thanked the young woman, paid her for her patience, and struggled back to the farming instructor's house, feeling like the frayed ends of a worn-out moccasin.

Yet how gently does the healing hand of time bestow the miracle of tranquillity! Through the long vista of the years that have passed since then, I can look back on that experience with equanimity, and even with relish, as I recall the ludicrous aspects of the scene when I attempted to paint the Cree mother and child.

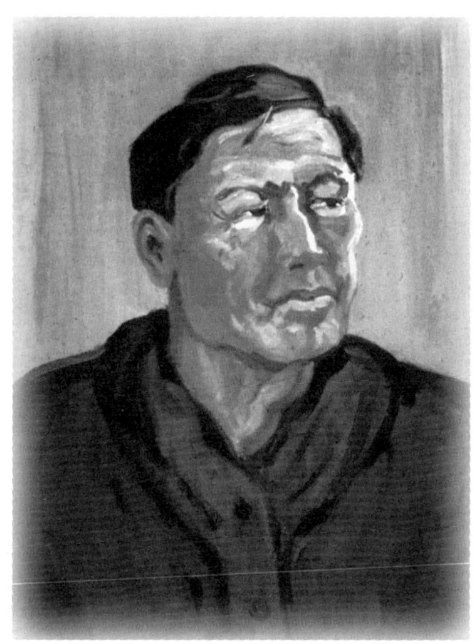

Stanislaus Almighty Voice

Autumn in Saskatchewan. The sun hung golden in a turquoise sky across which bright tufted clouds were tossed like tennis balls in the keen wind. The wind had gathered momentum over thousands of leagues of open prairie and the grass scurried away before it in rippling, gleaming waves of silver and gold that sparkled and shone in the dazzling light.

So vast a land and so good a land! It had belonged to a proud and fearless race since the time when the Great Spirit Himself had committed it to their keeping. From generation to generation it had supplied all their needs of food, shelter and clothing.

There was nothing meagre or stinted about the gifts of the Great Spirit. Abundance was everywhere. A man might wander where he would and his acquisitions were limited only by his skill and daring. The children of the plains were the offspring of freedom free as the air they breathed, as the winds that blew or as the eagle that soared above them.

Strange and portentous things had happened of recent years. Into this wonderful land had come another race of men, crafty, ambitious and greedy for profit. Like a plague they had swarmed into the country, disturbing the peace of centuries and effacing slowly and surely the customs that were rooted in immemorial tradition. Like frightened children the Indians had been driven from refuge to refuge until, at length, they had seen the very foundations of their existence disappear with the extermination of the buffalo. They knew not how to supply their needs nor where to find the succour they so desperately required.

Finally plans were devised by the new order with which all could live. Reserves were set aside for the use of the aboriginal. Law and order replaced confusion and destruction. Peace superseded murder and rebellion. One era had ended and another had begun.

Memory and pride in the old days and in the old ways struggled on in the breasts of the red men along with apprehension and fear of the new regime. Not easily were old habits forsaken, not without pain were the old links broken. Like derelicts tossed in a shoreless, stormy sea, the Indians groped for equilibrium and safe anchorage. It was a strange, incomprehensible new world.

Many Indians were ill-clothed; most of them were hungry. Old men shook their heads sadly and accepted the new order in stolid silence. The young men were restless and combative. No longer could they leap on their ponies, ride out on the prairie and take, with their own hands, the food that nature had provided for them on a land that had once been theirs.

There had been times, even within their memory, when they could look in any direction and see herds of buffalo grazing. Now only the empty stare of the lonely, silent plains met the searching scrutiny of their troubled eyes.

Ka-Kee-Man-I-Tou-Wayo and his girl-wife Con-Ne-Con-Pee-Te-Qua were heartily sick of it all. Better for them the old ways. Better the freedom and the open trail. The settled dwellings of the white man and the monotony of farming had no appeal for them.

He was a magnificent Cree, barely nineteen years of age. Six feet four, he stood, strong of arm, fleet of foot, and with a fierce pride in the history of his unhappy race.

His grandfather, Chief One Arrow, had named him Ka-Kee-Man-Tou-Wayo, meaning "Almighty Voice," because, as an infant, he cried so loudly that it sounded like the voice of the Great Spirit. Con-Ne-Con-Pee-Te-Qua was but fifteen, slender as a willow wand and pretty with the dark, exotic beauty of her race. The white people called her "Helen" in after years, but her Cree name meant "the first to go in."

It was weeks since there had been fresh meat in their larder. Why should they not have food? Why should they go hungry? In this mood they came across some cattle grazing, cattle that belonged to the government which, they thought, had usurped their heritage. The government owed them a living. Resolutely the young Indian raised his rifle and, with one shot, brought down a fine, fat steer. They took it home.

Somehow word of his misdeed came to the ears of the Mounted Police who immediately went to the reserve and arrested Almighty Voice on a warrant of shooting government cattle. He was taken to the guardhouse at Duck Lake, handcuffed and fastened by a chain to an iron ring in the floor.

Visitors to Duck Lake may still see this old building standing behind the local post office. The heavy iron ring is still in the floor; the table and chairs are still intact. Two policemen were in charge at the time. Almighty Voice asked when they intended to let him go. Old timers say one of them jestingly remarked that they were going to hang him in the morning. Little did the thoughtless man dream of the holocaust of trouble and bloodshed he precipitated by his careless words.

The incredulous Indian, not sharing the white man's sense of humour, believed what he had been told and secretly vowed that they would never carry out the threat. Late at night one of the policemen went away, leaving the other sitting at the table to guard the prisoner.

The tall dark form of Almighty Voice lay full-length upon the floor, his eyes watching every move of the constable from the folds of his blanket. A bunch of keys hung tantalizingly from the policeman's belt. If he could but get possession of those, his way would be clear.

As the long hours dragged by, the policeman's eyes grew heavy, his tired head sagged forward and finally rested upon the table. Soon his deep, regular breathing pronounced that he was sound asleep.

This was the moment for which the watchful Indian had been waiting. Stealthily as a cat he crept over to the sleeping man, deftly lifted the keys, and in absolute silence unlocked his chains. Another instant and he was out the door with the keen wind of the prairie in his nostrils. Exultantly he leapt into the night and, by the time his escape was discovered, many miles lay between him and the guardhouse at Duck lake.

To add to his first misdemeanour, Almighty Voice had now broken jail. For days the police searched the countryside for him, but in vain. At length Sergeant Colebrook, with a half-breed guide, came up with him and his young squaw on the open prairie. The young Indian couple had just killed a prairie chicken for food. When his pursuers came within hearing Almighty Voice swung his gun to his shoulder and warned the guide to tell the policeman to go away. "If he does not, I'll shoot," he said.

But the sergeant had been ordered to arrest Almighty Voice, so was duty-bound to go forward. He called the Indian to surrender and slowly approached. Through tense lips Almighty Voice hissed a second warning, but true to the traditions of the force, the relentless Redcoat came on, ignoring the threat. He paid for his action with his life.

The guide fled in terror with a bullet-shattered arm as a souvenir of the tragedy and a hole through the rim of his hat. It is said that "he ran so far and so fast that he has never been seen or even heard of again to this day." Be that as it may, news of the shooting soon reached the police.

Grim and sinister was the fate which saw the charges mounting. Almighty Voice was now a murderer. News of Sergeant Colewood's death swept over the plains like a prairie fire. With renewed intensity the countryside was combed from end to end, but no trace of Almighty Voice could be found.

He and his young wife were always hiding somewhere, on the plains or among their own people, many of whom doubtlessly befriended them. Sometimes in the dead of night Almighty

Voice would steal into the lodge of his mother, Spotted-Calf, and his father, Sounding-Sky, to obtain food and a little rest.

Many moons went by and on one of those nocturnal visits his young wife followed him into the tepee with a moss-bag on her back. It was a wee brown baby, Almighty Voice, junior, or Stanislaus Almighty Voice, as he is called today. With the stars for candles, the grass for a bed, and the police forever on the heels of his luckless parents, Almighty Voice and his young parents continued to avoid capture. Born on the open prairie, he had become the innocent offspring of disaster.

Over two years passed before Almighty Voice, finally wearying of his long outlaw isolation, made his last stand with two blood brothers in a protected copse in the Minnichinas Hills near Batoche. There they prepared to sell their lives dearly.

Now that the police knew where the fugitive was, they thought it would be a simple matter to apprehend him. Inspector Allen and a company of men went out to take the Indian, dead or alive. As they approached the hideout, crashing gunfire shattered the silence. The inspector was wounded in the shoulder. The fusillade continued and presently another policeman fell. The proposition suddenly did not look so easy.

A fire was started in the bluff in an effort to smoke the culprits out, but the green wood refused to burn.

Three policemen, seeing some openings in the bushes, began to crawl towards the outlaws, hoping to surprise them. Three more shots rang out with deadly accuracy and three more valiant men gave up their lives in the line of duty. Two more were wounded.

All that night the police guarded the bluff. Toward morning Almighty Voice called out to them, "Brothers, we have had a good fight today. I've worked hard and am hungry. You've plenty of grub. Send me in some and tomorrow we'll finish the fight."

It was the way of the Indians—no resentment, no plea for mercy—simply expecting a fair fight under fair conditions.

Another time, when the battle was at its height, he cried to his attackers, "You are doing well, but not well enough!"

Dismayed and chagrined, the police finally sent a message to their headquarters at Regina for reinforcements and, in that fledgling city that night was enacted a Canadian counterpart of the historic eve of Waterloo. The Royal Canadian Northwest Mounted Police barracks was a scene of light-hearted revelry as the elite of the capital had gathered to say farewell and Godspeed to a select detachment being sent to England to attend the Queen's Jubilee. The ball was at its height with "fair women and brave men" dancing in the gaily decorated hall when abruptly, the music stopped and the solemn strains of "God Save the Queen" rolled out to replace the sprightly dance tunes.

People stared at each other in dumb puzzlement as Colonel Herchmer, commanding officer, announced that plans for sending the contingent to England had been abandoned. Every available man was needed in the North and must prepare to depart immediately. News of the utmost gravity had been received from the outpost at Duck Lake.

Soon, two officers and twenty-nine non-commissioned officers and men with two field guns and seven nine-pounders [*sic*] were on their way to the blood-soaked retreat of the embattled Indians.

By this time many sightseers were on the scene: Indians, half-breeds and settlers. On a knoll nearby sat the wrinkled old mother of Almighty Voice, huddled in her blanket through the long ominous hours. Her tired body swayed in rhythmic harmony to the weird cadence of her quavering voice. Intermingled with the roar of the guns she could be heard singing her son's death song according to the custom of her tribe, enjoining him never to give in, to remember the bravery of his father and his grandfather and of all who had gone before, recounting his own deeds of valour and daring and calling on him to die as brave men do.

Few stories are so poignant, so fraught with stark tragedy and warring human emotions as that of the last stand of Almighty Voice and his devoted companions. The big guns of the white men soon put an end to the Indian's resistance. Then it was all over.

Four brave policemen had been killed and many others wounded. Three Indian lives had been lost—all because of the killing of a steer and a thoughtless jest in a guardroom.

Lest anyone be hasty in condemnation, be it remembered that many of us might have been guilty of just such an indiscretion. It is doubtful if anywhere in the world a group of men could have been found who matched in tact, courage and resourcefulness the Royal Canadian Northwest Mounted Police of those extremely perilous early days. To realize, in part, the enormous contribution they made, one has but to compare the history and treatment of the Indians in the United States over the corresponding years. Shocking indeed is the record of that shameful period. That the difficult transition period in Canada was abridged with so little friction is due chiefly to the intuitive understanding of the Indian mind and the almost uncanny wisdom of the hardy, brave and true men of the Royal Canadian Northwest Mounted Police, whose fame has gone out to the ends of the earth.

In the summer of 1942 I visited Duck Lake and Batoche to look over the historic ground. It was my desire to paint a portrait of Almighty Voice, junior.

The Indian Agent drove me to his home on the One Arrow Reserve, but the doors were locked and the family away. However I caught up with him a few days later on Duck Lake Sports Day when Indians from many miles around assembled for the races.

Stanislaus Almighty Voice was his father's own son, tall, broad-shouldered and handsome, with a keen eye, small hands and feet. I found him courteous and obliging, speaking excellent English. He told me that his mother was still living on the reserve and that she had been blind for twenty years.

"Do you think she would permit me to paint her?" I asked. "I am sure she would," was his reply.

The postman was going to Batoche that very afternoon, so I prevailed upon him to let me go along, and paid him to take me to where Old Helen lived with her niece some five miles beyond the village.

Mile upon mile, the reserve was deserted that day. I think Joe Paul's family were the only Indians who were not at the sports event. They stayed at home rather than leave Old Blind Helen alone. She was sitting on the edge of her bed in her bare little room and "looked" up inquiringly at the sound of a strange voice.

Her nephew sat down beside her and very gently told her, in Cree, who I was and that I wanted to paint her portrait.

She wanted to touch me, and when I took her slim little hand in mine, she agreed to let me paint her. Touch and sound told her that I was a friend.

Twenty years before she had shaken out a blanket that was lying on the grass. Pieces of foxtail, one of the prairie weeds, flew into her eyes. If they could have been removed at once, she would have suffered no permanent injury, but it was nearly two weeks before she was taken to Prince Albert Hospital, and by that time her sight was gone.

Helen was in need of various articles of clothing, and I promised to send her some items on my return home. Two large boxes were accordingly dispatched later in the year, and then began a very interesting correspondence. Mrs. Paul wrote and thanked me for Helen, who had dictated as follows: "I'm very much glad for you not forgetting me the clothes I ask from you. You make me think of my past life, also my grandparents. I name you Ows-Ka-Tau-Eskean; that means putting your most ability for us Indians, and hope you will never forget me and I will never forget you. Yours truly, Blind Helen."

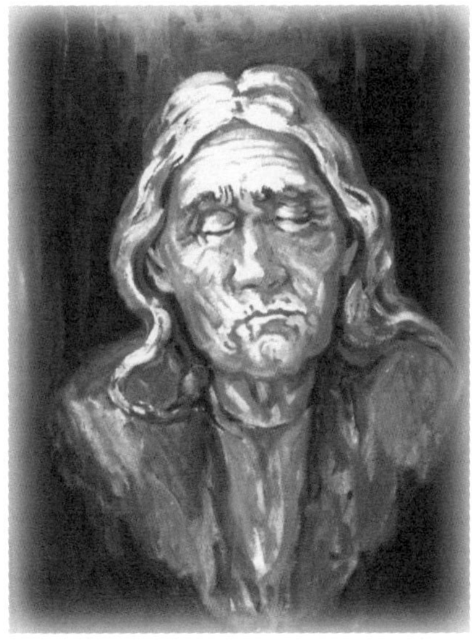

Old Blind Helen   ▸ *page 112*

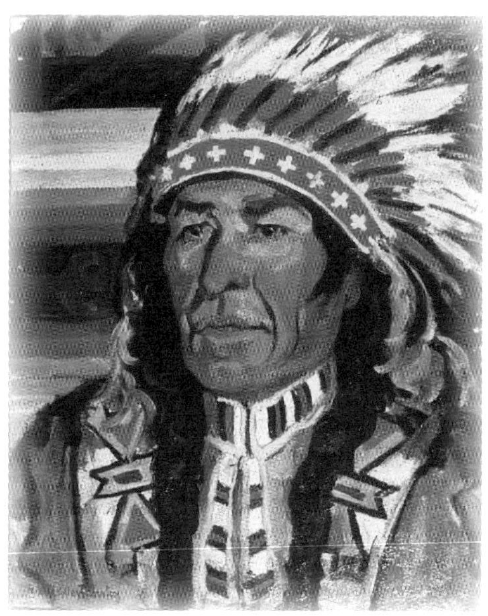

Nanepowiskh

Few parts of the world have such a colourful and romantic, though brief, history as the plains of Western Canada. To gaze out over the vast, immeasurable horizons is to wonder at the vivid panorama and realize anew that it was a country that bred courageous men.

It is a soul-testing land where only the stout of heart may survive and where weaklings fall by the wayside under the harsh unmitigated dictum of survival of the fittest. Once you have lived there and have felt the beat of its strong heart, the prairie will never let you go, though you may wander to the outermost parts of the world.

To the superficial eye it is a stern, unyielding land, devoid of beauty and barren of soul, but the treasures there must be sought; they must be earned, and the process includes love of the treasure and joy in the seeking. If you do not fall in love with these silent, immutable spaces they will mean nothing to you for you shall carry nothing away from them though you may search forever.

▸ *colour plate page 113*   50

Small wonder that the Indians loved this, their very own land, which had yielded them all the necessities of life centuries before it was discovered by the white man.

These and many other similar thoughts came surging through my mind as I drove through the beautiful Qu'Appelle country one lovely fall day. I was a guest at the home of Mr. and Mrs. R.C. Davis. Mr. Davis was the Indian agent at Muscow. They took me on many trips as Mr. Davis went about his duties in the valley, thereby enabling me to get valuable material and saving me much time and inconvenience.

It was autumn and no season is half so wonderful as autumn on the prairie. The air was crystal clear, the skies wide and windswept. The brilliant blue above intensified the deep, rich colour of the trees and shrubs, and there was that poignant hint of coming frost that makes every hour so precious at that time of year.

We drove to the home of Nanepowiskh on the Muscow-petung Reserve. It was a small, unpainted house, like all the rest, but looked clean and comfortable from what I could see of it.

The place was as silent as the great hills beyond it. Not a soul was in sight, so Mr. Davis strolled toward the house and called out in a loud, hearty voice, "Anybody home?" He was immediately answered by a varied assortment of grunts and salutations as several men came out to greet us. I was fascinated by the figure of Nanepowiskh when he appeared. He was of medium height, straight and dignified, and possessed the finest head of hair that I have ever seen. It hung in two thick, glossy, raven-black braids to his knees. Though he was sixty-seven years of age there was no trace of grey in it and his skin was as smooth as a child's, while his cheeks had a warm, rosy glow. His features were strong and regular. Altogether he was a most handsome man.

When he understood my mission, he pondered for a few moments, then decided to be painted. Slowly and solemnly he unbraided his shining tresses, combed them very carefully, and braided them again. Then he donned his gleaming buckskin suit, adorned with beautiful bead embroidery, and his splendid head-dress, to present a truly regal and dignified figure.

I never found out why Nanepowiskh did not wish to be painted under his own home, but the fact remains that he threw himself astride his nearby horse with more speed than I could pick up
a paint brush, and galloped off up the road toward the home of
the farming instructor, to which, he knew, we would eventually
follow. Since we were in a car we quickly overtook him and
arrived before he did. In a surprisingly short time we saw his
resplendent form turning in at the gate. And now the question
arose: where to paint him? It was too cold to sit outdoors for long
and I could not use the house of the farming instructor, as that
was the busiest place imaginable with the process of bread-mak-
ing going on and six husky farmhands to feed. Finally, I decided
on the granary. It was small and poorly lit there being but one little window, but it had a floor, a roof and four walls. One must not
be too particular on these occasions. There was a tiny hall which
happened not to be filled with wheat, and this I requisitioned as
my temporary studio. I hung up an Indian blanket, that chanced
to be handy, for a back-drop and got on with my work.

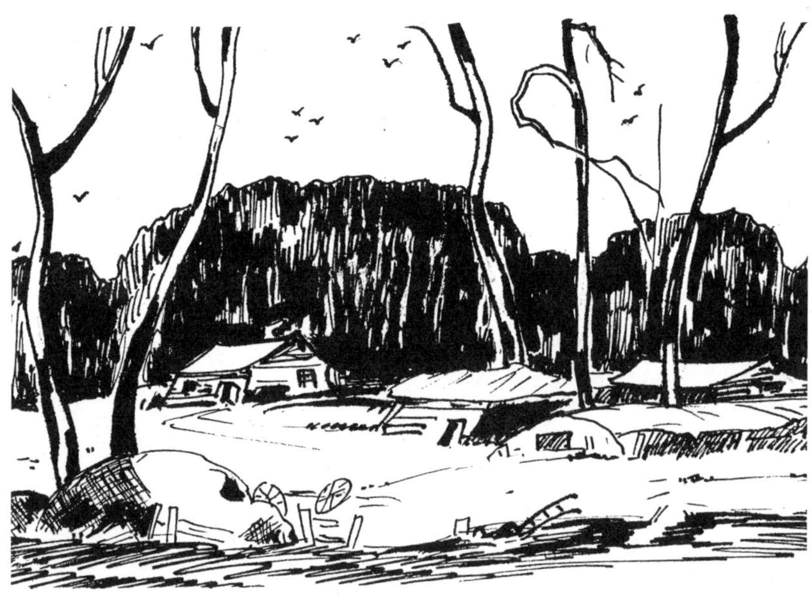

Nanepowiskh was an interesting subject and sat like a marble statue, as if conscious of the destiny of his portrait which would represent his race along with many others. When I had finished he wanted to know if he could have the painting. "You give him to me?" he asked. This request rather floored me, but I paid him for his time and told him that I would send him a photograph later on. I happened to have my camera with me and took a full-length snapshot of him and promised to send him a print and subsequently did so.

While I was working, several other Indians appeared, from goodness knows where, and hung about in intense curiosity. Three women came in and stood silent and absorbed, watching every move I made. They would bend over my paintbox and obscure my vision, saying, "Tsh, tsh, tsh," and shaking their heads as though completely mystified. The tiny place was soon packed with Indians. I had barely room to wield my brush and sometimes I painted the wrong object as they thrust their faces in front of me.

When I picked up my camera the women muttered something unintelligible to me, threw their shawls over their heads and ran for dear life.

Amazed and somewhat amused at this strange behaviour, I questioned a young Indian man about it. He explained that many of the Indians, especially the older ones, had a superstition about cameras. They believed that if their picture was taken they would die before the year was out. No doubt they thought that, in some mysterious manner, their souls became detached from their bodies and entered into the queer little black box which possessed supernatural powers.

And for that matter, we need not laugh. Not so long ago we of the white race had equally strange notions, such as thinking that tomatoes caused cancer, that toads caused warts and that it meant disaster to walk under a ladder.

The Saulteaux Indians

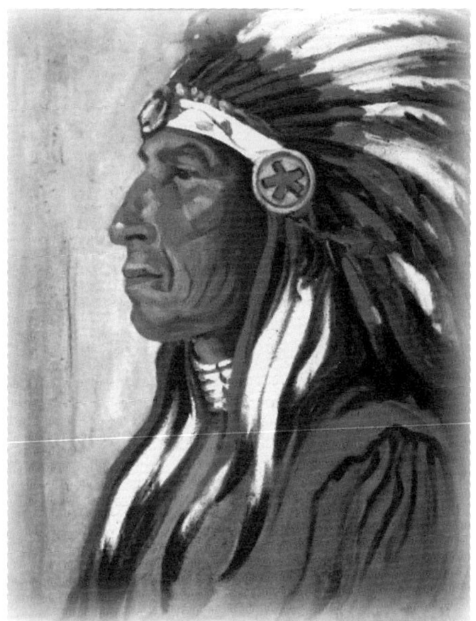

Pat Cappo

Pat Cappo was a member of the Saulteaux tribe and lived on the Muscowpetung Reserve in the Qu'Appelle Valley. He was a young man with the strong features so often found among the prairie Indians. The name Saulteaux was derived from the fact that the tribe used to live near Sault Ste. Marie. It is an offshoot of the Chippewa, who roamed the vast territory from Lakes Huron and Superior and Georgian Bay to the prairies.

They are "the people who wear puckered moccasins" and very beautiful moccasins they are, too, with fine designs and deft beadwork. The Saulteaux is almost the only tribe which sometimes uses naturalistic floral decorations in their beadwork and it can often be identified by this distinction. The best and most valuable beadwork from the collector's point of view, however, is conventional in design. Every part of the design had

▸ *colour plate page 115*

a definite meaning in the ancient days, but the record of its significance has long since been lost to modern Indians which is a
great pity.

Pat Cappo was a grand subject to paint and seemed to thoroughly enjoy the experience. His wife was a comely young
matron, so I painted her also as I thought the pair represented the
best of their tribe in modern times. They had taken kindly to
farming and worked diligently at it. Though some of the Indians
found the farmer's life dull and irksome, there were others who
were quite successful and contented working the soil.

The two daughters of the household, dressed in smart shirt-
waists and slacks, were busily engaged in breadmaking. The
kitchen was a very cheerful place with bright linoleum on the
floor and a big shining range. It was typical of the kitchen of any
prosperous farmer and probably better than most.

Our hostess took us into her parlour which was an attractive
room, well furnished in the latest manner, with healthy red gera-
niums blooming profusely in the window boxes. The men of the
household were threshing a bountiful harvest and big straw
stacks seemed to be looming up all over the barnyard.

The agent explained to me that the mother in this family was
aptly called a "go-getter." She was determined that her daughters were going to "be somebody" and that it would not be her fault if they were not. Each girl had her own horse, cattle, fowl and a share of the crop. Each trans-acted her own business and banked her own money. Both had been well educated at the Indian school and both were very good-looking.

The mother was a tall woman with a handsome, keen face and a pleasant, confident manner. In addi-

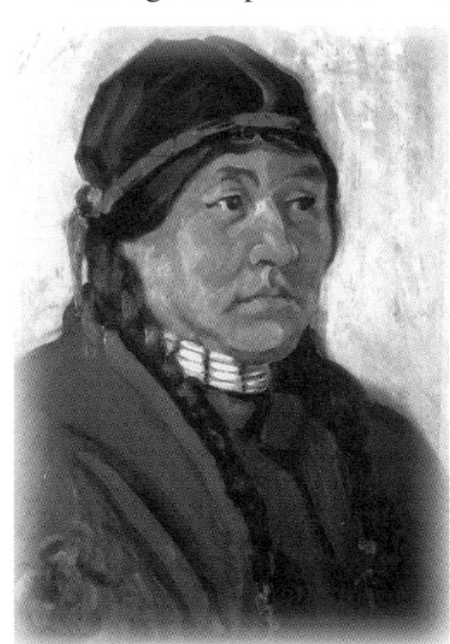

Pat Cappo's Wife   ▶ *page 114*

tion, she had the necessary *avoirdupois* to enforce the demands of her will.

When she said "Go," everybody "went"—and no fooling about! She fairly radiated industry and prosperity and it was plain to be seen that laziness would not be tolerated in her presence. She had brains that were not allowed to ossify through lack of use!

This was an exceptional family, but many Indian families do make a fairly good success at farming. I was surprised when told how much money the tribe had on deposit in the bank on this reserve.

Much credit for this must go to the government for its wise policy of placing competent farming instructors in each agency. The results are seen in such fine homes and people such as I have described, as well as others who are not nearly so conspicuous.

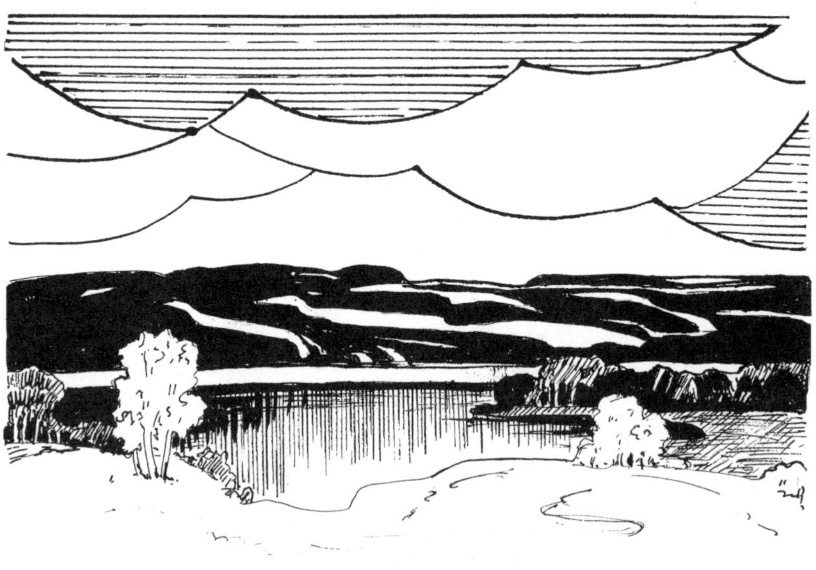

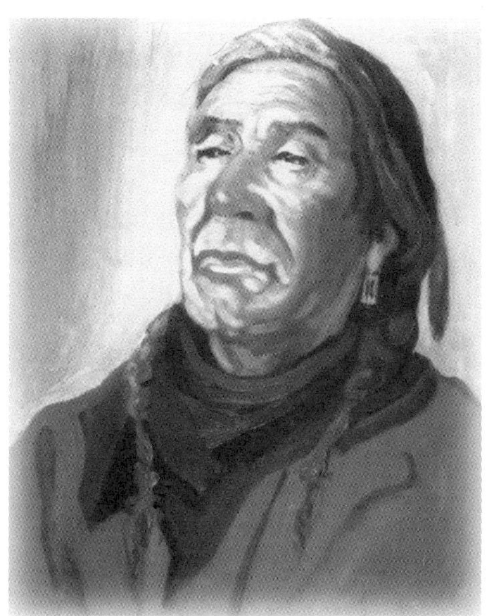

Chief Ben Pasqua

Ben Pasqua was the tall and burly chief of the Saulteaux on a reserve in the beautiful Qu'Appelle Valley of Saskatchewan. His little frame house nestled at the foot of the rolling hills which stretch for countless miles across the prairies of this region.

I had often heard of Ben and of his uncompromising, proud manner and his independence of spirit. He was the son of the famous Chief Pasqua who was one of the signatories of the Indian Treaty at Fort Qu'Appelle in 1874.

Ben's father was the first of the major chiefs in that locality to become a Christian. He, with his entire family, were baptized into the Roman Catholic Church by the revered Father Joseph Hugonard, who for more than forty years was principal of the Indian school at Lebret, Saskatchewan.

Ben succeeded his father as chief and was known as a man with progressive ideas who was eager to assist government plans for the betterment of his people.

In the early days the Indians, more restless and nomadic than they later became, were often on the move across the prairie.

They often camped near the city of Moose Jaw. When their supplies ran low Ben would visit one of the town's bakeshops for a
handout. Suddenly appearing at the door, he would demand, not
ask for, bread, and strangely enough, he was never either rebuked
or denied.

Possibly he felt that the white man had deprived his people,
not only of their land, but also of their means of livelihood with
the obliteration of the buffalo and, therefore, had a moral obliga-
tion to sustain them when necessary. So when he demanded
bread I expect he thought he was merely claiming a right.

I tried to paint him once at the Regina Fair but the lure of the
midway was too strong to permit him to loiter more than a few
moments and I was obliged to forego the attempt. Finally I went
to the reserve with the Indian agent who intervened on my behalf,
telling Ben that I wanted to paint "all the most famous chiefs" but
that bit of cajolery did not mean a thing to old Ben. He was quite
unmoved and in no way flattered as we hoped he would be.

After unsuccessfully trying several times to arrange a casual
and tactful meeting, we eventually drove to his home, hoping to
"beard the lion" in his den. Unfortunately Ben was not there. He
was "somewhere" on the prairie, we were told by neighbours and
"might be back after awhile." With this sparse and nebulous
information we had to be content.

Glittering autumn sunshine had set the foliage on fire with
colour and the crisp, cool air was a joy to inhale. We wandered
about to put in the time as we waited.

After what seemed an interminable period, Ben appeared and
I could plainly see that he was in no very acquiescent mood. It
was painfully evident that he had no use for white women who
packed curious little boxes of paint about the prairie and had
nothing better to do than paint Indians. This was not his idea of
a woman's place in the scheme of things.

Out of deference to the agent, however, he condescended to
sit for a short time, with his imperious head thrown back in reluctant silence. He sat stolidly, gazing through the window of his
tiny kitchen at the broad, sunlit valley.

It did not take much perspicacity to divine that he was sitting
on sufferance only and I had the uneasy feeling that he might bolt

at any moment, so I worked with all the speed of which I was capable.

After about thirty minutes of almost frantic brushing I noticed signs of impatience and Ben said that he must be getting back to his horses. He hitched his trousers and rose to go, but I begged him to remain a little longer. With a surly grunt he settled back again for another brief spell.

I toiled as long as his submission lasted, getting what I could—and grateful for that! When he got up a few moments later I knew that it would be futile to plead with him further though my work was incomplete. With an irritable yank at his trousers, he grabbed his ten-gallon hat and made for the door. "I got work to do," he muttered as he walked away, not even deigning to look at my canvas.

Ben was a man of magnificent stature, well over six feet in height, broad-shouldered and well-knit. He acted as though conscious of his chieftainship, having the air of one who is born to command. While he was most impressive in his bearing, he seemed to lack the kindliness and good humour that I so often found among his people.

But for all his gruff, bristling appearance, Ben must have had a vulnerable spot somewhere beneath the veneer of his rough manner. When it came to dealing with "the opposite sex" he must have had a perfectly devastating way with the ladies of his tribe, for, if rumour was correct, it was his fifth wife who sat nearby, observing with placid but smiling indifference while I strove desperately to capture the features of her unwilling spouse. What the fate of her predecessors had been I was not able to discover. In any case, the reasons left no shadow on her calm brow, for she had a sweet expression which argued well for old Ben's felicity—all rumours to the contrary notwithstanding.

Under the circumstances it was something of a relief to gaze upon this smiling and attractive woman and suddenly I felt that I would like to paint her also, if she were willing.

Surmising what I wanted, she brought out her best red shawl and some heavy black beads to hang around her neck. She was as patient and obliging as Ben had been restless and irritable, making ample compensation for the strain I had endured painting

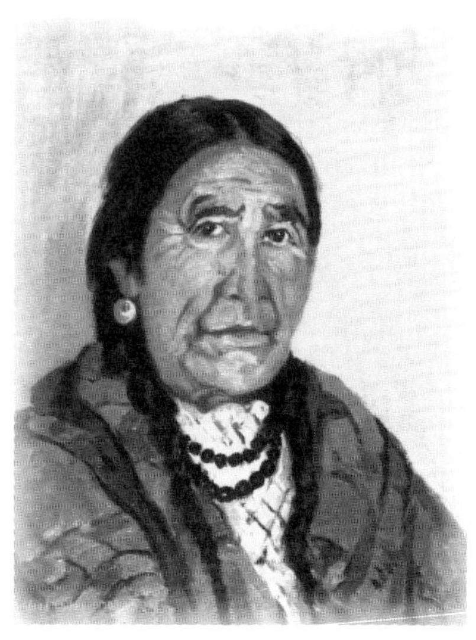

Chief Ben Pasqua's Fifth Wife ▸ *page 116*

him. Not a word of English could she speak but we got along very well and I thought her one of the most pleasant women I had met on the prairies.

A young neighbour came in with a little child and became an interested spectator of the proceedings. The baby was a beady-eyed little chap with a jolly grin on his smooth, brown face. He looked healthy and very clean. The mother told me that there were few Indian babies alive on the reserve under one year of age. When I asked the reason she said that an epidemic of whooping cough had been raging that fall which had been fatal to all very young children. The agent said that this was true, as the mothers did not know how to care for their babies in such an emergency and the mortality rate had been dreadful. He had witnessed a most pathetic incident in this connection on another reserve. A little child, who was greatly loved by many relatives, had died and their grief was overwhelming. They had made a shallow grave and buried the baby not far from where the agent was staying. Thereafter, morning after morning for many days, the relatives had come at sunrise to walk with averted heads and melancholy incantations toward the hallowed spot. Their wailing had been most pitiful and, upon leaving, they did not turn about but, with heads still bowed, backed away toward their homes.

Though he had witnessed many interesting ceremonies among the Indians, he said few things had touched his heart as this had done.

It was while painting such portraits as that of Ben Pasqua and his pretty wife that I stumbled upon many fascinating legends, customs and ceremonies of this rapidly changing breed.

The Stoney Indians

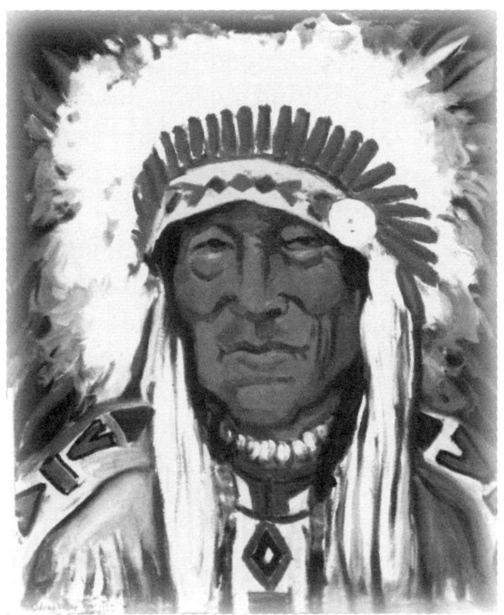

Chief David Bear's Paw

People have often asked me if I have ever had any trouble getting the Indians to sit for me. As a general rule, no. I have found them most courteous and obliging and it is indeed seldom that I have been turned away in disappointment. Many of the older people are superstitious about the camera, but when it comes to having their portraits painted they are usually curious, interested, indifferent or sometimes frankly flattered.

Indians are very shrewd and it does not take them all day to measure your intentions. If you are patronizing or superior in your attitude they know it immediately and you will not get far with them.

They are exceedingly psychic by nature and sense many things much more quickly than others. This, I think, is because they live close to nature and to the spiritual world and because of this they are acutely intuitive. They have not bartered their souls for so-called progress and the doubtful assets of commercial life. Hence they seem to be alive to the prompting of an inner spiritual voice.

If you go to them with an open mind, recognizing their talents and traditions, you will find a warm quick response coupled with a willingness to co-operate. There have been only three portraits that I wanted to paint that I did not succeed in obtaining and there was a valid reason in every case.

The Indian does not expect to get something for nothing. Neither does he expect to give something for nothing, and I never dreamt of taking up his time without making some compensation. Treat him as you would like to be treated. Nothing more is needed.

Portrait artists become very perceptive of the characters of their sitters. The trouble with painting people of my own race is that one frequently observes too much. With the Indians it is different. They have nothing to hide. You take them just as they are, or leave them, and no questions will be asked, no protests made. You will never be asked to erase a wrinkle or delete a blemish. The way God made them is good enough for them and they do not attempt to improve on his plan. They ask no favours and expect no flattery. The story that life has etched on their faces is there for all to see and to record. A stirring, worthwhile story it is too, in many cases.

Take the fine, strong features of Chief David Bear's Paw, venerable head of the Stoneys, who was a great hunter and warrior sixty years or more ago. When I visited the Calgary Stampede I had been told that he was the oldest Indian of his tribe in attendance and I was eager to meet him.

The indispensable and ever-reliable corporal of the RCMP took me to his teepee and, to my great joy, he was perfectly willing that I should paint him. He was sitting cross-legged by his fire and preferred that I work inside as he was over eighty years of age and not as vigorous in health as he used to be. He put a circlet of bears' claws around his neck, adjusted his beautiful headdress and buckskin shirt, and settled himself comfortably on a fur rug before me and filled a much-used pipe upon which he puffed contentedly from time to time.

Chief Bear's Paw could not speak very good English and I knew even less of his tongue, but we conversed in the language of the heart and somehow got along very well. He came from the reserve at Morely, which is between Calgary and Banff, and appeared to derive such enjoyment from the stampede that I asked him if he travelled from home very often.

"Just to hunt," he replied.

"Hunt what?" I asked, revealing my abysmal ignorance.

"Hunt bear," he answered and smiled as he reminisced. "Hunt bear in mountains."

I wanted to know what he did with the bear when he got it. He answered me with a broad grin, in which I read both tolerance and pity.

"Eat bear, bear meat good meat, yes, good meat." I was in no position to contradict him, so I suppose it is true.

As I continued with my work, the chief's wife, Peggy, crawled about the rugs and quilts making the place tidy. Occasionally she replenished the fire in the centre of the tepee over which some meat was cooking in an iron pot suspended from a tripod of branches. Thin, blue smoke curled up gracefully to the vents at the top of the tepee. The scene was one of comfort and colour.

She seemed unconscious of my presence or at any rate, she considered me harmless for soon she began to sing in her native tongue some of the tribal songs and chants. Though she was no longer young, her voice was pure and sweet and I felt that I had been privileged to hear something of unique interest and beauty. Very ardently I wished that I was able to document what she was singing, or that I could record, in musical script, the pensive notes of her song.

While I was in the midst of my pleasant project we were rudely interrupted by the most obnoxious individual imaginable. He was a short, dark, fat little fellow who blew in with a boisterous, patronizing air and a manner of unspeakable vulgarity. I can tolerate flies, mosquitoes, snakes and fleas as well as a wide

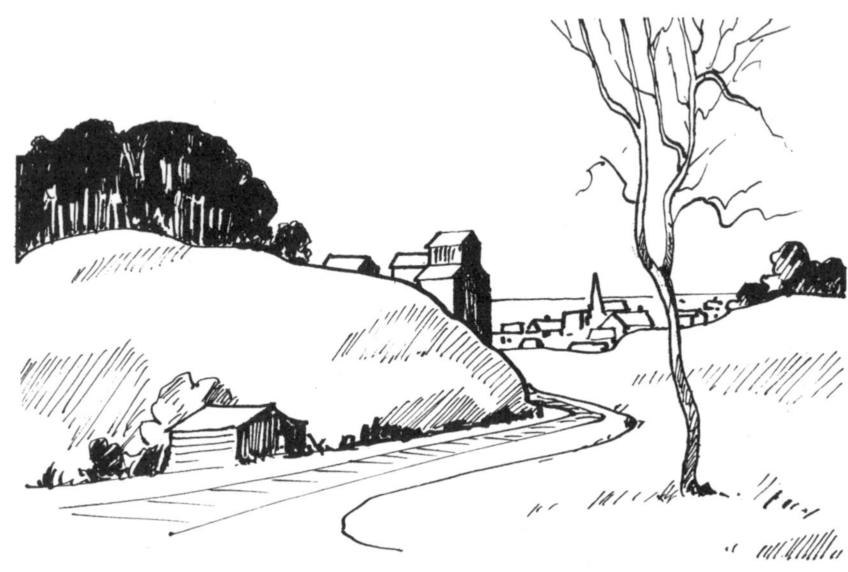

assortment of disagreeable sounds and odours, but I find the manners of some of my own race hard to take.

This particular pest was a publicity man from over the border who, for some mysterious reason, had evidently been in Calgary previously with a large quantity of beads which he had bartered with good effect to curry favour with the Indians. He seemed to be totally oblivious of the fact that he was rudely interfering with my legitimate business.

The chief's son and his grandson, a dear little fellow of about three, were also in the tepee and the repugnant little intruder conversed with them loudly and incessantly. I should more accurately say that he spoke "at them" for they never had a chance to utter a word, and with natural Indian politeness, did not attempt to do so.

He grabbed the tiny lad and bounced him about, finally making him cry and then laughed triumphantly about his achievement. After submitting to this insufferable annoyance for some time, I was at long last compelled to ask him bluntly to leave and not to obstruct my work any longer as I was paying the chief for the sitting. Only then did he depart and peace and quiet were once more restored under the gaily painted canvas of the tepee.

When I finished the portrait I showed it to the chief. He studied it long and earnestly before making a comment. I could see that he was pleased with my effort. His wife signified her approval with a silent smile.

Later that summer I happened to be on a coastal steam ship returning to Vancouver from Powell River, BC. There were many people onboard who had taken advantage of the lovely weather and spectacular scenery for a day's cruise. Countless happy voices blended in a rather pleasant monotone through the strains of a dance-orchestra. Half-consciously I heard a radio above the hum around me. Suddenly a familiar name caught my ear "Bear's Paw!" Yes, the announcer was talking about the old Stoney chief! It was the day on which the late Duke of Kent visited Banff and, in recalling the events of interest, the announcer said "His Royal Highness met and conversed with the aged Stoney chief, David Bear's Paw and listened attentively when the chief told him that he had seen his brother, the King, at Calgary in 1939. The Duke had been impressed with the beautiful beadwork on the Indians who were on hand to greet him."

The Indians, for their part, take great interest in these occasions when they are recognized as valued and honoured participants in the colourful diorama which such events are able to present to visiting celebrities. At such times, we can readily see how much the pageantry and traditions of the Indians contribute to Canadian identity and culture and how drab it would be without them!

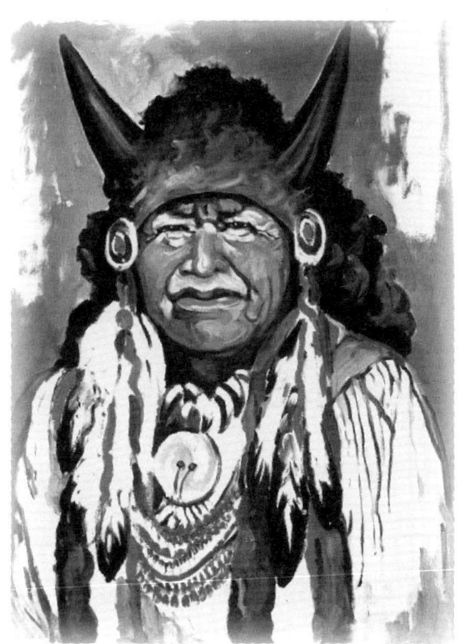

Chief Walking Buffalo

In popular imagination the Indian is regarded as a man of brave deeds but few words. Yet there have been those among them who, when aroused, could soar to heights of superb oratorical eloquence. Some, indeed, were born orators.

One has but to recall the history of Tecumseh, Joseph Brant and Chief Crowfoot to realize that, when moved to express himself on matters that vitally concern his tribe, the Indian does not lack for appropriate words nor for the emotional power to expound his views. He is not given to superficial verbosity, but speaks in clear, concise language, accompanied by immense dignity of bearing and natural gestures. His eloquence comes from the heart and should not be judged by the standards of academic criteria.

George MacLean of the Stoney Tribe was one who had that natural gift to an unusual degree. Providence had not been over-generous to him in the matter of physiognomy. In fact it had been somewhat chary, but it made ample compensation by the bestowal of a ready flow of language. He told me that for twenty-five years he had borne the proud title of Chief Walking Buffalo, but he did not disclose why he became just plain George MacLean. His Indian name was Tatanka-Mani.

The memory of those years must have been exceedingly precious to him and I am sure he was able, without much effort, to recapture some of their glory when he donned the strange and wonderful buffalo skin headgear from which he had derived his name.

The buffalo occupied a prominent place in Indian legends and was an object of more than ordinary veneration, especially among the prairie tribes to whom it was food, fuel and raiment. What the cedar tree was to the British Columbia coastal tribes, the buffalo was to the Indians of the plains. Their whole order of life centred around it. Its skin, worn in a headdress, was believed to possess inherent virtues and it was believed to endow its wearer with wisdom and power.

Chief Walking Buffalo took special pride in his peculiar apparel and walked proudly at the head of every procession of his tribe. His own physique was rather "buffaloesque" in character. He had a large head, huge, burly shoulders and seemed to taper off in distant parts!

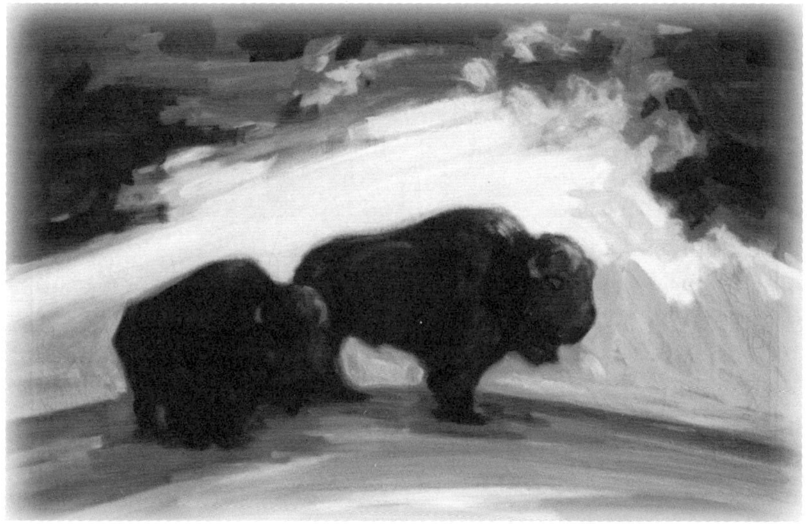

Buffalo on the Plains

▶ *page 135*

Only upon one other Indian have I observed a buffalo headdress such as his. That belonged to a Sioux from the United States who was quite the handsomest Indian I have ever seen, very tall, of magnificent physique and with a face that the gods might envy. I saw him first in the Calgary Stampede parade and sought out his tepee at the earliest opportunity inasmuch as I would have staked anything to paint him. At first he gave partial consent. It was 9:30 in the morning and he indicated, in a rather hazy sort of way, that he would sit for me at 10:00, then went inside his tepee, calmly sat down and commenced to smoke.

To me there was no apparent reason under the sun why he could not have allowed me to paint him there and then, unless it was because he wanted to keep me on tenterhooks and enjoy my discomfiture. I knew better than to argue, however, and was on the spot punctually at 10:00 A.M. when he informed me he was not ready yet. Another half hour went by and I again made my humble presence known. Still he was not ready, but muttered what sounded like "11:30." Very patiently and hopefully I hung around, but when the fateful hour arrived he was still sitting cross-legged in his tepee and still smoking his pipe.

To my query he announced with the utmost finality, "Me not come." So that was that and there was not a thing I could do about it.

For many long years I have retained remorseful visions of the portrait that I almost painted—which would have been the "Beau Brummell" of the lot, so it can readily be understood that I was thrilled when I encountered another Indian wearing a similar headdress and costume. Chief Walking Buffalo had none of the big Sioux's prepossessing attributes but he had the same kind of headdress and that was something!

When he strolled into the Royal Canadian Mounted Police headquarters where I made my wishes known to him, George was very non-committal at first. It was just not compatible with his dignity to be considered an easy conquest. I engaged him in conversation and when he saw that my interest was genuine he began to warm up a little. I spoke of several things pertaining to my work among the Indians and then the floodgates opened wide. George had a very large mouth and when he burst into oratory it animated his face. He stood, with his hands in his pockets and his stout shoulders thrown back, and bespoke a torrent of philosophy.

He was nobody's fool, this man with the ready tongue and flashing eyes. He had been about a good deal and considered himself a "man of the world." I was impressed by his sincerity, logic and sound sense.

He kept me in suspense for several days before he finally consented to allow me to paint his portrait. First he said he was sick, then he had business to attend, and then he "expected company." When he ran out of excuses he decided to submit to the inevitable and told me to come to his tepee at a certain hour. His buxom wife greeted me, smilingly though silently, and while I prepared my paints George prepared himself for the ordeal.

He opened a huge trunk which was full of beadwork. His wife got down on her knees and they both began throwing things about, right and left. Of course, his regalia was at the very bottom and before they reached it there was buckskin, beadwork and feathers all over the place. I commented on the great beauty of some of the designs and George said, "Hundreds and hundreds of dollars worth in trunk." I asked him if he ever sold any. "Mostly at Banff," he replied.

Chief Walking Buffalo was an astute business man. Because of his unusual headdress many people wanted to photograph him wearing it. He hung around where the crowds at the Calgary Stampede were thickest and would pose at twenty-five cents a snap and there were many takers.

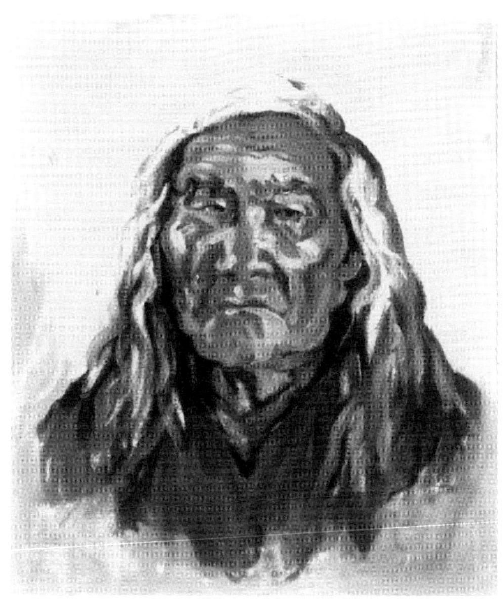

William Hunter or Yellow Bear

William and Joshua Hunter or Yellow Bear and Spotted Eagle

You ought to paint our famous Stoney twins, old William and Joshua Hunter or, in other words, Yellow Bear and Spotted Eagle. They are in their ninety-fourth year."

It was Mr. Iredale, agent on the reserve at Morely, Alberta, who gave me this exciting suggestion. We were in the office of RCMP Inspector Schmidt at Calgary.

"Indian twins and ninety-four!" I exclaimed, "Of course I want to paint them! When is the best time to do it?"

"Be sure to come on a Thursday," I was informed. "That is ration day when they always come in for supplies if the weather is fine. If it is stormy they get some of their friends to fetch the supplies for them, as they live quite a distance from the Agency."

After painting a number of portraits in Alberta and Saskatchewan I returned to Calgary, planning to paint the twins on a certain Thursday on my way back to Vancouver where I was now living. Again I appealed to Inspector Schmidt, who had

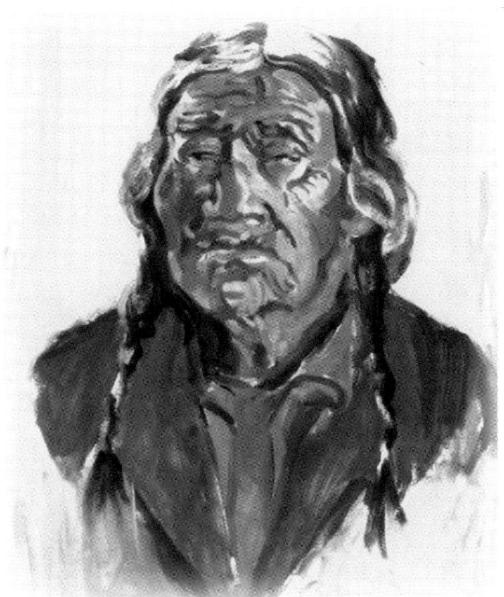

Joshua Hunter or Spotted Eagle

already assisted me very generously. I told him that I wanted to go to Morely, paint the old twins and return the same day.

"Oh, you can't do that," he said. "The evening train does not stop there."

I must have looked very crestfallen for, after some hard thinking, he exclaimed, "I have it! The doctor from Sarcee goes to the hospital at Morely every Thursday. You can go and come back with him."

He called Dr. Murray who was both Indian agent and doctor at Sarcee on the phone and asked him to pick me up at the CPR station at nine o'clock.

I awoke on Thursday morning to the steady patter of rain on the roof. Why the gods, who had blessed me so abundantly with fine weather on the rest of my trip, should choose this particular day for a deluge, I could not imagine. Ruefully I recalled Mr. Iredale's warning that the old twins did not come in for rations in bad weather but instantly I dismissed the perilous thought. I would go to Morely anyway and somehow I would paint the twins.

When Doctor Murray and I reached the Agency Mr. Iredale pointed to the ration house a short distance away. "There are a

71

few Indians around," he said, "but I doubt if the old twins are among them. We shall go and see."

His assistant was handing out supplies when we arrived. "Oh, there's William," said Mr. Iredale, pointing. I beheld a man of rather less than medium height, clad in ordinary clothing except for his hat. That was a faded sun helmet of the Woolworth variety. Its wide brim provided an excellent run-off for the rain which fell in glittering droplets all around his shoulders.

With the Indian's inbred love of decoration, William had draped the fur of a small animal around the helmet so that it hung down the back in two long pennants whilst a shorter piece swung jauntily from the middle of the crown.

Approaching William, Mr. Iredale asked, "Where is Joshua?"

"Oh, Joshua, he no come," was the answer.

"Well," I said, "I shall paint William anyway, if he will allow me to do so."

William consented and was ready for the ordeal at once, but Mr. Iredale was not satisfied. "It's too bad," he said, "to have come so far and not get them both." He then intimated that he thought, for a consideration, one of the young men might go after Joshua and bring him in.

Joyfully I took the hint, delved into my purse, and in a moment I saw a strapping young fellow galloping off on his horse to Joshua's house, some seven miles away, to bring in the other half of the fascinating pair.

Meanwhile I hustled William along to the agent's office. I must not lose a moment, as Dr. Murray had warned me that he must be back in Calgary before the banks closed at three o'clock. Hoping for the best, I began at once on William. He looked at me apologetically, saying, "I did not comb my hair this morning."

Then, thinking that it might remedy matters somewhat, he commenced unbraiding his grey locks and shook them out over his shoulders. I always like to paint the Indians the way they want to be painted, so I did not ask him to braid his hair up again.

In the midst of my work, Mr. Iredale looked in to say that I was to go to the hospital for lunch with Dr. Murray and the nurses, and that William would be a welcome guest in the kitchen. I was loath to take the precious time for this interlude and would have much preferred going without lunch if it meant finishing my work, but courtesy demanded that I accept the hospitality offered. I enjoyed the lunch and was much impressed when the head nurse showed me over the hospital. It was beautifully appointed, clean and well-equipped and the view from its windows, looking toward the mountains, was glorious.

Soon I was back in the office working on William again, and just as I put the finishing touches on the canvas, up rode my young Indian emissary with old Joshua in tow. Thrilled beyond measure and hoping against hope that Dr. Murray would not show up too soon, I began my second portrait.

Joshua made no excuse for his hair. I could just take him as he was which I was glad to do. He sat placidly in the warm room with William quietly looking on. We were a silent trio and I worked intently. As the painting neared completion, Mr. Iredale came in with an interpreter, Dan Wildman, a very fine-looking Stoney Indian who was well known to visitors at the Calgary Stampede.

By an act of mercy, which I considered nothing less than providential, a very sick Indian woman had been brought into the hospital, so the good doctor had to remain to administer to her the rest of the afternoon, thus enabling me to finish my work in peace and without undue haste.

The rain was still coming down heavily. It was cold and miserable outside but warm and comfortable within. The two old men responded to the genial atmosphere and were eager to talk as an excuse to remain in such cozy quarters. For nearly two hours Dan plied them with questions in their own language, while I wrote furiously to record what he told me.

William was the most talkative, but occasionally old Joshua would check him up or break in with a word or two. Then they would look at each other squarely, confer earnestly, and presently William would be off again. Joshua managed to get in a few words quite frequently, however, so William was not permitted an entire monopoly on the conversation.

While they talked they used sign language freely and I was fascinated to watch the swift, graceful movement of their dark, knotted little hands. I wrote down verbatim Dan William's translation of the conversation and I give it to you, word for word, knowing that it would lose much colour and character if I put it into conventional language.

"William told of a buffalo being rounded up by an old man. It turned and charged and caught him on its horns in the pit of the stomach, and threw him high in the air, then caught him again the second time in the back and tore his body open. The man's lungs and organs came out of his side, and that night towards morning, the man was dead.

"When the man's wife saw the buffalo killing her husband, she wanted to get killed herself, and she attacked the buffalo, which meant sure death for her. She rushed in with an axe, making a full charge, because she was so furious about what the buffalo had done to her husband. She hacked the cords of the buffalo's hind legs and it collapsed, and she cut it all to pieces, she was so angry. William believed that if the buffalo was still alive and had the cords of its hind legs cut, it would fall and not be able to charge."

After a short pause, Dan continued translating: "Broken Leg was the name of a very old man, they remembered, who hid in a badger hole to attack the buffalo. The smallest herd in those days would have from one to three hundred animals in it and the largest up to ninety thousand or more.

"The Indians used to lie down with their ear to a badger hole to hear the echo of the buffalo's hooves many miles away, like a radio. They could tell exactly how far away they were, from which direction they were coming, how fast they were travelling and how many there were in the herd."

Another anecdote followed: "William was in New York over forty years ago in 1899. The Indian agent got a letter from people in New York who wanted every tribe represented there at a big exposition. He was the only Stoney to go. He was in full costume with red flannel leggings, a coat with lots of beadwork and a fringe of weasel skins. He wore an old timer's hat and put two eagle feathers on the back. He appeared before the public twice to imitate the call of the moose. He called and called, demonstrating as he talked and everybody was pleased. Next he was asked to imitate a grizzly when it was angry. He took a horn that he had made of birch bark and did his best and everybody was pleased. He was well looked after on this trip but the huge city and its strange sights frightened him and he wanted to go home.

"When they were boys they were very hard up. A Cree tribe was nearby, and they came at night and stole their dogs and took them away and ate them. Often they had to eat their own dogs when they were hungry, but they never did this unless they had to.

"At this point I asked if they ever had their horses stolen. They thought I asked if they ever stole horses, and rebuked me solemnly by saying that the Stoneys were good, religious people and never stole anything.

Dan continued: "Once they sliced the hide of a bull moose with hair on it, intending to make a shaganappi with it. They oiled it with grease to make it soft to tie on their wrists, but then they grew so hungry that they had to boil the shaganappi a long time and eat it for they could get no other food.

"In the old days they ate just plain buffalo meat and drank only water. Sometimes they had fish and berries.

"Long ago the Indians wore buckskin clothing. Only "clever," independent Indians wore white man's clothing. Nowadays they can wear any clothing they wish and feel safe, but when a person has nothing to eat and is awful cold, it's terrible what hardships they endured."

This statement seemed somewhat convoluted but I think it made sense. "Often they would have to wade through ice and the cold water trying to get food and their clothes would be frozen on their backs. Many times they had nothing to eat and but little to wear. Now they have flour in their home and food enough to go around. And at the present time they all have saddle horses, even the little children." To an Indian of the plains, to possess a horse is to have his dearest wish fulfilled.

"They knew the famous pioneer Methodist missionary John McDougall well, and used to go to Fort Benton, over one hundred miles away with him on horseback, for supplies.

"Long before McDougall came, they used to see groups of white men with "collars" around their chests, pulling boats on the Saskatchewan River near Rocky Mountain House." These were, undoubtedly, Voyageurs.

William sighed and began carefully to braid his hair. Asked about burial customs, he said, "For fear that wild animals would eat a body, they made a log house just big enough for it. They had no prayer service, just crying over the body, and then came away and left it there. If old or young took sick upon the trail they would not leave them, as has often been wrongly charged, not the Stoneys. They never left them to die alone, but stayed with them 'til the end.' The Stoneys are very religious and tell the truth."

Then followed an amazing tale: "Once a man told a story to his tribe that he had seen something that had more power than human [*sic*]. Asked to prove what he had seen, the next day he went out onto the plains and he came back riding a cow moose, one of the finest and most dangerous of animals. "He went out to hunt moose and he rode a cow moose home! We saw with our own eyes. We saw him travelling. sometimes he would walk slowly with the moose and around his body was light, brighter than daylight. He came across the timber ridge, riding the cow moose home. Then he tied its foot with grass and the animal made no effort to get away. Everybody saw the wonderful light. One of the braves said that when he saw the moose tied near the camp, he took his gun to shoot it for the tribe, but the shot fell to the ground and did not hurt the moose, which stood, still tied to the grass. We saw this with our own eyes."

Another legend followed: "Once man lived without woman. There were hundreds of thousands of them and one time they got lost as they were going south and they camped near a buffalo pound. The chief was a magic man and no one knew how long he had lived. He advised some of the best hunters to approach three buffalo which were sleeping on a hill. When they got near to them they saw somebody else crawling near a nearby creek intending to kill the buffalo also. They watched to see what would happen. The person took a bow and arrow and shot one of the buffalo. They noticed that the person was 'made different' from what they were, and that was how the Indians found woman and that is how things started."

I was very reluctant to say goodbye to William and Joshua when Dr. Murray finally arrived to take me back to Calgary. The painting session had turned into a fascinating diary of history and legend.

The Sarcee Indians

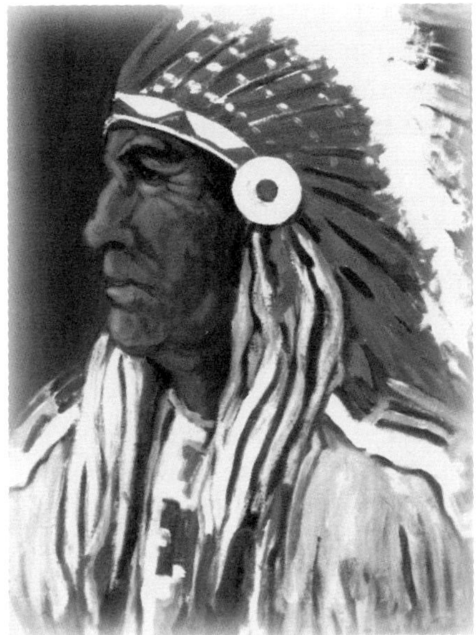

Chief Joe Big Plume

The Sarcee Indians are an offshoot of the Athapaskans who used to roam the vast area now known as the MacKenzie River Basin. Eventually they drifted out into the open prairie and linked up with the Blackfoot, with whom they have been on friendly terms for many generations, just as they have been forever the sworn enemy of the Cree, though strangely enough, they closely resemble the Crees in custom and manners.

The Sarcee is reputed to be the oldest of all the tribes of the Plains Indians. To this claim may be added the distinction of being the most audacious and haughty. They were a very warlike people and much feared by other tribes. Next to hunting and fighting they loved feasting, gambling, dancing and singing to the throbbing syncopation of the tom-tom. During the old days they took great pride in their beautiful headdresses and buffalo skin lodges.

▸ *colour plate page 124*

The Sarcee were sun worshippers but, like the Blackfoot, they could not celebrate the Sun Dance except upon the fulfillment of a woman's vow. The woman, whose purity and self-sacrifice permitted them to do this, became an object of much veneration during the remainder of her life.

Like all Indians, the Sarcee are exceedingly fond of children and exert great care in their upbringing.

They are a distinct nation and have a different language from any other tribe on the plains. It is guttural and throaty in character and, it is said, few outsiders have ever been able to master it.

Until recently (circa 1940) the Sarcees were dwindling rapidly in numbers until only about one hundred and fifty remained on the reserve near Calgary which had been ceded to them at the signing of the Indian Treaty. Largely due to better living conditions and improved medical care that lamentable state has been greatly remedied. Now there are over two hundred in the tribe and their outlook for survival is much brighter.

Their head chief was Joe Big Plume, an intelligent and capable man. It was he who some years ago performed the colourful ceremony investing Sir Charles G.D. Roberts an honourary chief of the Sarcees when the title "Na-Kee-Tlee-Se-Ah-Kee-Tcha," Chief Big-Tribe, was conferred upon him. Other notables who have been similarly honoured by the tribe were His Royal Highness, The Prince of Wales, later the Duke of Windsor and Sir John Martin Harvey.

Big Plume had a manner which fairly impressed all who beheld him. Tall, sturdy, handsome, self-assertive and confident, he would attract attention anywhere. I caught a glimpse of him one morning at the Calgary Stampede and could not rest until I had captured him on canvas. This was not the easiest thing in the world to do, as you might imagine. People like Big Plume, I was warned, must be approached with the greatest discretion. It is not a simple matter of asking a frank question and getting a definite answer. No, indeed. One requires the diplomacy of a politician, the patience of Job and the negotiating skills of a barrister.

A Royal Canadian Mounted Police constable conducted me to his tepee, but Big Plume was nowhere to be found. No doubt he was trying his luck on the midway, but it was hopeless looking for him there. As we stood discussing the matter, I noticed a tourist, unmistakably American, staring at the Mountie with an eager look in his eyes. He was a good-looking, middle-aged man with several cameras festooned about his neck. Approaching us he said to me, "I have taken thirty films of the Indians but that is what I really want," dropping his voice and pointing at the resplendent figure of the RCMP constable in a tone replete with admiration and awe.

"Well that is easy to get," I said. "Step up, constable, and take your place among the immortals." With a smile he acquiesced and the delighted American began to snap away. For several days he had been longing to photograph a Mountie and had hung around the encampment in awestruck hesitation, fearing to ask such a great favour. Such is the name and fame of the Mounties!

Returning to the Sarcee camp later on, we found Big Plume at home. I had been told that he was the most important man of his tribe, so I judged he was the one to paint, if possible. Hitherto I had found most Indians very obliging and affable, and recalling the warning, I hoped Big Plume would be the same. I was soon to adjust my views on the subject. When he emerged from his tepee I could read pride and condescension written all over his face. Meekly I stated my mission. At once he wanted to know how much I would pay him. He was inclined to haggle about the matter and wanted to know what was wrong with artists who did not have much money. That, alas, is one of the great unsolved mysteries of the ages and I was unable to enlighten him. He thought that an hour of his valuable time was worth at least five dollars. I quickly assured him that it was not worth that much to me and, as I turned to go, he grudgingly said that he would sit the next morning. I did not feel at all certain about this, in spite of his promise, so I made sure of being there the next morning promptly at the hour designated. Sure enough, he was there. Acting as though he was insufferably bored, he accompanied me, with an air of vast indifference, to what I guilelessly thought was a secluded corner of the encampment.

Big Plume had a very striking costume which he took care to bring along, telling me as we walked, what a hard time he had to provide for his large family of seven children, a problem which is not by any means peculiar to the Indians.

Once the chief got settled at the chosen location, he put on his good humour along with his beaded coat and fine headdress. He was now full of jokes and gay banter and I felt that he was secretly laughing at me for my efforts. As he spoke excellent English we had no difficulty in conversing.

My secluded outdoor studio soon became less secluded. An Indian man in his early twenties soon stretched out on the grass beside me and showed a most intelligent interest in what I was doing. He stayed right there, without shifting position, until I had finished.

I talked to Big Plume as I worked and it was not long before other curious folk converged on us like a swarm of bees to a honey pot. I was delighted with the effect this had on the chief. With imperial dignity he waved them off in no uncertain manner. Swinging his husky arm in a gesture of dismissal, he roared, "Get out of here, all you people! This is no free show! I am being paid to do this. Get out, I tell you!" They went in a hurry, to my intense satisfaction and amusement but, alas only to make room for fresh contingents who were likewise sent on their way as soon as they assembled. I had been longing to say the very thing that Big Plume was saying, but did not have his imperious courage. He was not hampered by the conventions into which I had been born, so deigned to be absolutely forthright about the matter.

A couple of women came by and wanted to take a snapshot. "It will cost you a quarter," he told them. Not only did they pay his price cheerfully, but they came back later and presented him with a bottle of ginger ale and a fat cigar. He accepted the gifts as though he were doing them a great favour and sat waiting for more.

All in all, we had a very active and rather exhausting session, the chief and I, and it was with a sigh of relief that I paid him and turned to go.

As I departed, I saw a very old Indian sitting in the sunshine by one of the tepees and thought that he looked interesting. Since he could not understand a word of English I had to find an inter-

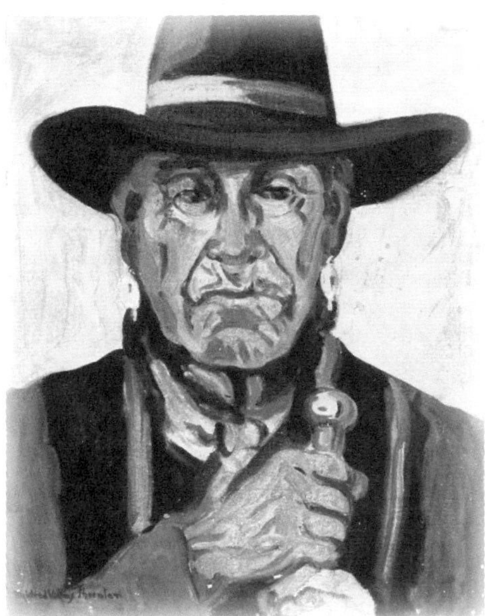

Pretty Young Man ▸ *page 125*

preter who told me that he was the oldest Indian in the Sarcee camp. Nearly ninety years had passed his weary brow and now he just sat and dreamt of the past.

I thought his name ill-chosen. "Pretty Young Man" did not fit this patriarch who was no longer young and certainly had never been pretty. He was gentle in manner and obliging, however, and a very unusual character. I was delighted to add his countenance to my collection. I also painted a portrait of "Turning Rope," another Sarcee who would never take a prize in a beauty contest.

I did not paint as many members of this tribe as I had intended. Their attitude seemed somewhat aloof compared to the others and I soon discovered the reason. They were possessed of a pronounced superiority complex. When I returned there again the next day a very ugly looking fellow ordered me off the premises, saying that he did not want his people painted. I tried to mollify him and to assure him that my intentions were strictly honourable, but my protests fell on deaf ears.

Hearing the commotion, Big Plume appeared and seemed to catch some of the other man's ill will. He told me that he and his tribe were "high class" and that all the other Indians were "low class" and "just no account at all." I think that I would have stood high with him if I had scorned the others and only painted Sarcees, but he discovered that I had also painted some of the Stoneys and Blackfoot, and that was a blow to his vanity.

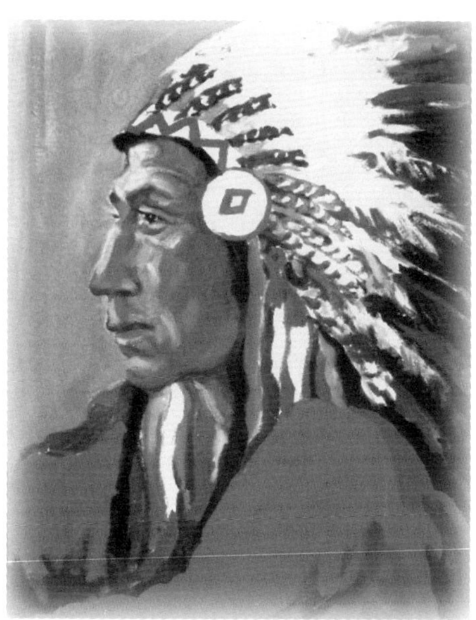

George Big Belly

It was his scarlet shirt that first attracted me, that and his long, regular features. He was tall too, and handsome as he stood grooming his horse against the dazzling white canvas of his tepee.

"Are you Blackfoot?" I inquired.

"No, I am from the Sarcee Reserve."

"Then I have painted your chief," I said, "and would like to paint you. What is your name?"

"George Big Belly," he replied as he carefully brushed his horse's mane.

I looked him up and down with renewed interest and inspected his circumference with a critical eye. Nothing was there to suggest why he had been so tagged. Indian names are supposed to mean something and are always given for a specific reason. Big Belly certainly did not apply to a man who was tall and slim, and I was puzzled to account for it, but dismissed the matter by concluding that he probably looked more corpulent when he was named in the first place. It was a good name anyway and robbed him not one whit of his native dignity and stature.

George was a man after my own heart who did not waste precious time angling for favours. He said he would sit for me and was prepared to do so at once. Going into the nearest tepee, he donned a beautiful headdress of eagle feathers with beaded band and calmly sat down on a blanket that lay on the ground.

I dropped down a few feet from him, propped my canvas against a pile of saddles and harness, and went straight to work. We were alone in the tepee and I was laying the paint on thick and fast when suddenly a shadow darkened the opening and a big, stoutish man came bustling in like a miniature cyclone. It was Chief Joe Big Plume, just returned from the Stampede parade.

"Hello there, Chief. I didn't know this was your tepee," I apologized, feeling as though I had been caught red-handed in a neighbour's house.

"Oh, that's all right," he boomed, "Keep right on working, you can paint here."

He stood straight and tall, towering above me, and no one could be more resplendent than the chief in his gorgeous native costume.

The July sun was very hot and little trickles of perspiration wriggled down his cheeks. He pulled off his headdress with a flourish and flung it on the floor, then he unfastened his beaded belt and laid it beside the headdress. Next he bent over with a grunt and began pulling his buckskin shirt over his head. These are snug-fitting garments and the chief had to give it a few vigorous yanks before he got it off. He put it with the other discarded apparel. He then removed his moccasins, unfastened his buckskin trousers, pushed them down and stepped out of them. These, too, were added to the rapidly growing pile on the floor.

Big Plume then stood beside me, big and bulging in his underwear, which I noticed were covered with many neat patches and were spotlessly clean. Gasping with the heat, he bent over me again and from the corner of my eye I saw him grab the tail of his undershirt and pull it over his head. I accelerated my painting and kept studiously to my work.

When Big Plume's undershirt came off there was revealed another one under it, equally patched and clean. A quick glance and I saw him unbutton his drawers, preparatory to removing them also. "This is no place for a lady," I thought wildly, and commenced to gather up my things for a hasty retreat.

"That's all right," the chief assured me, "Go right on with your work. It's all right, I tell you."

As he spoke his drawers came down, and there, sure enough, was another pair right under them. With a sigh of relief I settled back to finish my portrait. Once more the burly fellow bent over and off came the undershirt.

By this time I was beginning to understand why he had perspired so freely. He yawned and stretched and began to divest himself of the second pair of drawers. I made another move to go but he stopped me again, "Don't be scared. It's all right, finish your work, it's all right." I was assured.

At that point I fell back on my philosophy of non-interference and picked up my brushes, grimly resolved to finish my painting, come what might.

I did not know for sure whether there were any more layers yet to come off or whether the chief intended going right down to hard pan, but I was determined to see my mission through to the finish.

Big Plume went over to an old suitcase and extracted a coloured shirt and a pair of khaki overalls. He got into these with considerable satisfaction, reached for his pipe, and sank to the floor with a sigh of great contentment.

Meanwhile, George Big Belly just sat there, clasping his knees and gazing straight ahead of him as though he were in a Sunday school class, completely indifferent to the little comedy transpiring right under his nose.

Big Plume and I conversed serenely until I finished the portrait. Then he bid me a polite adieu and wished me well. I staggered over to the Mounted Police headquarters, dragging my equipment in one hand and my wet canvas in the other, feeling triumphant but greatly in need of an hour's repose and relaxation.

The Sioux Indians

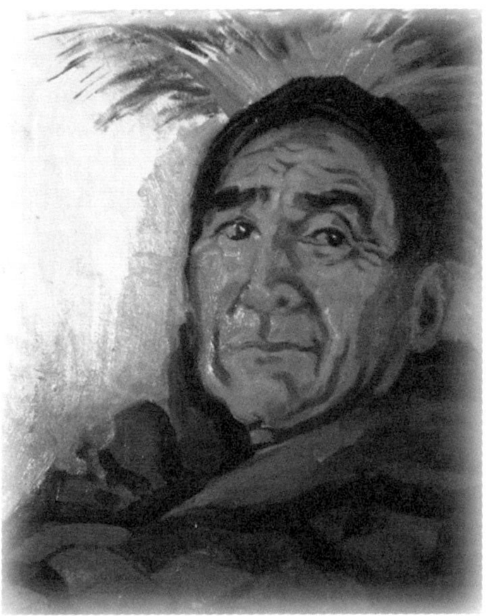

Chief Julius Buffalo

Everyone who is familiar with the history of the West has heard of Sitting Bull, warrior chief and medicine man of the Sioux Indians. After the Custer massacre the Sioux fled from the United States to the safety of Canada and there they remained for a long time, a source of embarrassment to the authorities of both countries.

Their leader, Sitting Bull, claimed that his ancestors had lived in British territory and that they had never forsaken their loyalty to Britain. As evidence of this, some of them had medals in their possession bearing the likeness of George III, which had been presented to them for their allegiance to the British Crown. Though it was a great relief to the Canadian government when Sitting Bull and his followers eventually became repatriated, it was a sad day for the indomitable old chief. Disappointment and

▸ *colour plate page 129*

further conflict awaited him, but there was one bright interlude in store for him with his association with Buffalo Bill's Wild West Show. In the end he was treacherously and brutally done to death even as he had feared.

Quite a number of Sioux remained in Canada and they are considered among the most intelligent and industrious of their race. Many settled in Manitoba while the Amdo-Wapuskiyapi Clan were allotted large reserves of land by the Canadian government where they have lived happily and peacefully ever since. The Sisseton Sioux pitched their lodges near Fort Qu'Appelle, Saskatchewan. Naturally they were not Treaty Indians, but eventually, in recognition of their good behaviour, the band that settled in Saskatchewan was under the leadership of the fine old Sioux chief, Standing Buffalo. When he died he was buried on the crest of the Sioux Hill overlooking the magnificent Qu'Appelle Valley.

Julius Buffalo succeeded his father as chief and now he, too, "sleeps the long sleep that knows no waking."

Some years ago (circa 1937), when I was looking for interesting characters on the Qu'Appelle Reserve, the Indian agent drove me to the home of Julius. His house was rather small and sparsely furnished, yet it had all the essentials and was spotlessly clean.

The chief's wife was one of those solemn Indian women who are absolutely noiseless in their movements. She glided about the house like a shadow and spoke not a word. Only her smile told that we were welcome and signified her interest in what I was doing.

Julius had been painted before, so he knew what to expect. He chose his own raiment, producing a huge blanket which he swung over his shoulders with a lordly air, folded his arms and sat down with an expression of intense satisfaction which said, as plainly as if he had spoken, "Can you beat that?" I could not, so got on with my work at once.

The chief's wife and the Indian agent stood behind me, watching the countenance emerge from the canvas. Strangely enough, they did not disconcert me as many people would have done.

In answer to my query, Julius said his headdress was made of badger hair. I was consumed with curiosity as I watched him put it on. He picked up a lock of hair on the top of his head and braided it tightly with a few deft movements. Next, he adjusted the headdress to its proper position, reached down through a small opening in the top of it and pulled his little braid through. Then he picked up a small stick from the wood box and thrust it through the braid at right angles, thus holding his unique millinery securely in place.

It was a joy to paint Julius. He was warm and comfortable and had no urge to be "up and doing," so was content to sit in perfect peace until I had finished.

I had a friend who had a summer cottage at Fort Qu'Appelle. She knew Julius for many years and had a thorough understanding of the workings of his mind. She bought a great deal of beadwork from the Indians and Julius looked upon her as a trusted ally. One day he drove up to her cottage with a load of wood, which he offered as a friendly gift. Now the lady had plenty of wood, but she knew Julius. It was beneath his dignity to exact payment from a friend, yet he confidently expected that the friend would not abuse his courtesy by withholding some manner of compensation. He sat down and rested his arms upon the kitchen table. With infinite tact, my friend casually dropped a bank note near his lean, brown hands, as she discussed the weather and thanked him for his generous "gift." Julius deftly slipped the money into his trousers and said it was a joy to present his friends with anything that was in his power to give, then drove away with an empty wagon, cash in pocket and dignity intact.

The Blackfoot Indians

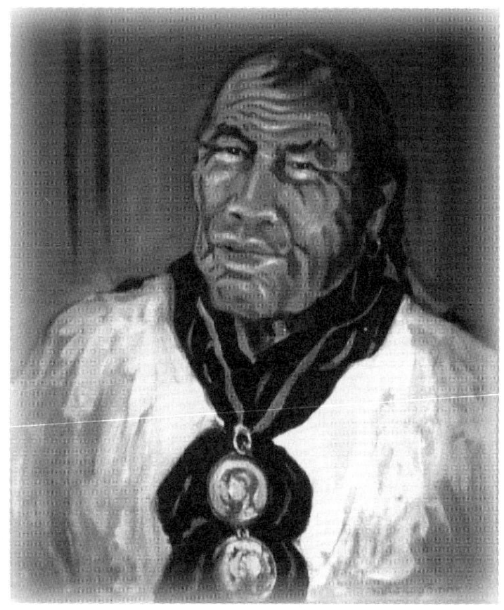

Duck Chief and His Medals

The pinnacle of the year for Alberta Indians is the Calgary Stampede. They prepare for it months in advance and live it over in memory long after it has passed.

Knowing that I should find excellent material for my brush, I was glad, when at length, I was able to attend that famous exhibition. Above everything else, the Stampede meant Indians to me, and my most fervent dreams did not exceed in colour and romantic appeal the scenes which awaited me there. Naturally, I went straight to the Indian encampment for the sole purpose of my visit was to paint as many Indians as possible in the time at my disposal.

The headquarters of the Royal Canadian Mounted Police were located protectively in front of the wide circle of tepees, and I knew from long experience that no one could be of so much assistance to me as the scarlet-coated keepers of the peace. A corporal and a young constable comprised the detachment. The building they used had been the original Mounted Police headquarters in Calgary and therefore had much historic interest.

In front of it stood an enormous, beautifully mounted, specimen of a buffalo which, the corporal told me, aroused the curiosity of many visitors, especially Americans. Some of them thought that it was alive and would not have been at all surprised to see it charge suddenly into the crowds. Inside the building were many fine robes, the soft brown fur of which had once protected the bodies of its brothers.

Almost all tourists wanted to be photographed beside the buffalo and the most enthusiastic wanted a Mountie thrown in for good measure. The burly corporal was an old hand at adapting himself to the whims of humanity, but the young constable blushed rosily every time he acceded to the tourist's wishes.

People came to the Mounted Police for everything but the moon. Women came looking for their lost children, others to ask the location of exhibits, and still others chanted advice about what to do for a headache or where was the best place to eat. The Mounties treated them all with equal good humour.

They seemed to enjoy their duties though some phases were not pleasant. One morning I arrived on the scene very early as I had been told that the best time to catch the Indians was before they started off for the daily parade. The corporal was in his trousers and undershirt, vigorously rubbing his face with a coarse towel. He had arisen a little later than usual, he told me, because he had been up most of the night. At about two in the morning he had heard some rowdies doing something to the buffalo.

"I jumped out of bed," he explained, "and ran out on the gravel in my bare feet just in time to grab one of them. 'And what do you suppose you are doing?' I demanded. They had cut off the buffalo's tail! Oh, I got one of them, all right, and threw him to the ground, but the others got away with the tail. I would know them if I saw them again!"

Tail or no tail, I should not care to meet the corporal if I were one of those lads! There was thunder in his eyes as well as in his rich Scottish brogue at the mere thought of them desecrating the symbol of his proud force. A buffalo head is incorporated in the badge of the RCMP.

In the corner of the building was a cell which, if it could speak, could tell many stories of the past. Seldom in use when I visited, it contained saddles, suitcases, boxes and other paraphernalia to which I was permitted to add various pieces of my equipment. I was at liberty to go in and out at will for my supplies.

Upon inquiring about the best subject to paint in the camp from an artist's point of view, the first man mentioned was Duck Chief, head of all Blackfoot tribes in Alberta, so I sallied forth with the constable in search of him. We located him sitting in front of his tepee. Duck Chief readily agreed when he heard my request and disappeared into his tepee to get prepared. However, he soon came out again and quietly announced that he would not pose. Extremely disappointed I turned away, knowing the utter futility of argument.

It was not long before I was busily engaged in painting someone else. The next few days were full of the most intensive work for there was plenty of marvellous material at hand.

Then one morning, quite unexpectedly, Duck Chief signified his willingness to be painted. Joyfully I seized my kit and hustled off to his tepee. I was curious what had made him change his mind. So was the Mountie, who started making inquiries. It seemed that the venerable chief had wanted me to paint him all the time, "But," he said, "my wife wouldn't let me." Alas, how the mighty had fallen! Here was the proud leader of a brave and warlike race, strong and fearless in his six feet of bone and muscle, yet meekly yielding to the will of the fat, black-braided little woman who swept his hearth and embroidered his moccasins. So it appears that the hand that rocks the cradle is also the hand that rules the brave.

Duck Chief preferred being painted in his tepee, for which I was thankful, as it shielded me from the curious gaze of dozens of passers-by who delighted in watching the process.

I liked the chief as he was, in his ordinary clothes, and wanted to paint him that way. But he had ideas of his own. He sat on the ground fumbling with two enormous medals suspended from sleek satin ribbons. Very carefully and deliberately he adjusted them around his neck, turning them this way and that, fastening and unfastening several large pins with which he made them secure. Quietly and patiently I sat waiting until the solemn ritual was over. Finally, everything was arranged to his satisfaction. Then he suddenly looked up and smiled like a pleased child which was his signal for me to begin.

Sunlight and shadow followed each other in dancing little waves over the white tepee. All was very quiet within. I was completely immersed in my work when suddenly the flap of the tepee opened and a small girl of about eight came tumbling in, struggling under the weight of a fat, brown baby. She did not glance at me, but walked straight over to Duck Chief and, without apology or explanation, dumped the infant on his lap and turned to go. Foreseeing grave complications in regard to my portrait, I called her back and persuaded her to remove the squirming little child. Duck Chief supported my appeal and soon we were alone again.

I saw so much behind his stolid bearing. His features were open and generous and slightly Mongolian, which is unusual in the Blackfoot. One does not paint portraits year in and year out without learning something about human nature if one is even remotely observant. In the face of Duck Chief I read good humour, patience, tolerance and wisdom. Added to these sterling qualities was a simple, childlike directness of manner, coupled with immense and appealing dignity.

I was so pleased about painting the portrait that I did not miss my sweater until I was back in my room that evening. I had not the faintest idea where I had left it, as I had been all over the encampment. Next morning I asked the Mounties to be on the lookout for it but I could tell that they were not very hopeful that I would ever see it again. Then I went to Duck Chief's tepee to ask if he had seen it. His face was absolutely impassive as he countered my query with a question of his own.

"Was it blue?"

"No," I replied. "It was tan."

Whereupon he turned on his heel, went into his tepee and came back out immediately, not only with my missing sweater, but also with a brush which I had overlooked. Smiling broadly, he handed them to me.

I was very curious to know more about his medals. He had many others besides the two large ones he wore when I painted him. The Mountie procured an interpreter for me when I had difficulty understanding him, but he was not able to elicit much information, so my curiosity remained unappeased. When I returned home, however, I looked up literature about the recent Royal visit and found much of what I wanted to know.

In a newspaper dated May 29th, 1939, was the following: "During the five-minute stop in front of the thirty teepees, His Majesty greeted Duck Chief, 75-year-old head of the encampment and a direct link with the final peace treaty that made all Canadian Indians wards of Queen Victoria.

"Duck Chief wore the medal given shortly after the signing of Treaty No. 7, the Blackfoot Treaty, and another to celebrate the visit in 1901 of the Duke and Duchess of Cornwall and York, later King George V and Queen Mary, parents of King George V1.

"Duck Chief told His Majesty that he had always wanted to meet the Great White Father, particularly after he had heard that the King was coming across the water to see his Canadian children."

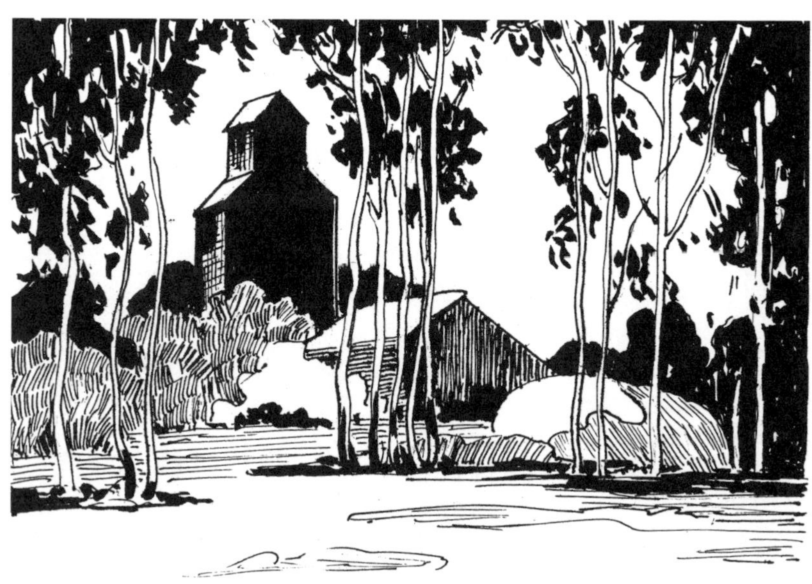

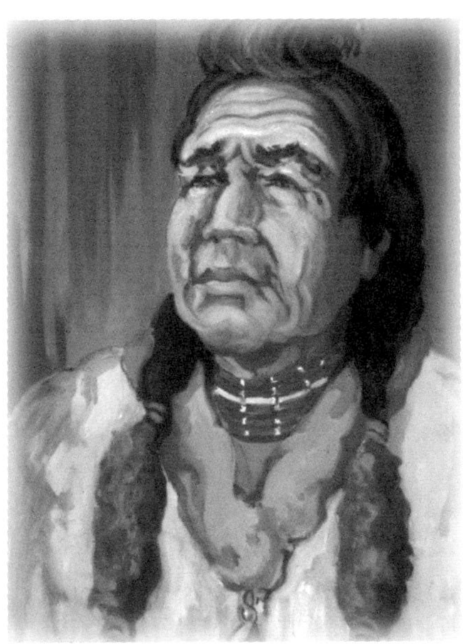

Chief Fish-Wolf-Ofe

One morning when I was attending the Calgary Stampede, a very old Indian, Joseph Sitting Top, from the Morely Reserve, came hobbling into the Mounted Police office.

He had lost a horse over a week before and had perfect faith in the ability of the Mounties to "corral" the beast at a moment's notice.

He was well over eighty and in his youth had driven dog sleds between Calgary and Edmonton for the Hudson's Bay Company and had many other links with the old fur-trading days, so it was suggested that I paint him.

I was not enamoured of his "good looks," but because of his historic background I thought he might be an interesting subject. He consented to sit for me, so we went off together and I managed to pilot him to a secluded part of the encampment where I fondly hoped to work in peace.

While I was getting my materials ready, a couple of old squaws, who were seated on the ground nearby, engaged Joseph in conversation, which, of course, I could not understand. I soon sensed, however, that they were asking him how much he was getting out of the transaction. When he told them, a wicked look came over their faces and they burst into a torrent of invective.

Presently this took effect and he informed me that they thought I ought to pay him five dollars an hour. I replied that I could not possibly do so and sat waiting further developments. Meanwhile, the temperature in my immediate vicinity was rising with an absolutely dizzy momentum. The air was getting blue, the volume of their voices louder and my enthusiasm rapidly diminishing in direct ratio to the ominous portent of the barometer [*sic*].

Perhaps they misinterpreted my silence for consent, or even for weakness, because they decided to push their claims still further. This time Joseph announced that his price had soared to eight dollars.

It did not take me very long to decide that he was a very ugly old man and that I was not keen on painting him anyway, so I picked up my things and abruptly walked off, leaving the trio gaping after me in open-mouthed astonishment.

When I went into the Royal Canadian Mounted Police cabin, the corporal looked up in surprise. "You haven't painted him already, have you?" he asked. "No," I replied. "His price was too high. He wanted eight dollars an hour for the job." It was a treat to watch the corporal's face. "Eight dollars?" he sputtered, his eyes fairly popping out. "Eight dollars! Why I wouldn't give that much for his whole blankety-blank carcass!"

Taking this episode as all in the day's work, I cheerfully looked around for more amiable prospects which I was sure would be forthcoming.

At the edge of the encampment I discovered several fine luxury cars which had been there the night before. They were owned by American Indians who had driven up from Montana to see the big show.

No brow-beaten, crestfallen, defeated race were these. They had money, plenty of it. They were well dressed and well fed, so I surmised that they were likely to be good-natured.

A tall, fine-looking man with a far-off look in his eye, attracted my attention, so I engaged him in conversation. When I thought the psychological moment had arrived, I broached the matter of him posing for me, to which he consented, saying that he would be ready for the ordeal at one o'clock. Promptly at that hour I appeared, with my materials, ready for work.

I thought it would be more private if I painted him near the high board fence which surrounded the fair grounds, so my subject took the seat out of his car and made himself comfortable for the sitting. I settled myself in what I thought, was a strategic position, with my back to the fence where I could command a view of the grounds and could easily see approaching trouble in the form of curious passersby. Located as I was, they would not find it quite so convenient to loiter and watch me work.

I liked the way this man posed. He was obliging, good-natured and courteous. He held his head erect, not so much in conscious pride for that was an innate quality with him, but as though he were lost in reflective thoughts that were pleasant and harmonious. He had a deep, husky voice that sounded like the rustle of tissue paper, only more musical.

Occasionally I heard a soft, throaty chuckle. Presently he grunted and then laughed outright. I laughed too, in good fellowship, and then he pointed to a loose board in the fence behind me where inquisitive and precocious boys and girls were gaining free admission to the grounds.

"While I sit here, seven boys and four girls come through," he said, then added with more grunts and chuckles, "It's all right. Got no money, no pay. It's all right."

I agreed with him, so we shared the dark secret together, while he continued to chortle from time to time as fresh newcomers swelled the day's attendance to record proportions.

When I asked him his Indian name, he held out his hand for my pencil, then slowly and labouriously, but very legibly wrote "Chief Fish-Wolf-Ofe" on the back of my canvas. I inquired his tribe. "Blackfoot of Montana," he said.

He liked the picture when I had finished, but called attention to the fact that I had omitted something which was evidently of great importance to him. It was an enormous claw suspended from a ribbon around his neck. It had been hidden in the folds of his yellow shirt so I had overlooked it. Carefully I painted it in to his intense satisfaction.

Then he told me about it. "Great chief, named Big Bear, gave it to me when I'm little boy," he said. "Oh, he was a great, great chief, and I always wear it around my neck ever since."

I asked him what sort of claw it was and he replied that it came from a very large grizzly bear. "Lots of people want to buy it. One man say he give me sixty dollars for it but I don't sell. I don't sell to anybody, no matter how much they give me, because I NO GET SICK!" And a truly magnificent man he was, with his long grey braids encased in mink skins which fell over his broad chest, while his hair swept back in a wide curve from his brow. More sophisticated folk might well envy his simple faith that was sufficient to keep him in excellent health which, quite obviously, he enjoyed, so he was perfectly right in not parting with the token.

It is interesting to recall that Big Bear, who gave him the charm, was the Cree chief who, with Poundmaker and Piapot, had listened to the fiery exhortations of the misguided Louis Riel and became enmeshed in the rebellion of which Riel was the author.

Government forces had to exert the utmost effort to prevent Poundmaker and Big Bear from joining the rebellion, which would have meant much additional bloodshed. Eventually, both surrendered and were sentenced to long prison terms. They were released when it was found that their confinement had broken their health. The pitiful victims of events they could not foresee and of a civilization that they could not understand.

Though they were bold and fearless foes, they were also valiant and honourable. At the time of the Frog Lake Massacre, when grave fears were held for their captives with many women among them, it was found that Big Bear had been most careful and considerate of them.

Often I read of those stirring days, and here in the light-hearted revelry of the Calgary Stampede, so many years since Big Bear had laid down his arms forever, I had stumbled upon this homely little incident revealing the kindly and human side of his nature. Small wonder that Chief Fish-Wolf-Ofe treasured the charm that the brave old warrior had given him so long ago.

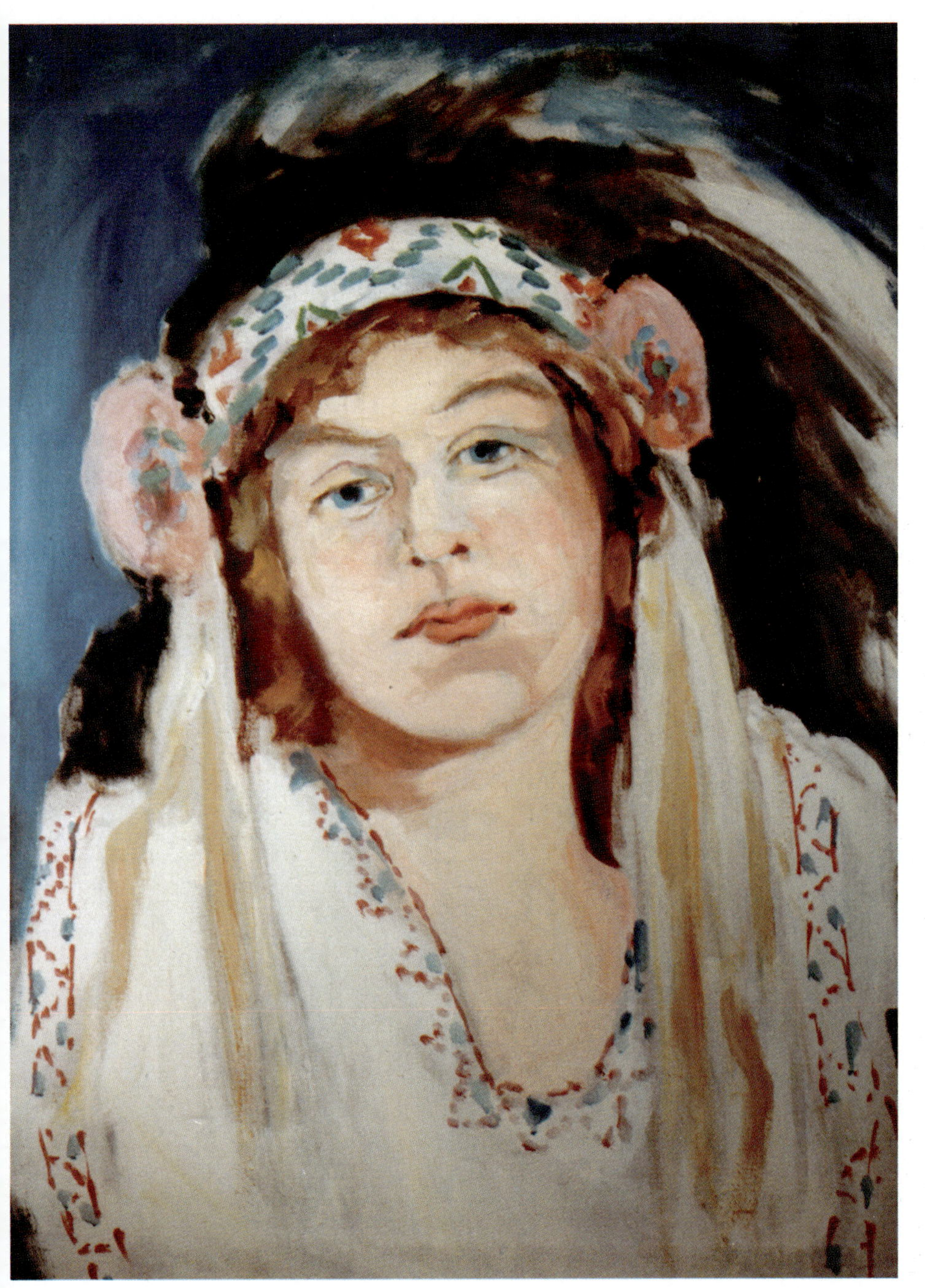

Mildred Valley Thornton, self-portrait.   ▶ *text page 9*

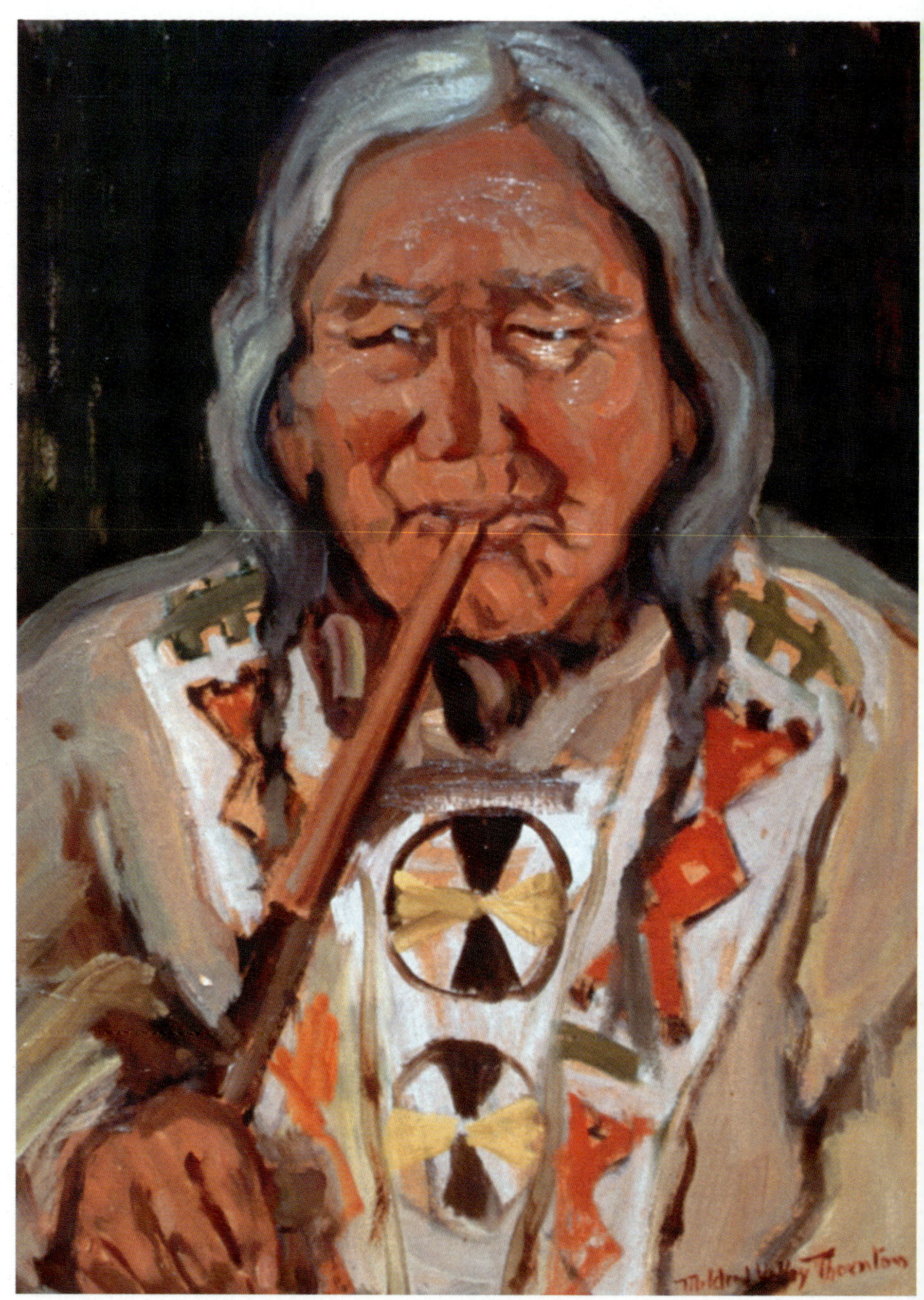

Manitouwassis "Child of God" (sketch) ▸ *text page 17*

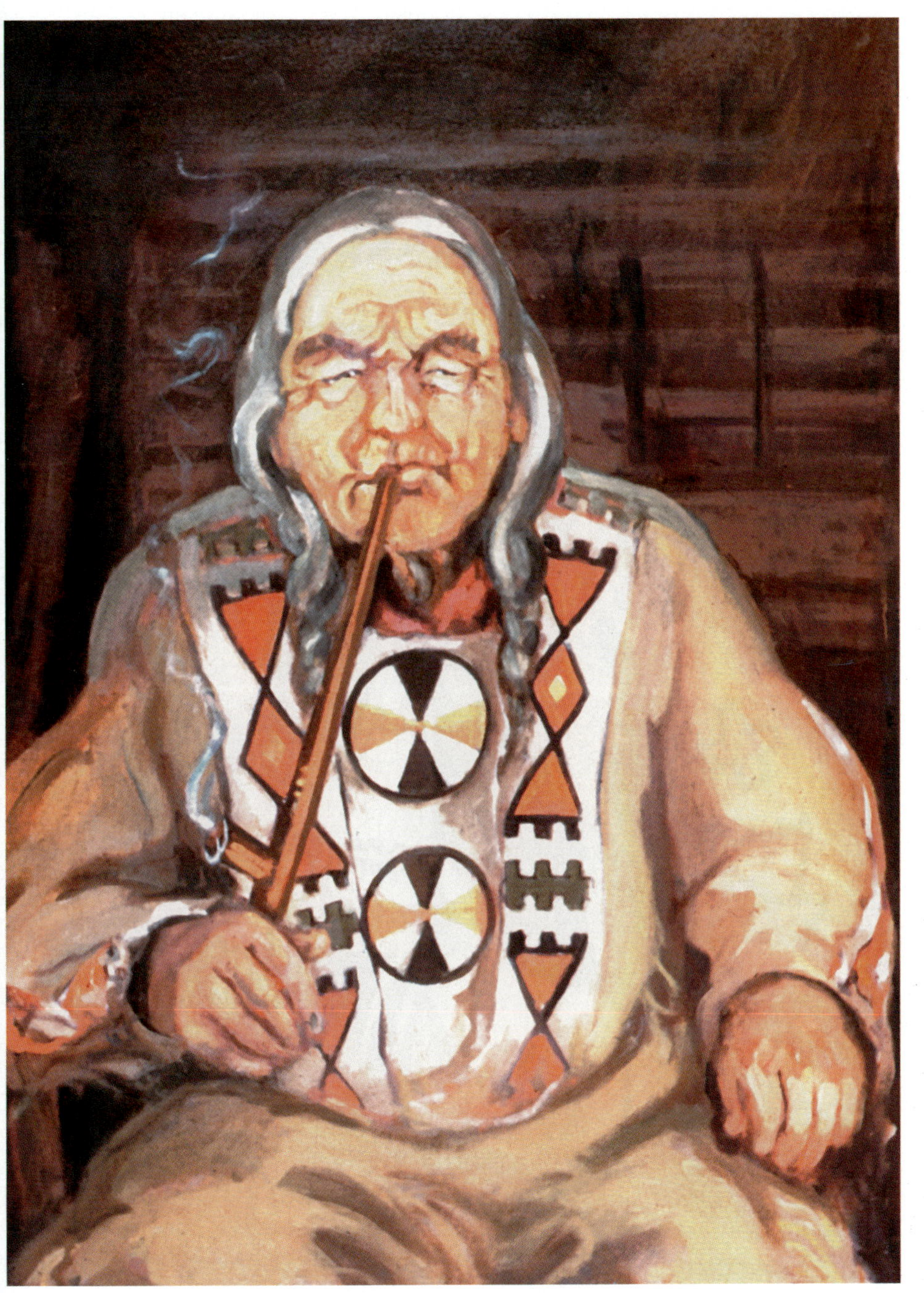

Manitouwassis "Child of God"   ▸ *text page 17*

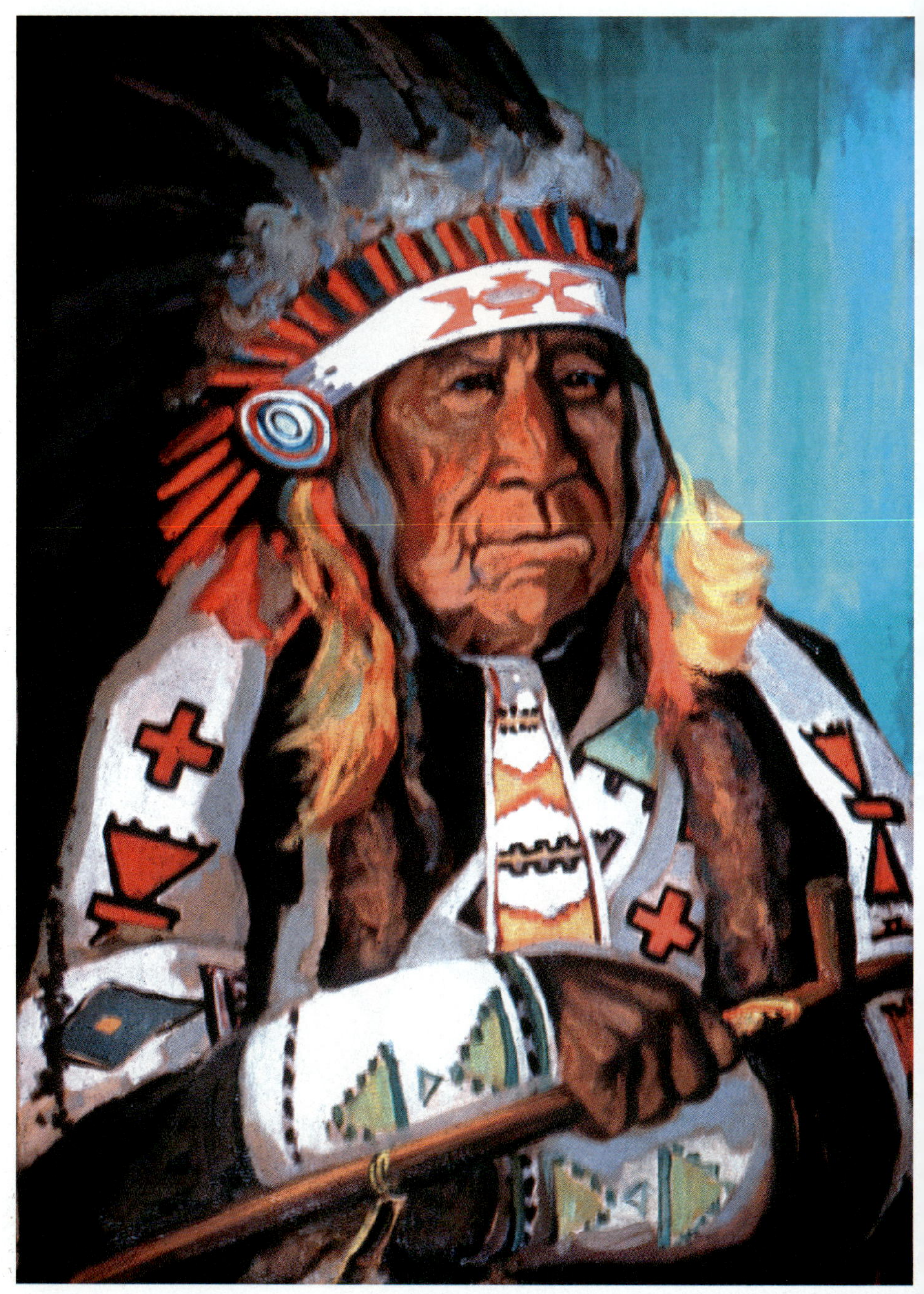

Buffalo Bow

▶ *text page 21*

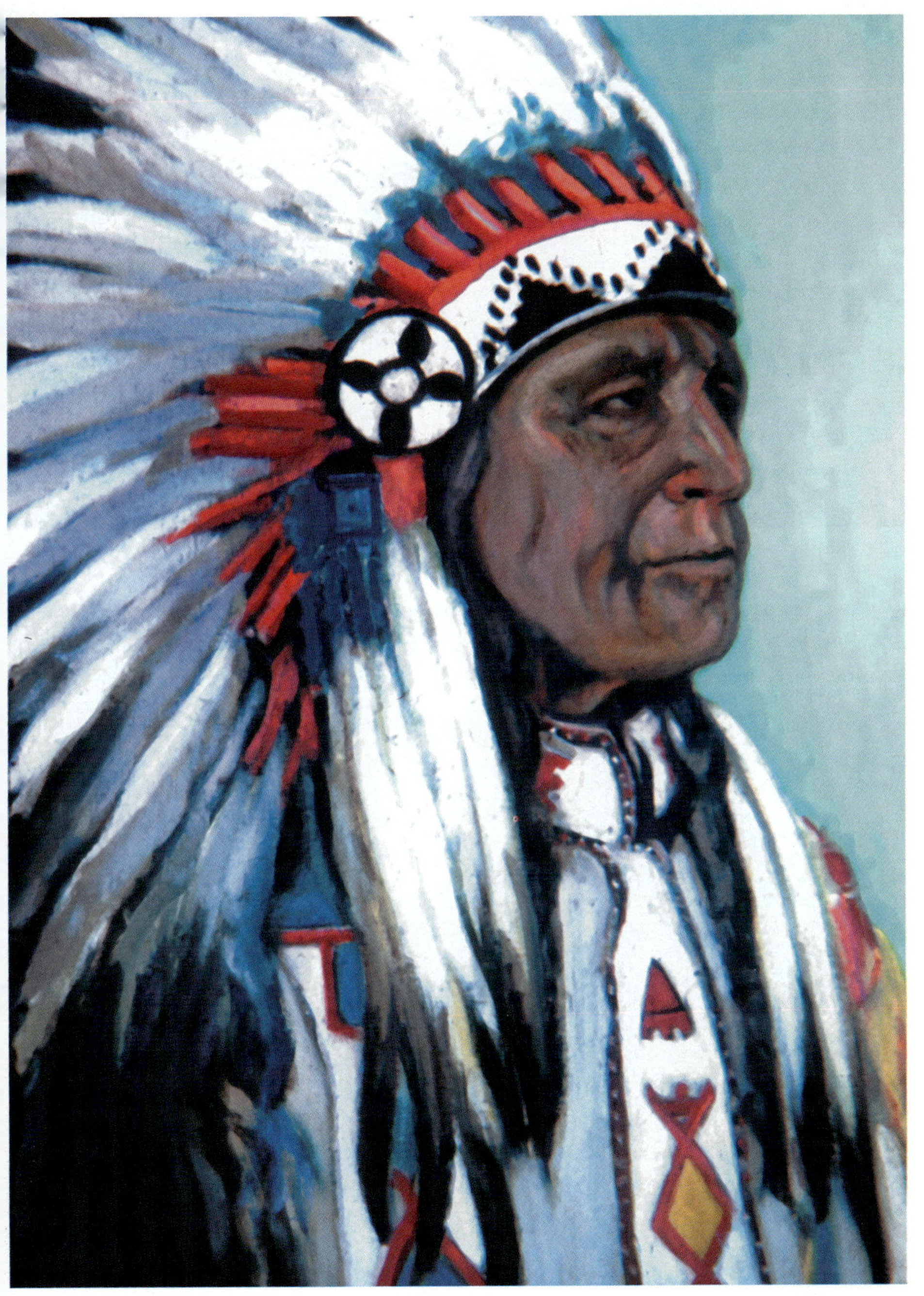

Chief Red Dog ▶ *text page 26*

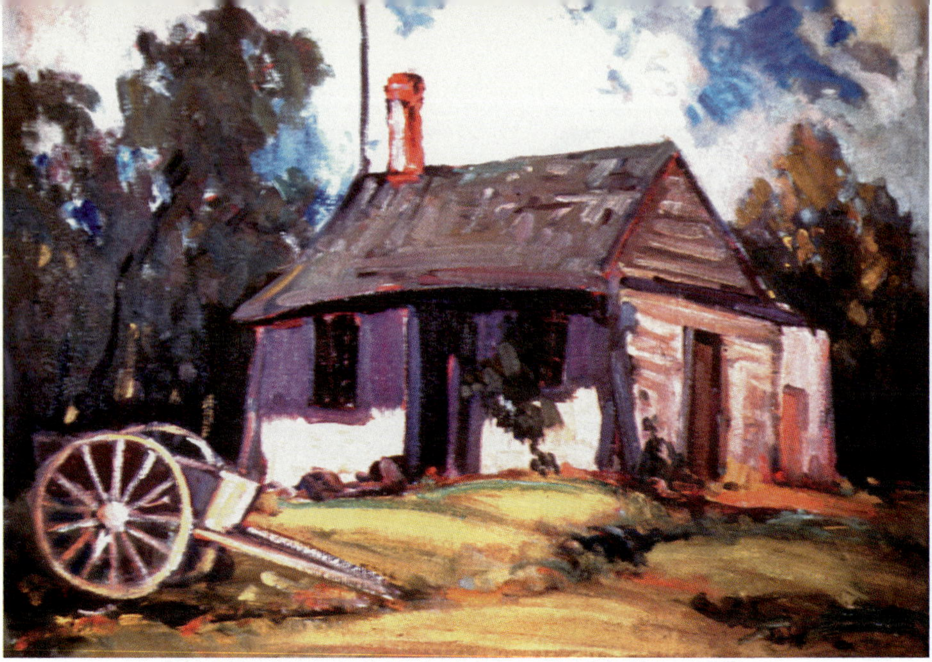

Old Hudson's Bay Trading Post, Fort Qu'Appelle

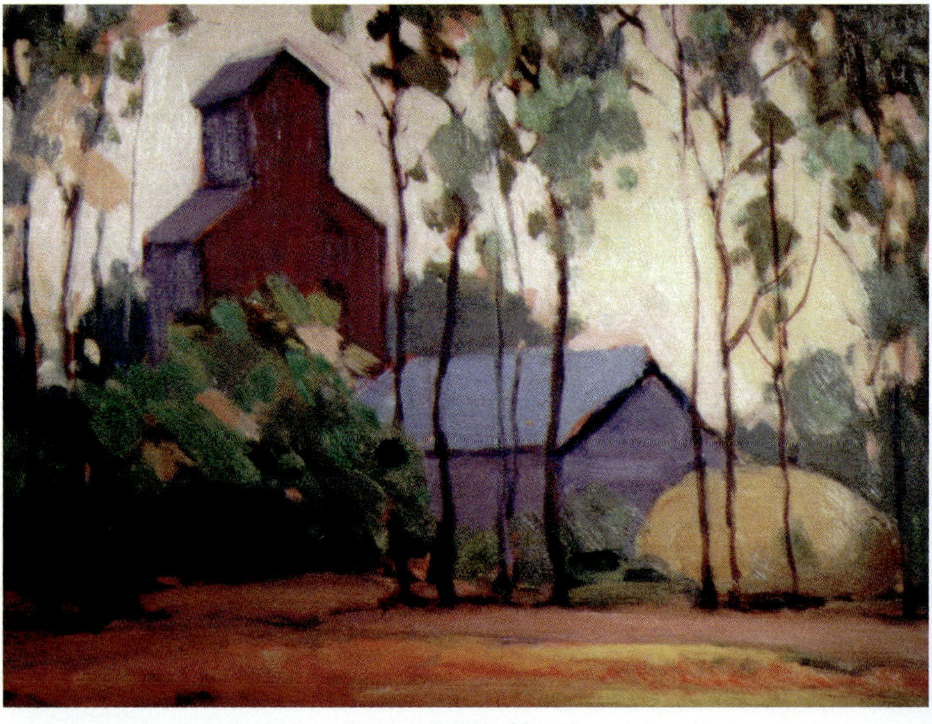

Farm and Grain Elevator

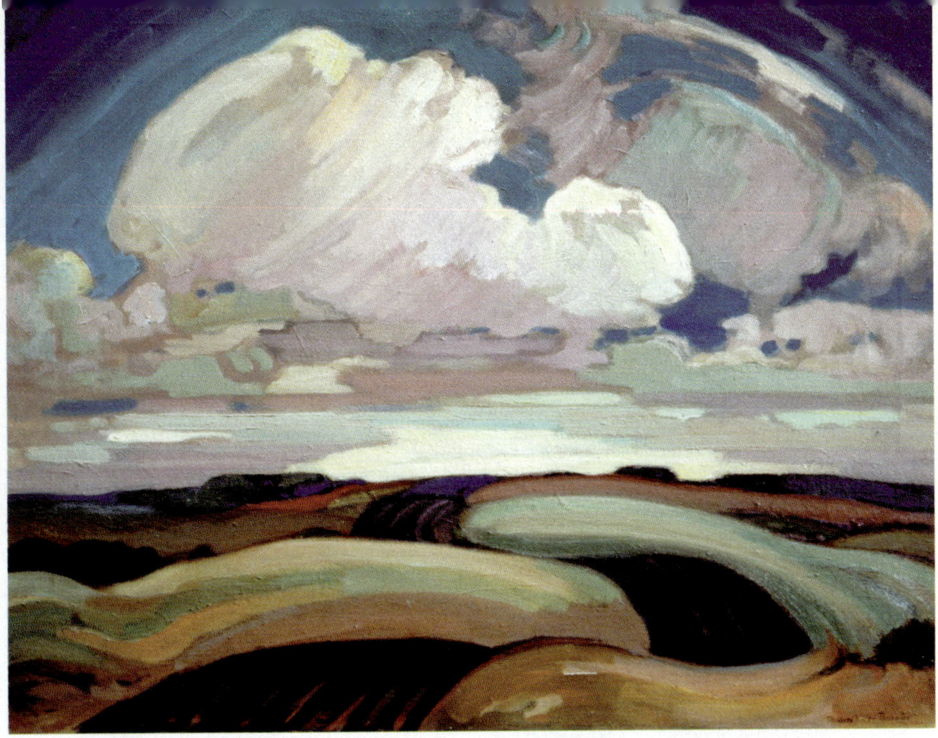

Fireguard, Saskatchewan

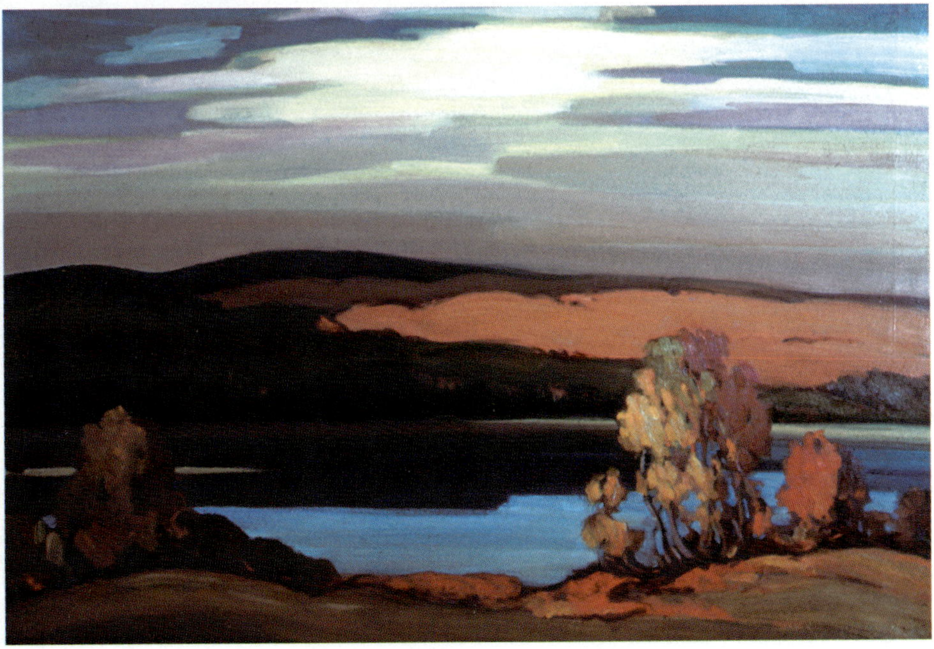

Evening at Touchwood Hills, Saskatchewan

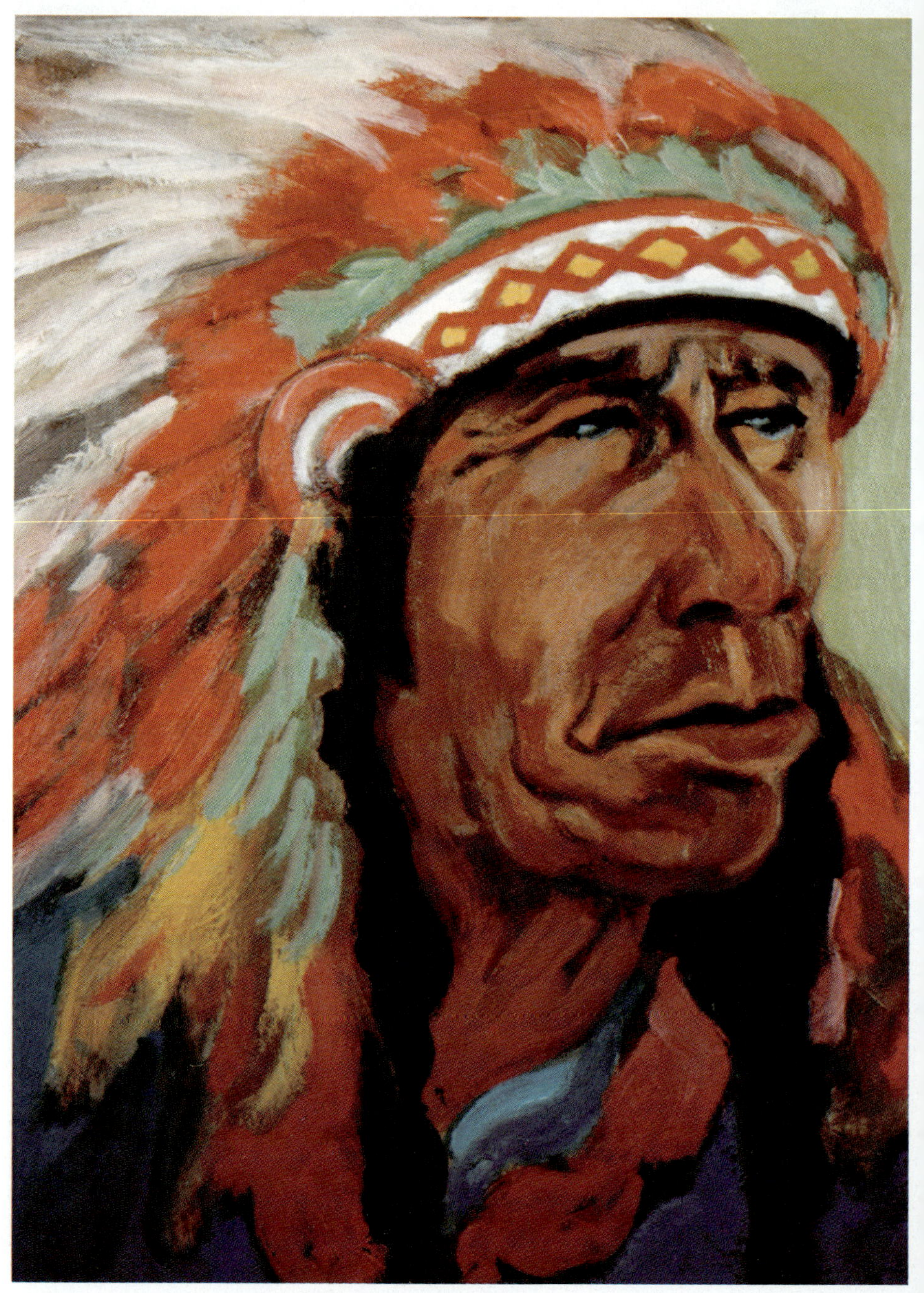

John Sugar   ▸ *text page 30*

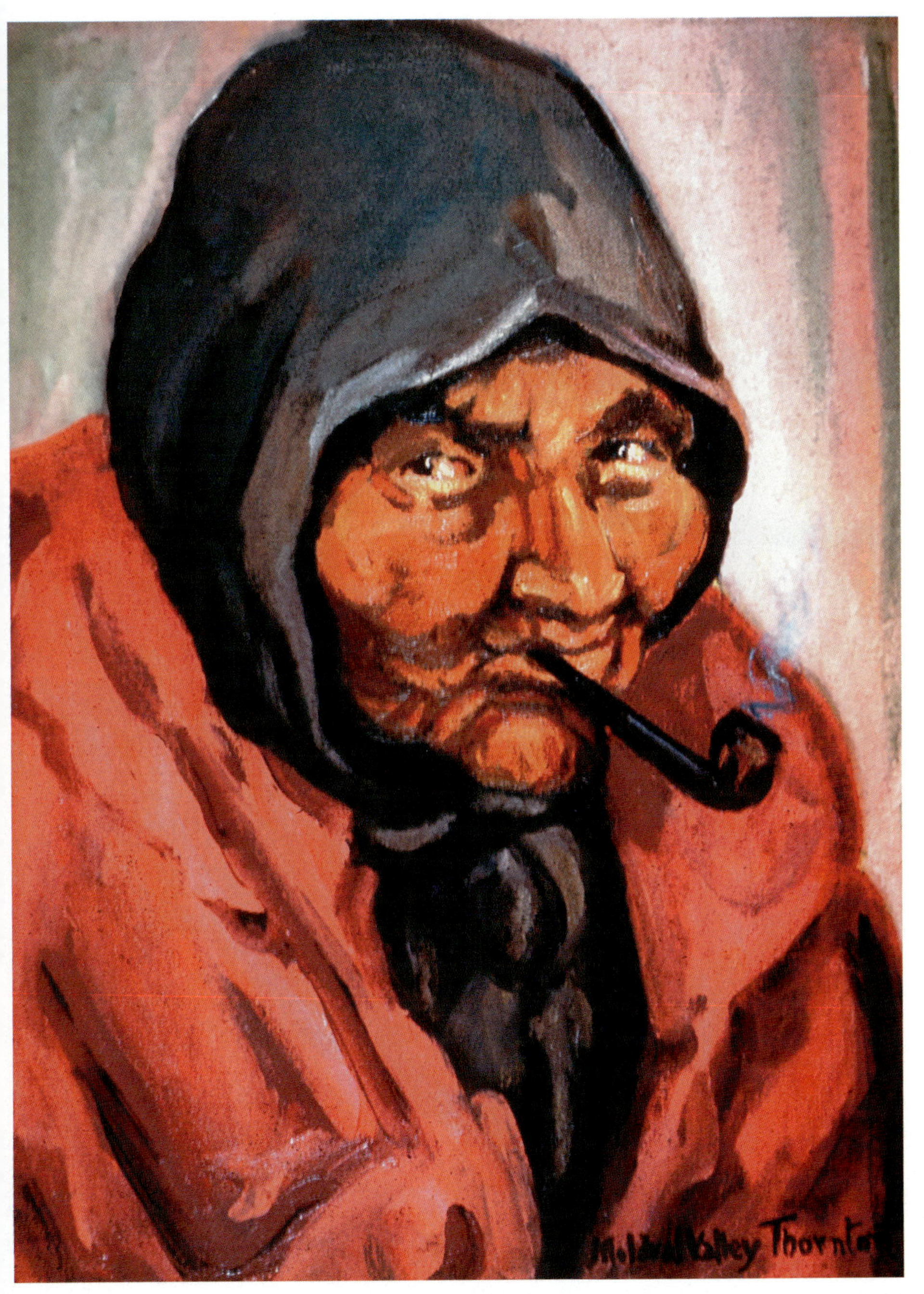

Mrs. Rock Thunder   ▸ *text page 30*

105

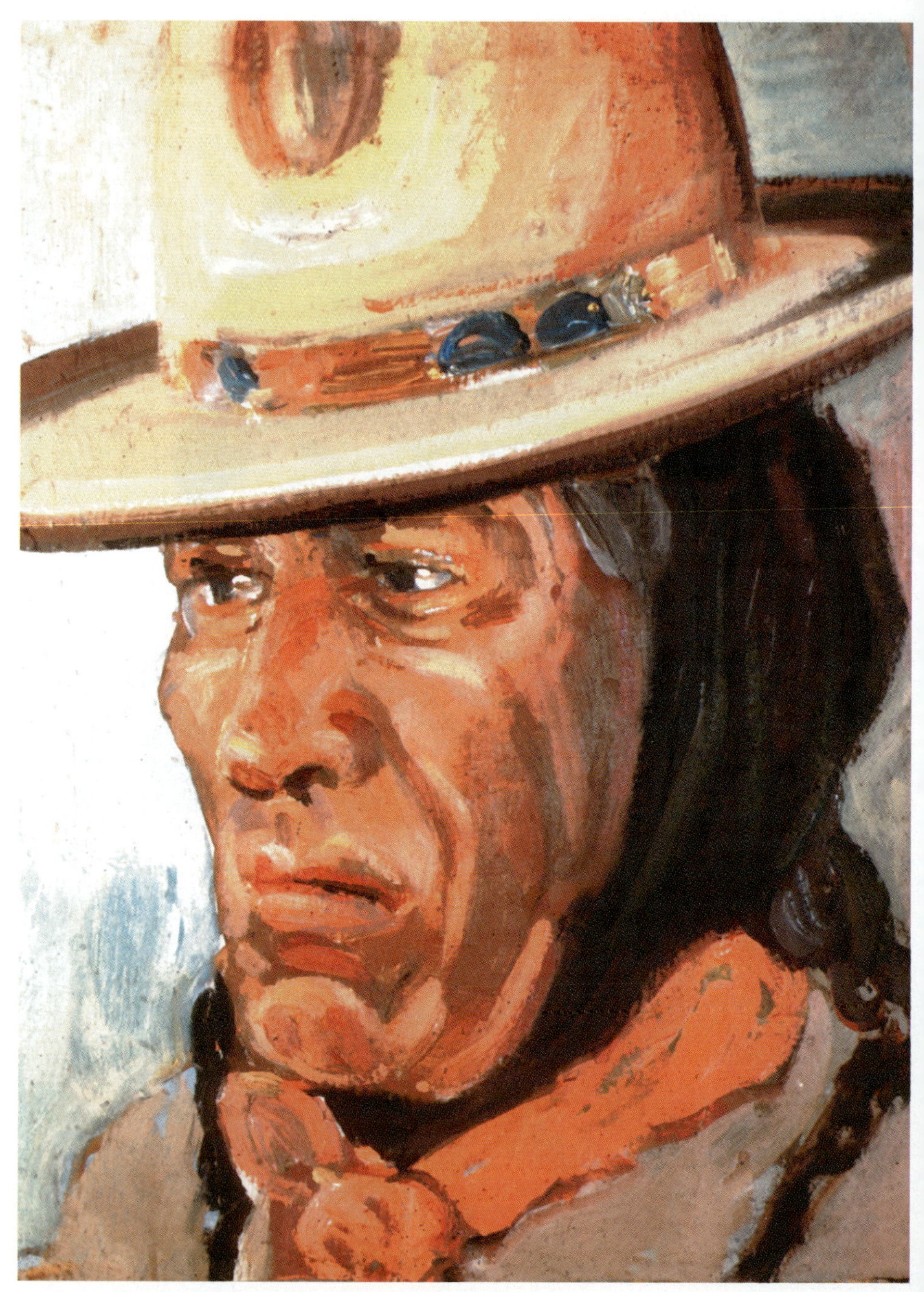

No Name   ▸ *text page 30*

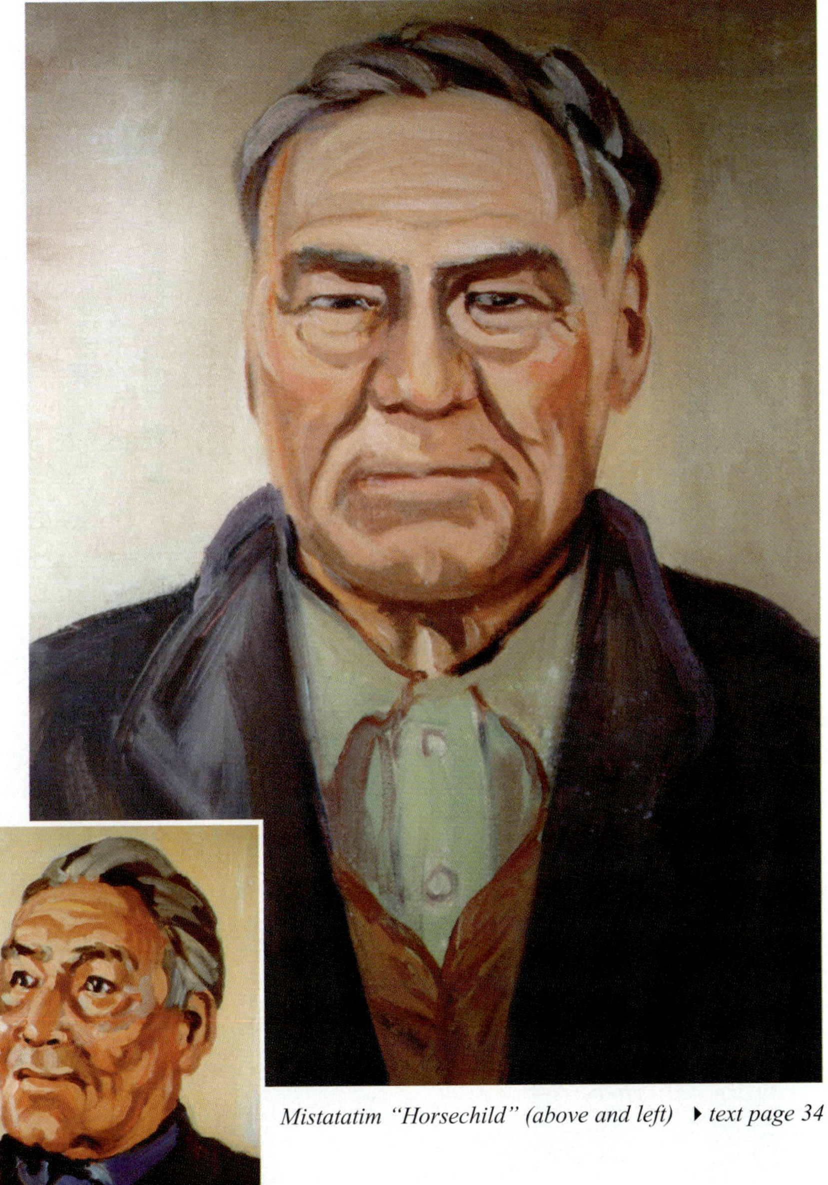

Mistatatim "Horsechild" (above and left) ▸ *text page 34*

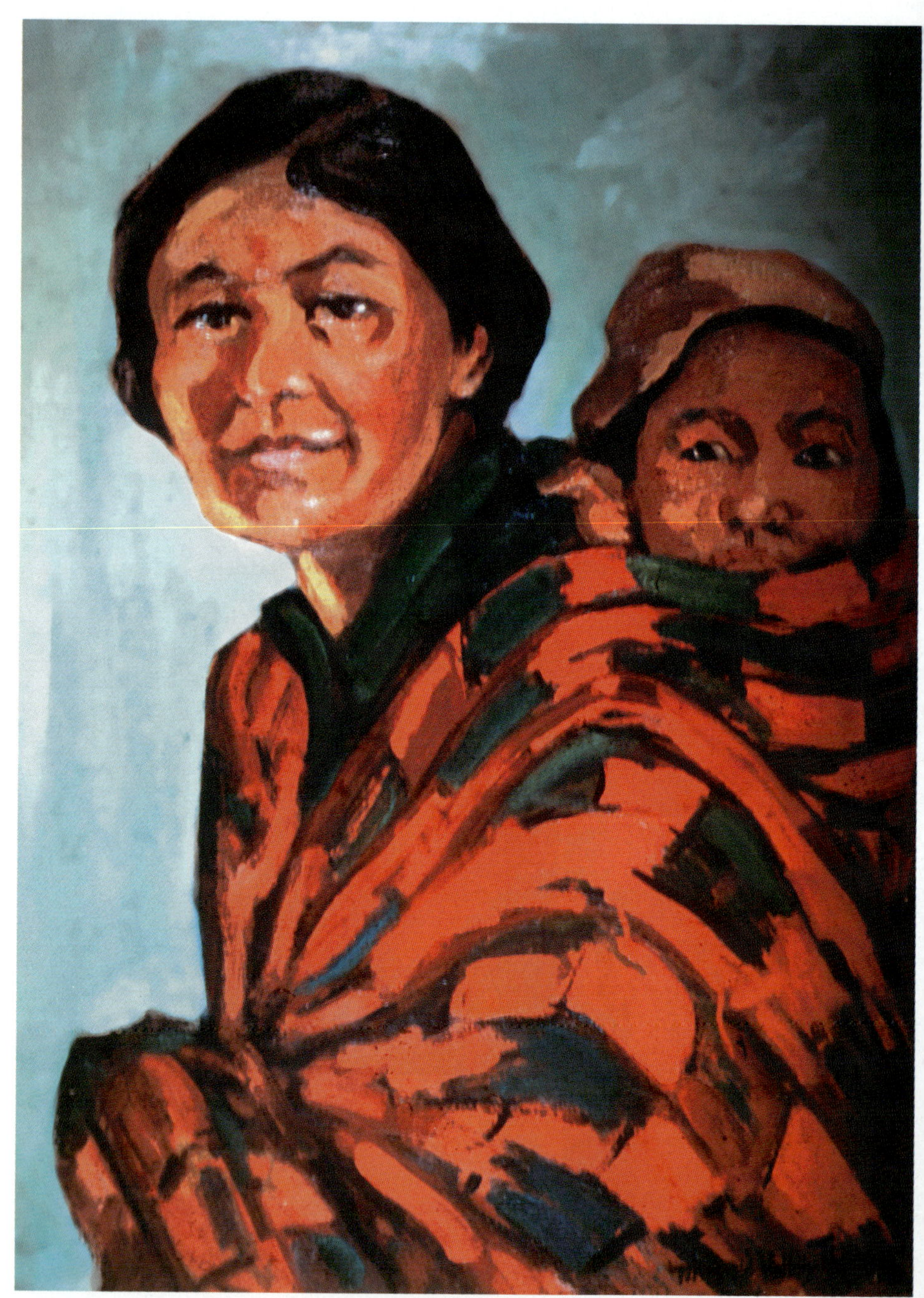

Cree Mother and Child   ▶ *text page 39*

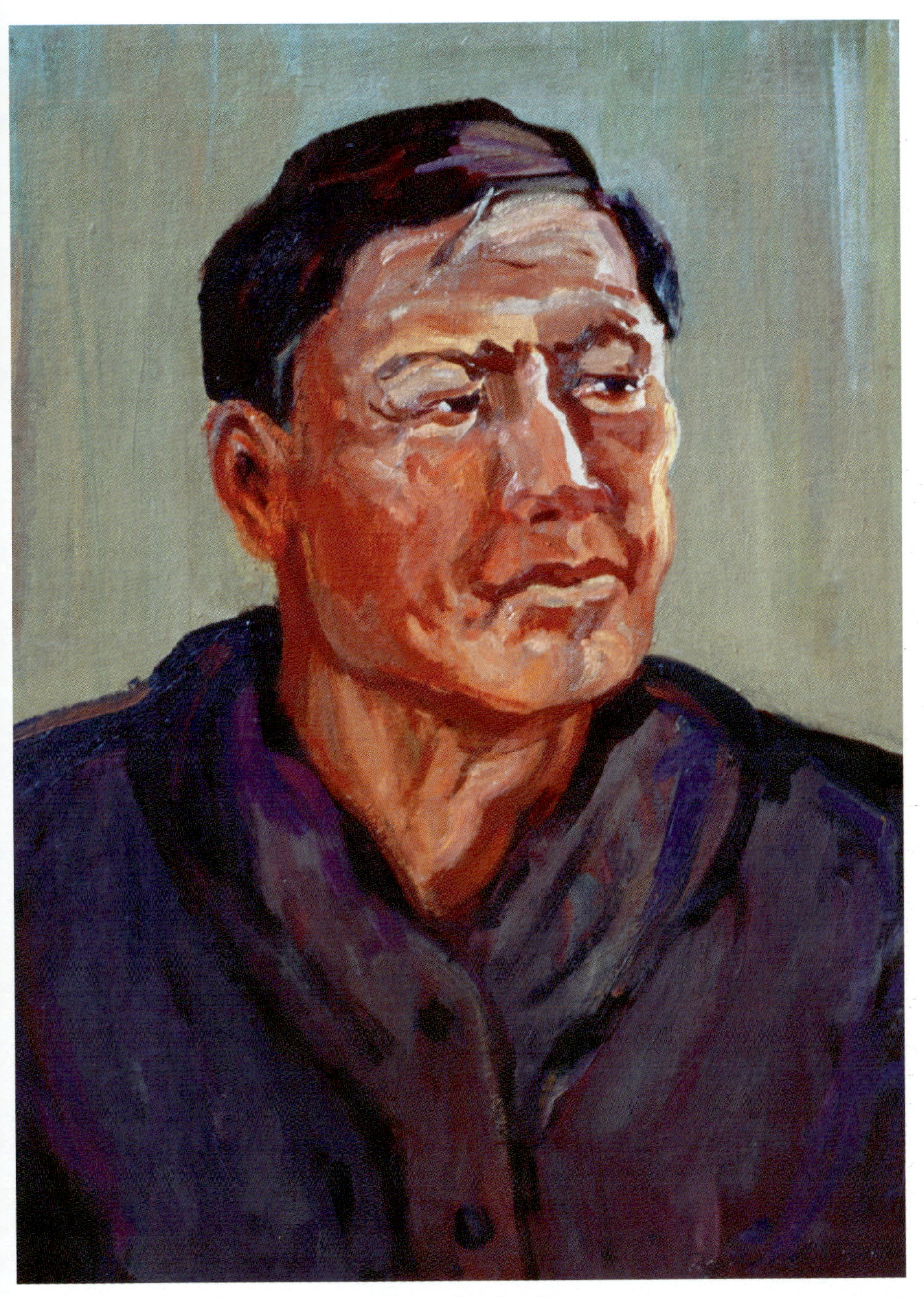

Stanislaus Almighty Voice   ▸ *text page 42*

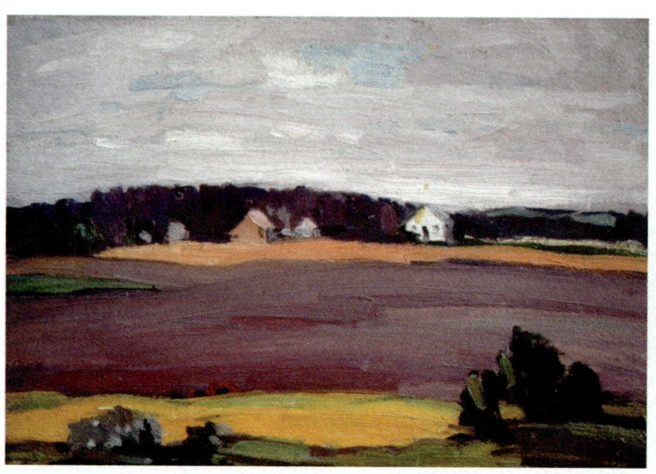

Saskatchewan Landscape (sketch)

In developing the finished canvas (below) Mildred Valley Thornton put more emphasis on cloud and field formation. She also intensified colour and increased depth through the furrows in the field and the addition of fields beyond the trees to the left of the horizon.

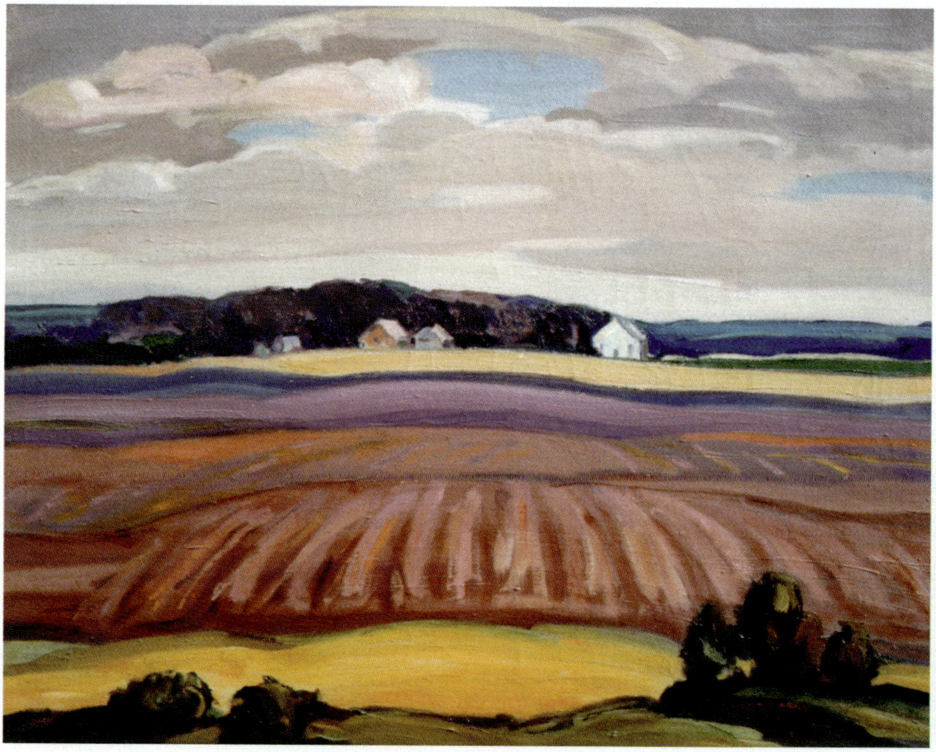

Saskatchewan Landscape

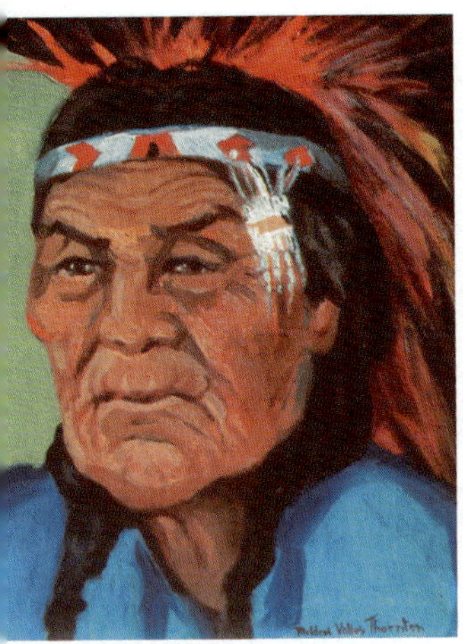

Eagle Hunter

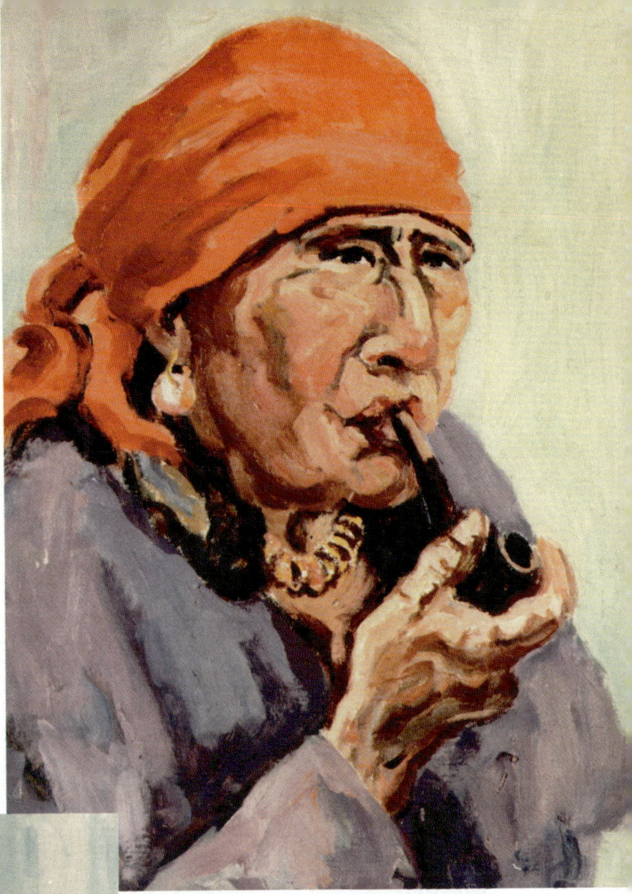

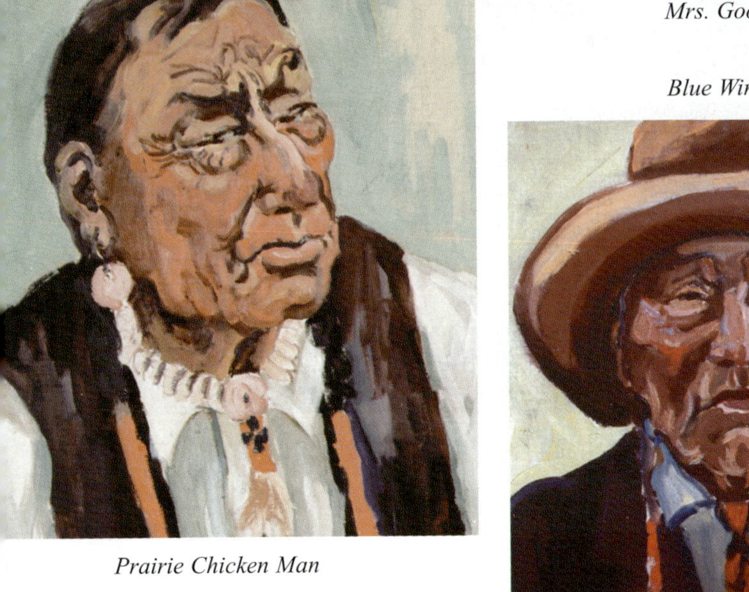

Prairie Chicken Man

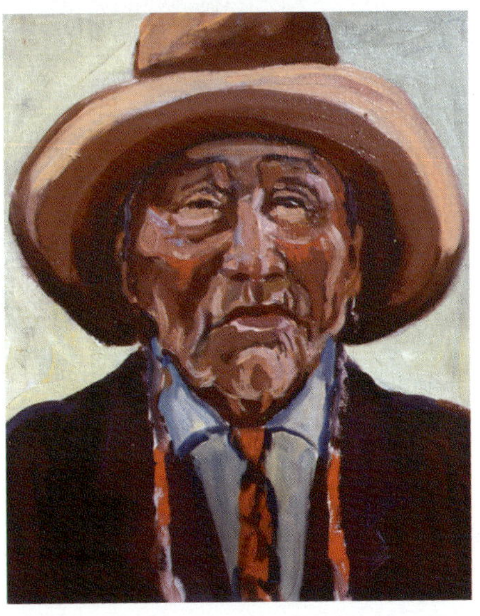

Mrs. Goodrider

Blue Wings

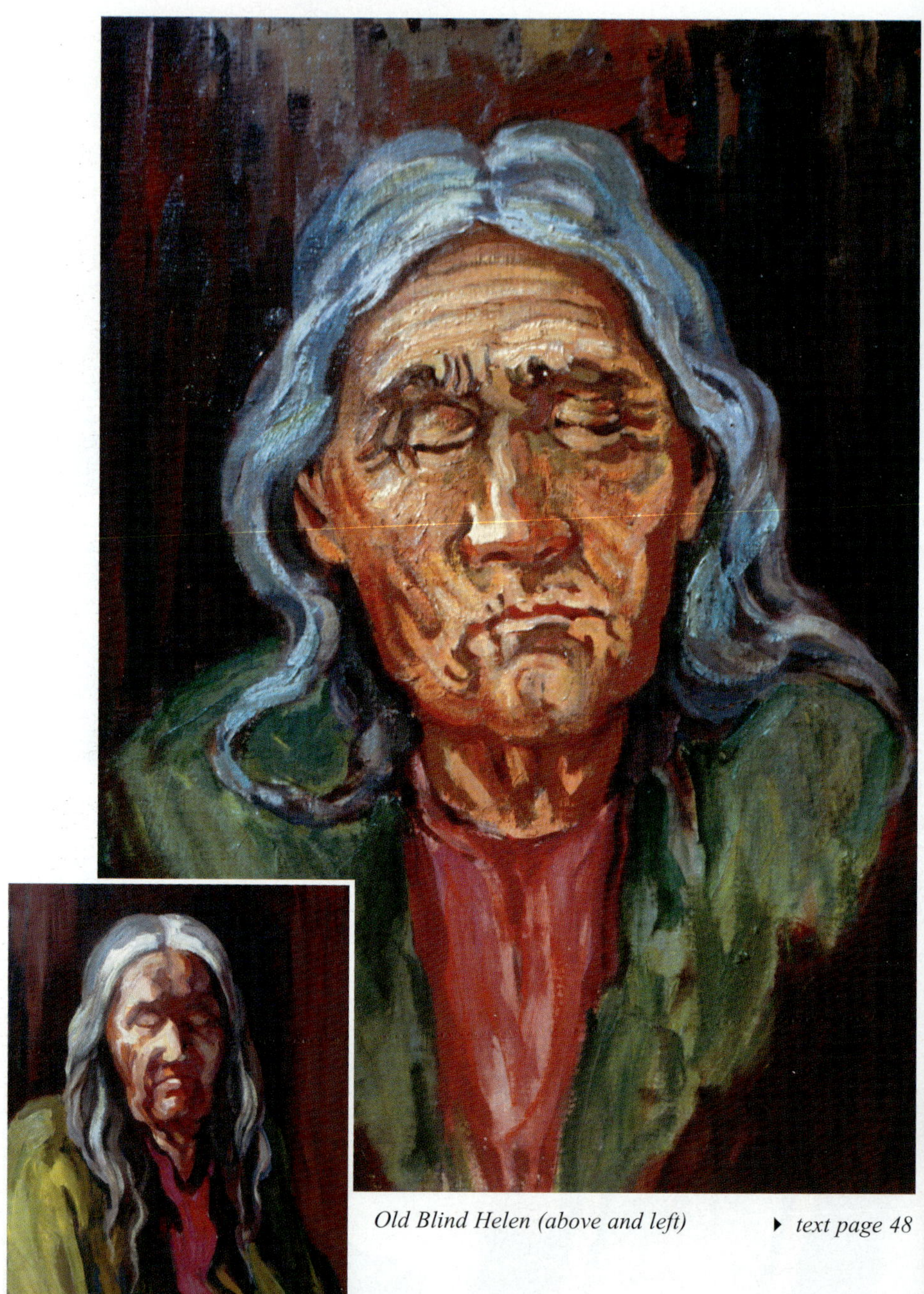

Old Blind Helen (above and left)   ▸ *text page 48*

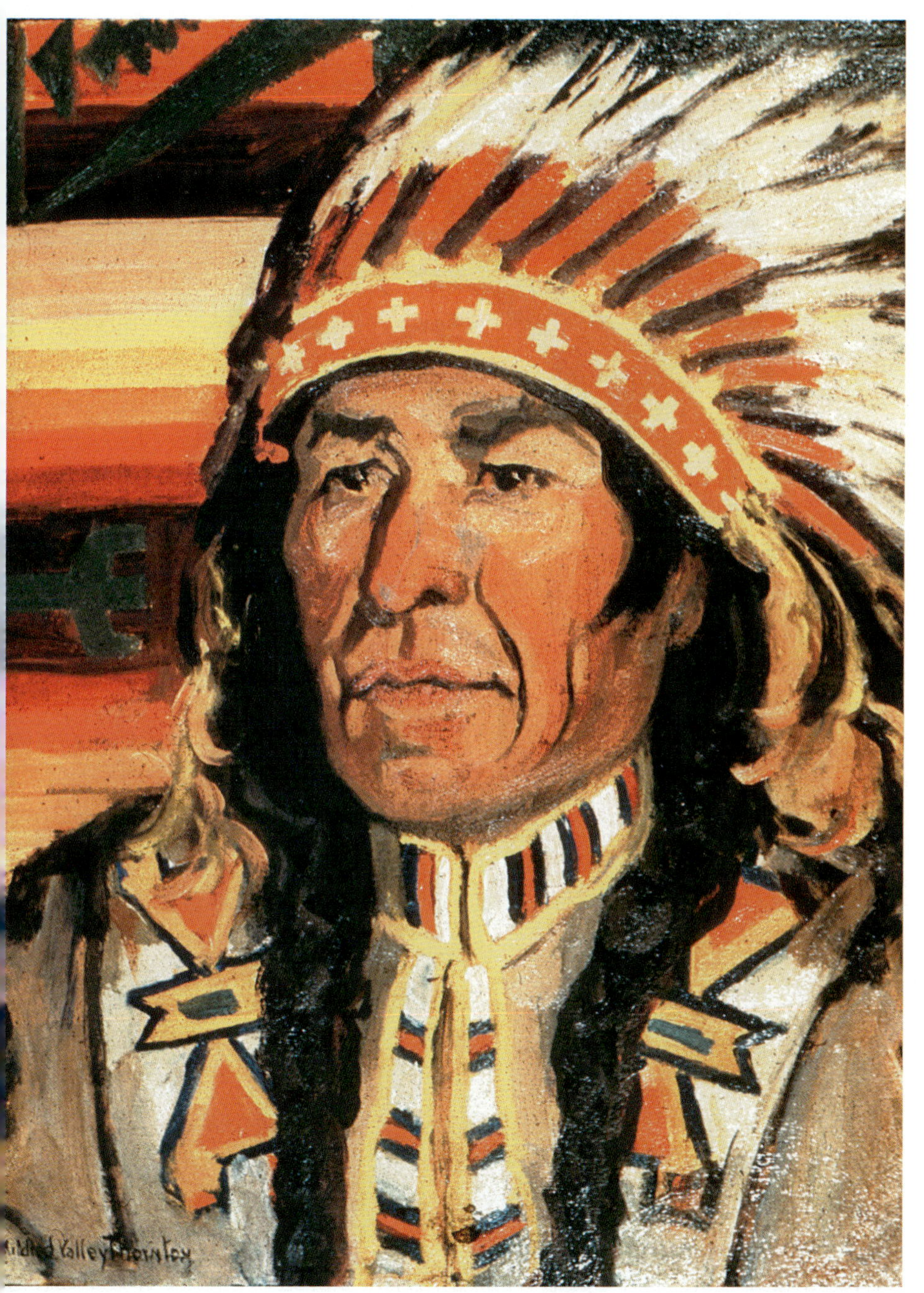

Nanepowiskh ▶ *text page 50*

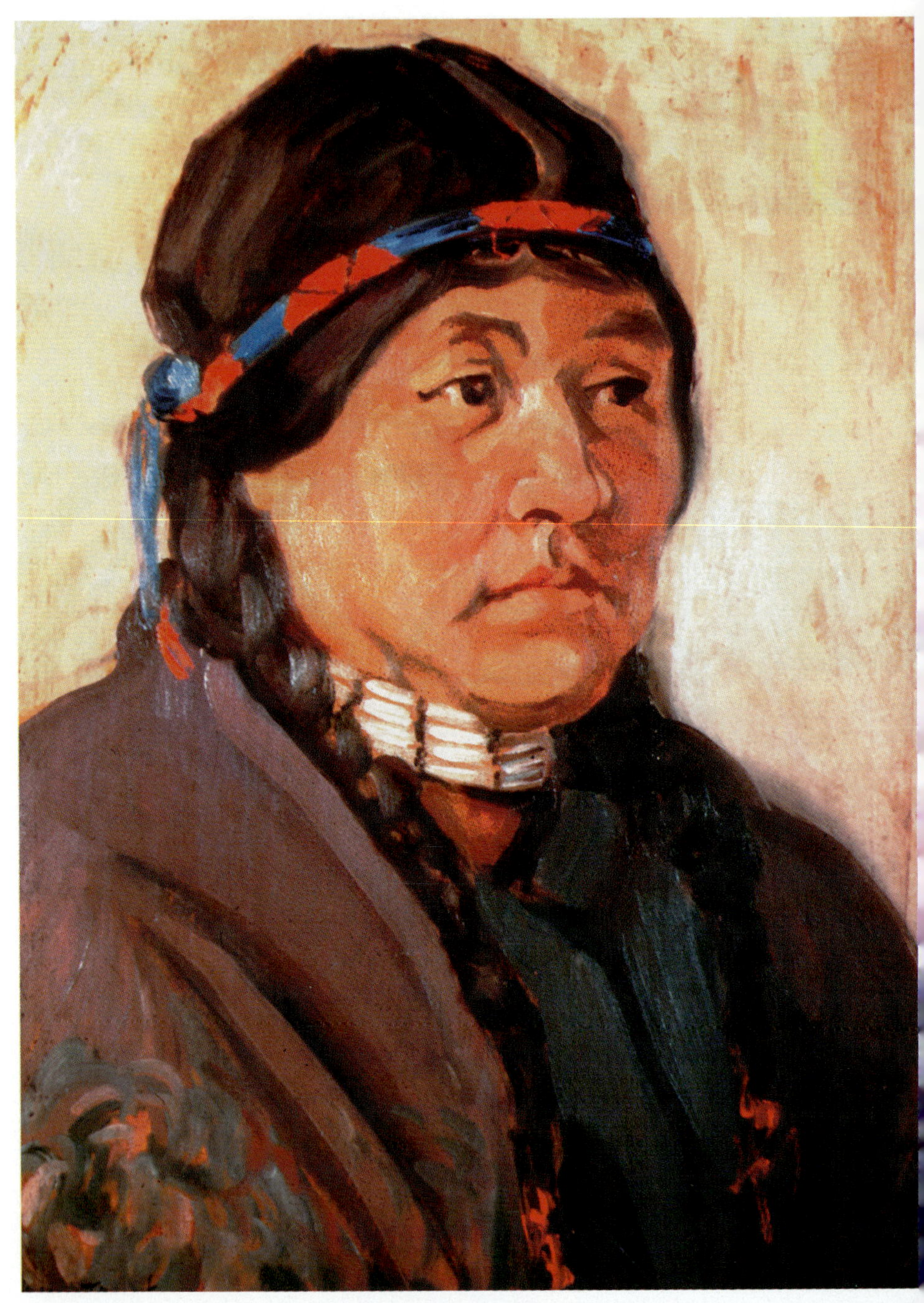

Pat Cappo's Wife

▸ *text page 55*

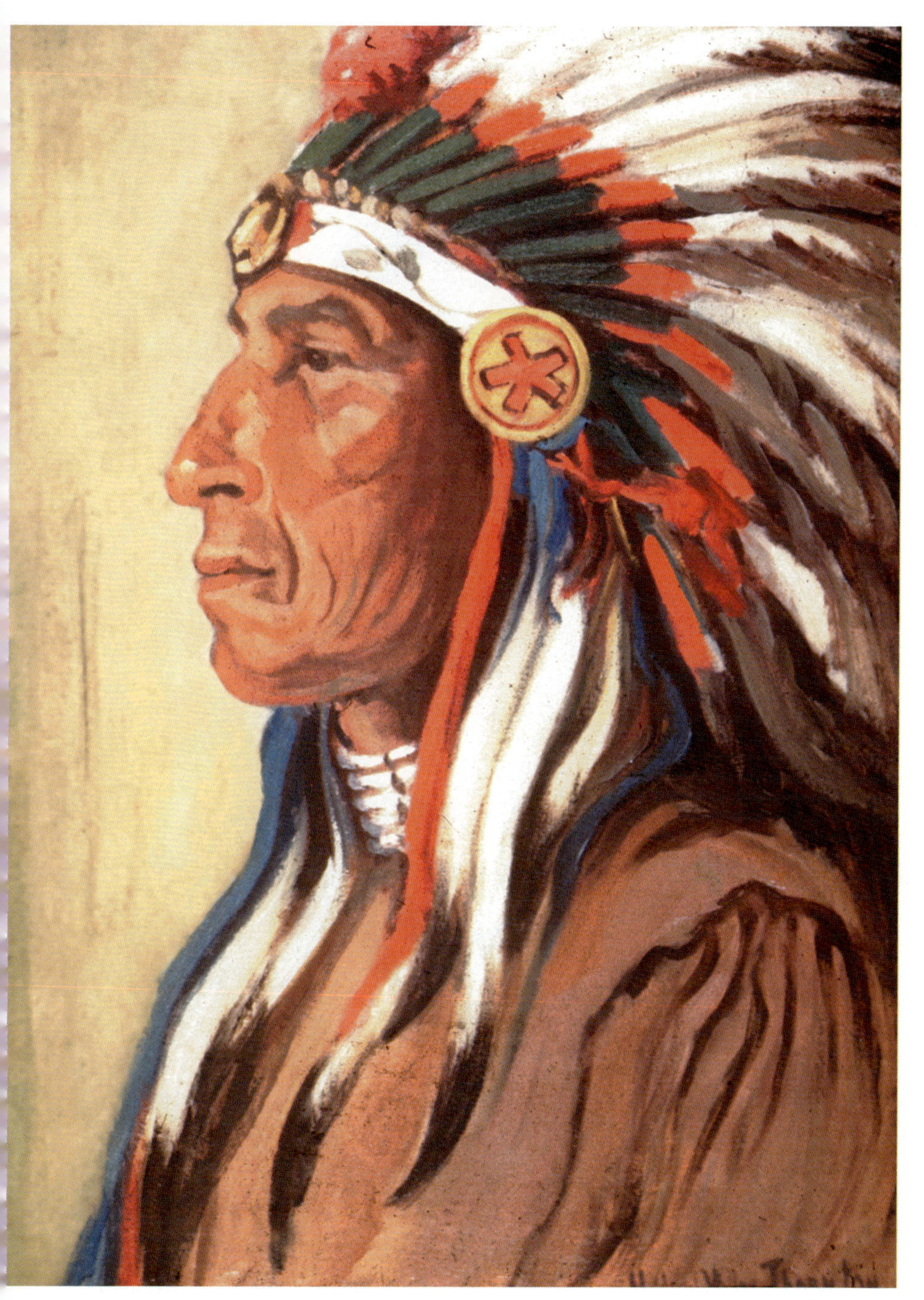

Pat Cappo   ▸ *text page 54*

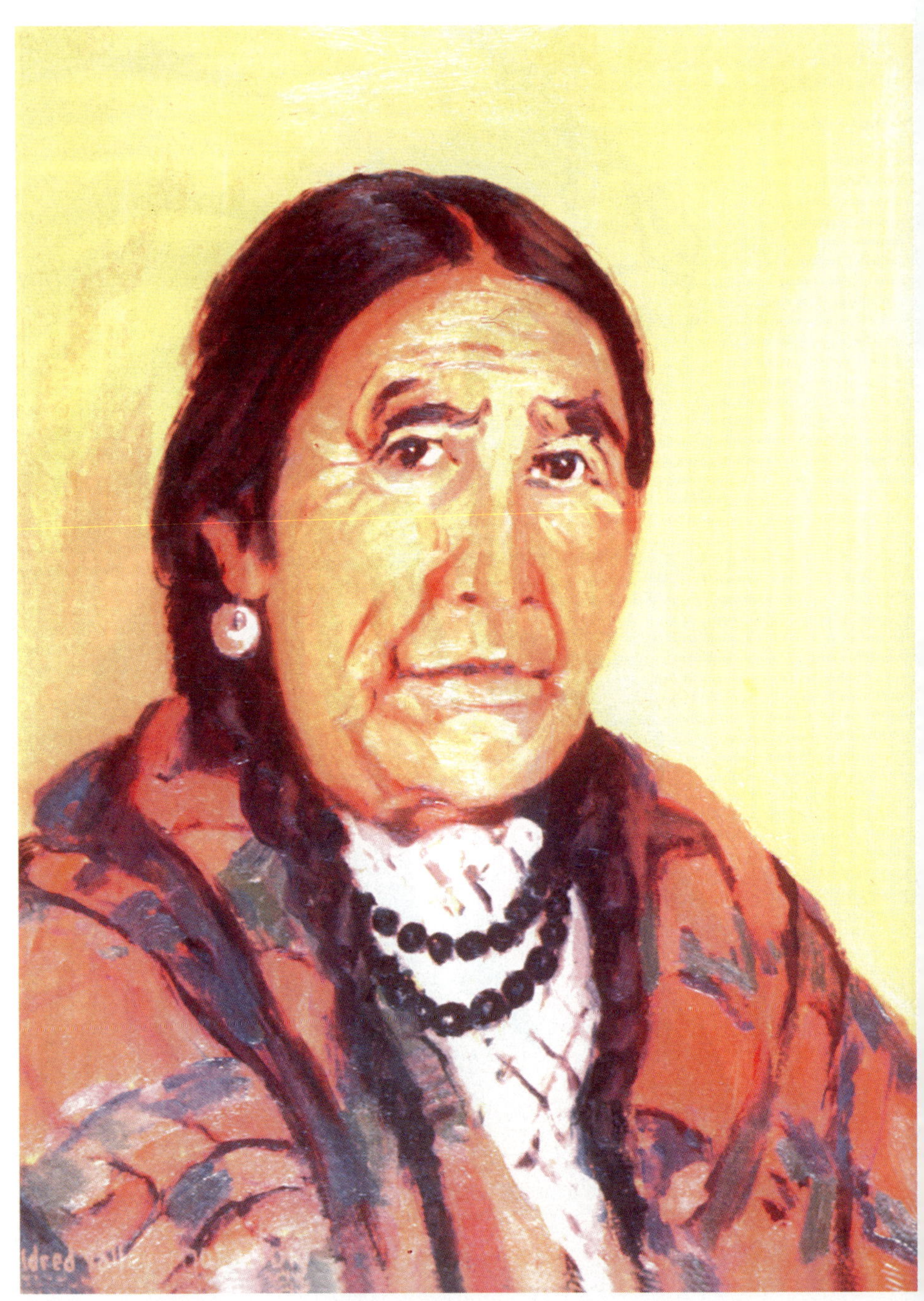

Chief Ben Pasqua's Fifth Wife   ▸ *text page 60*

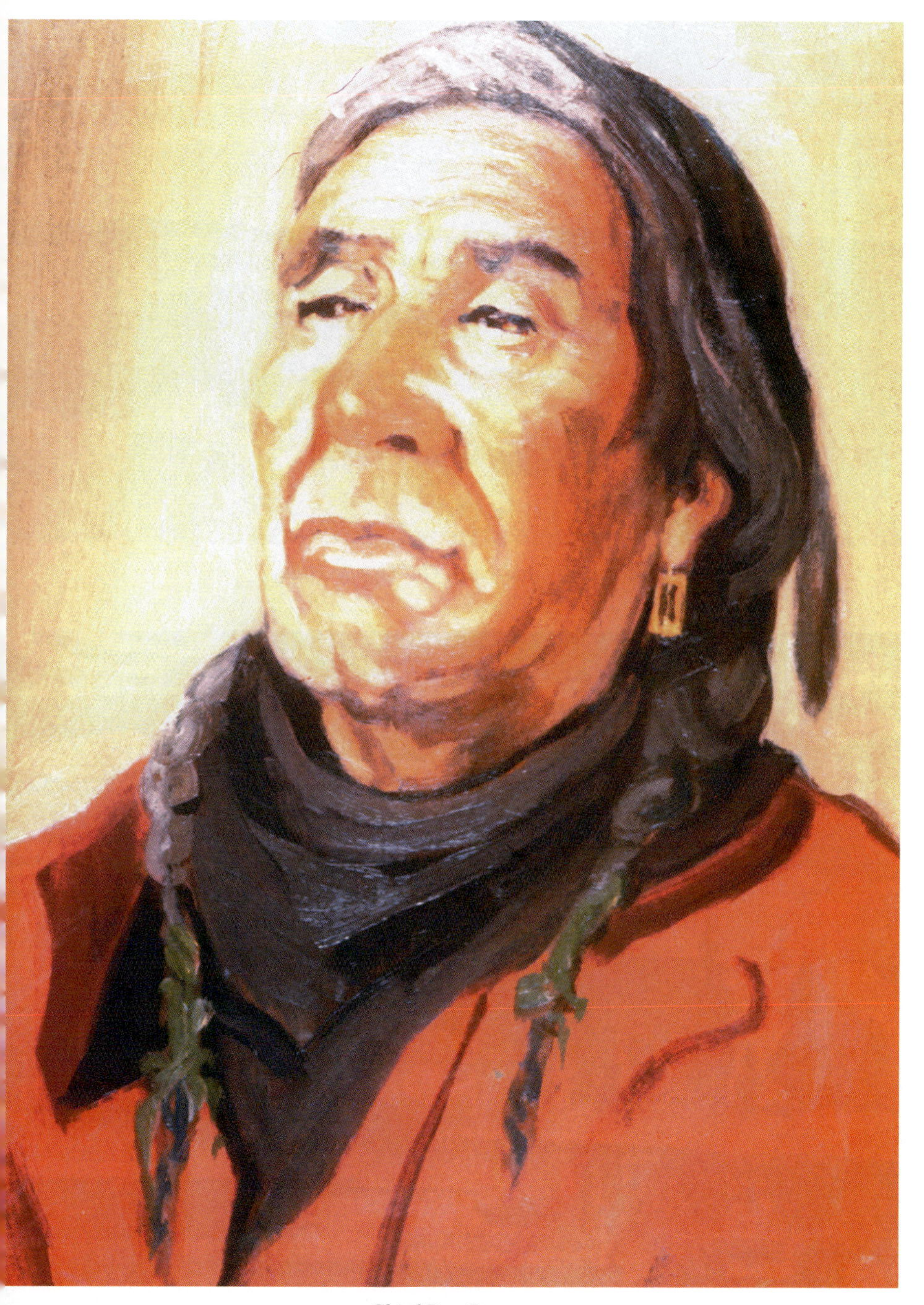

Chief Ben Pasqua   ▶ *text page 57*

117

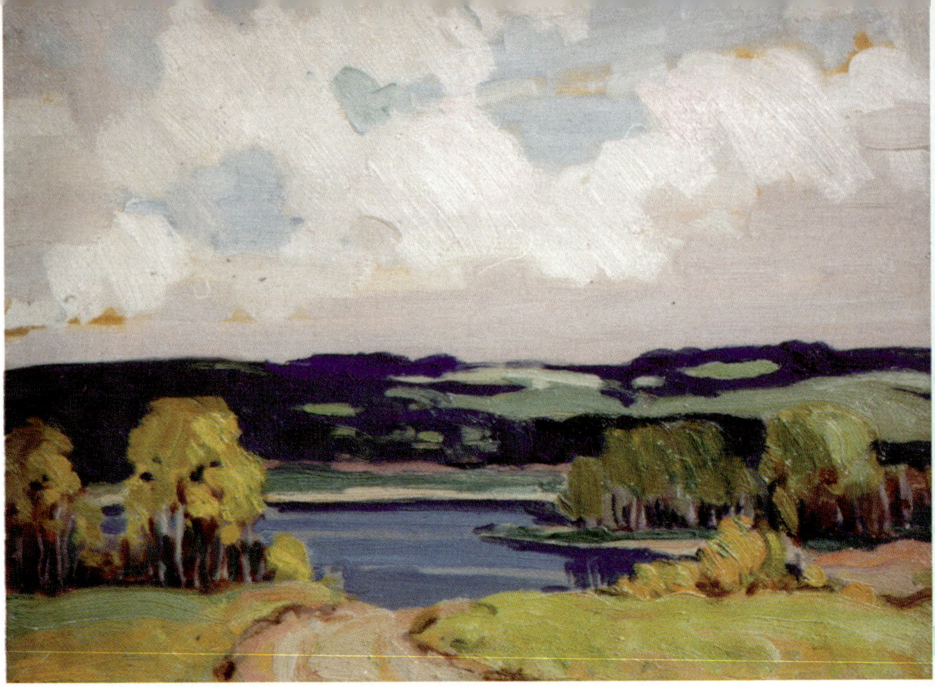

Lowland Landscape, Qu'Appelle Valley

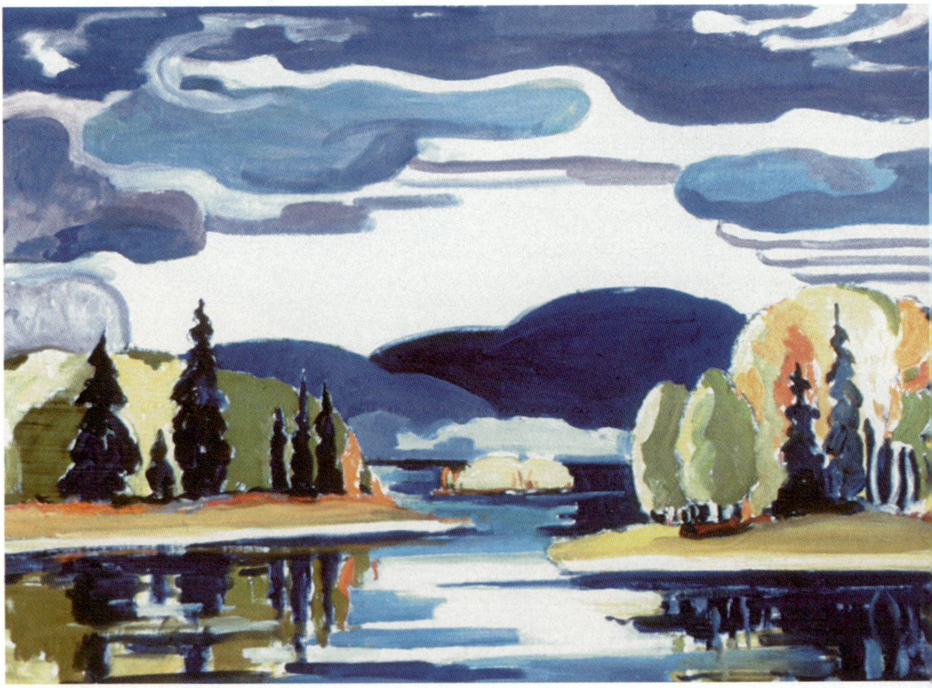

Qu'Appelle Valley

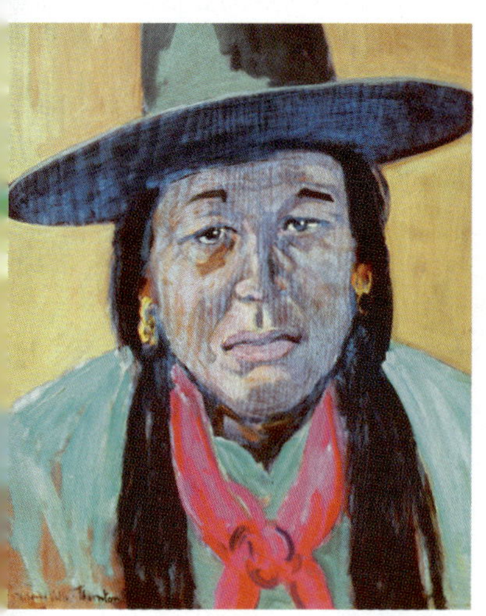

Achim

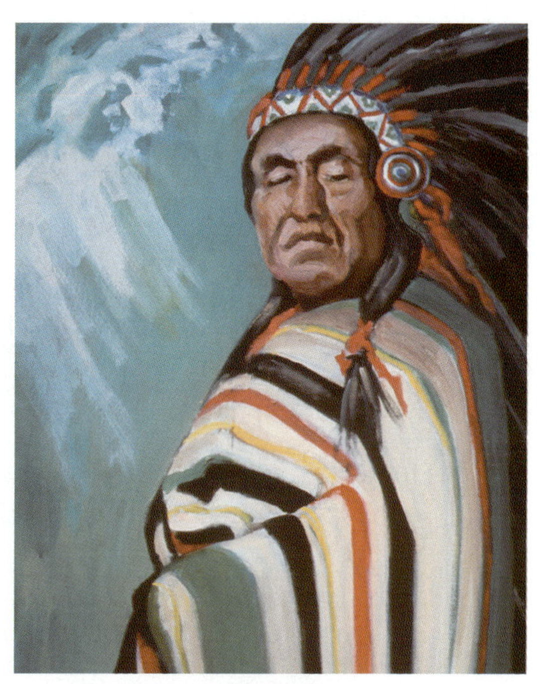

Cree Chief

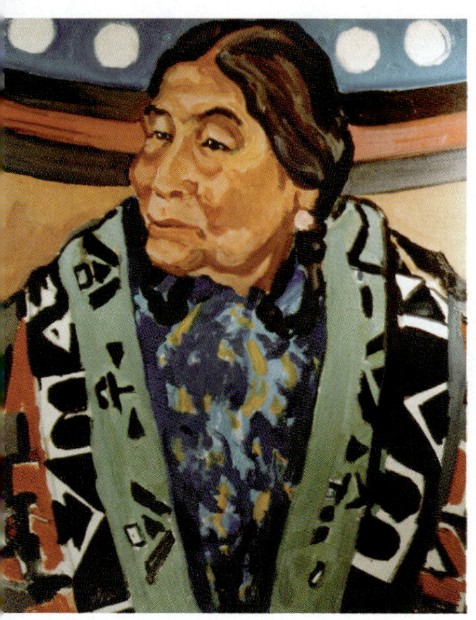

Mrs. Bruised Head/Yellow Squirrel

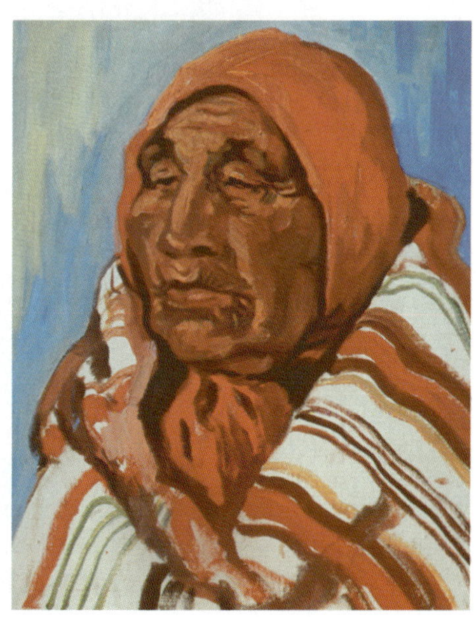

Mrs. Little Walker

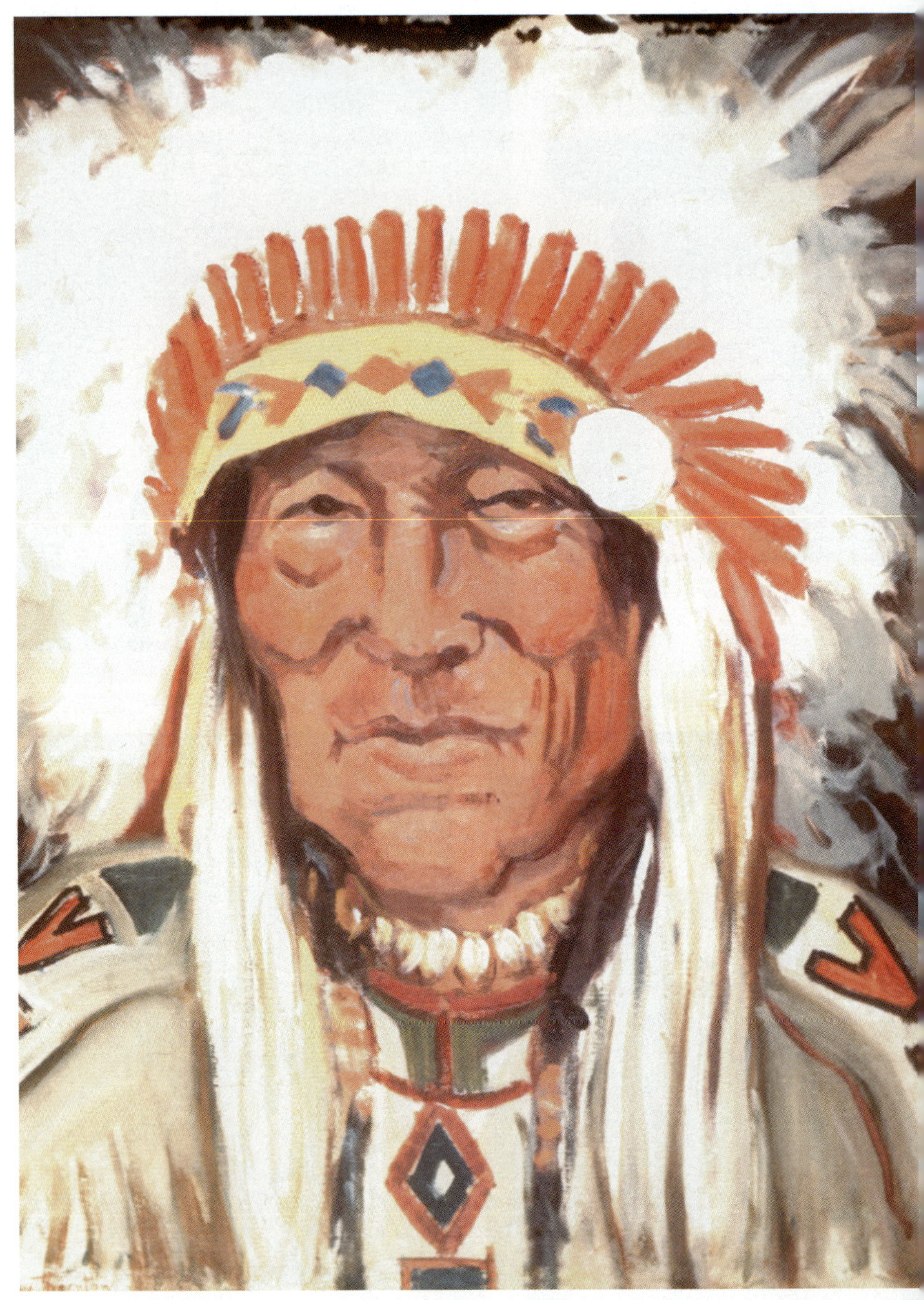

Chief David Bear's Paw ▸ *text page 61*

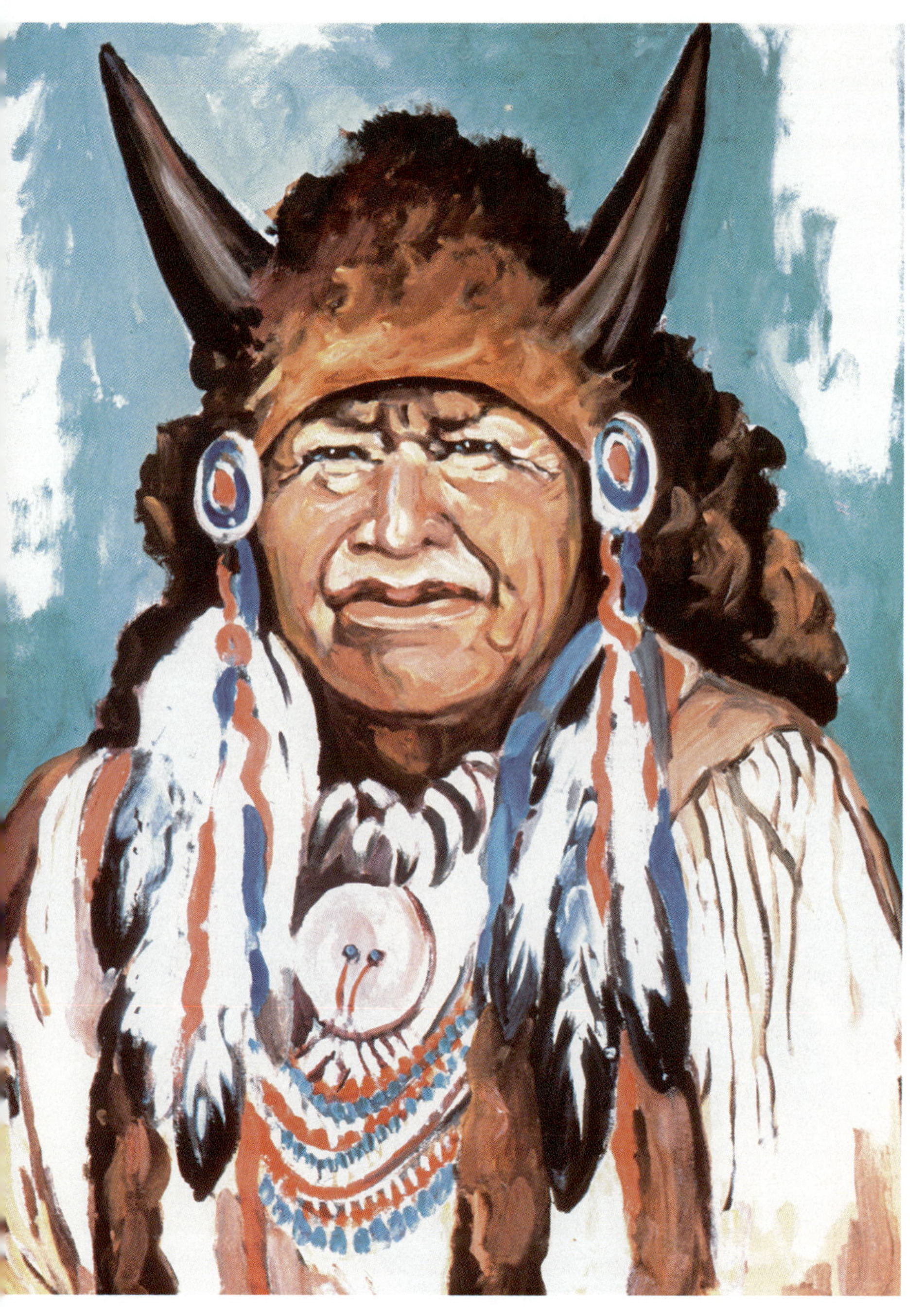

Chief Walking Buffalo   ▸ *text page 66*

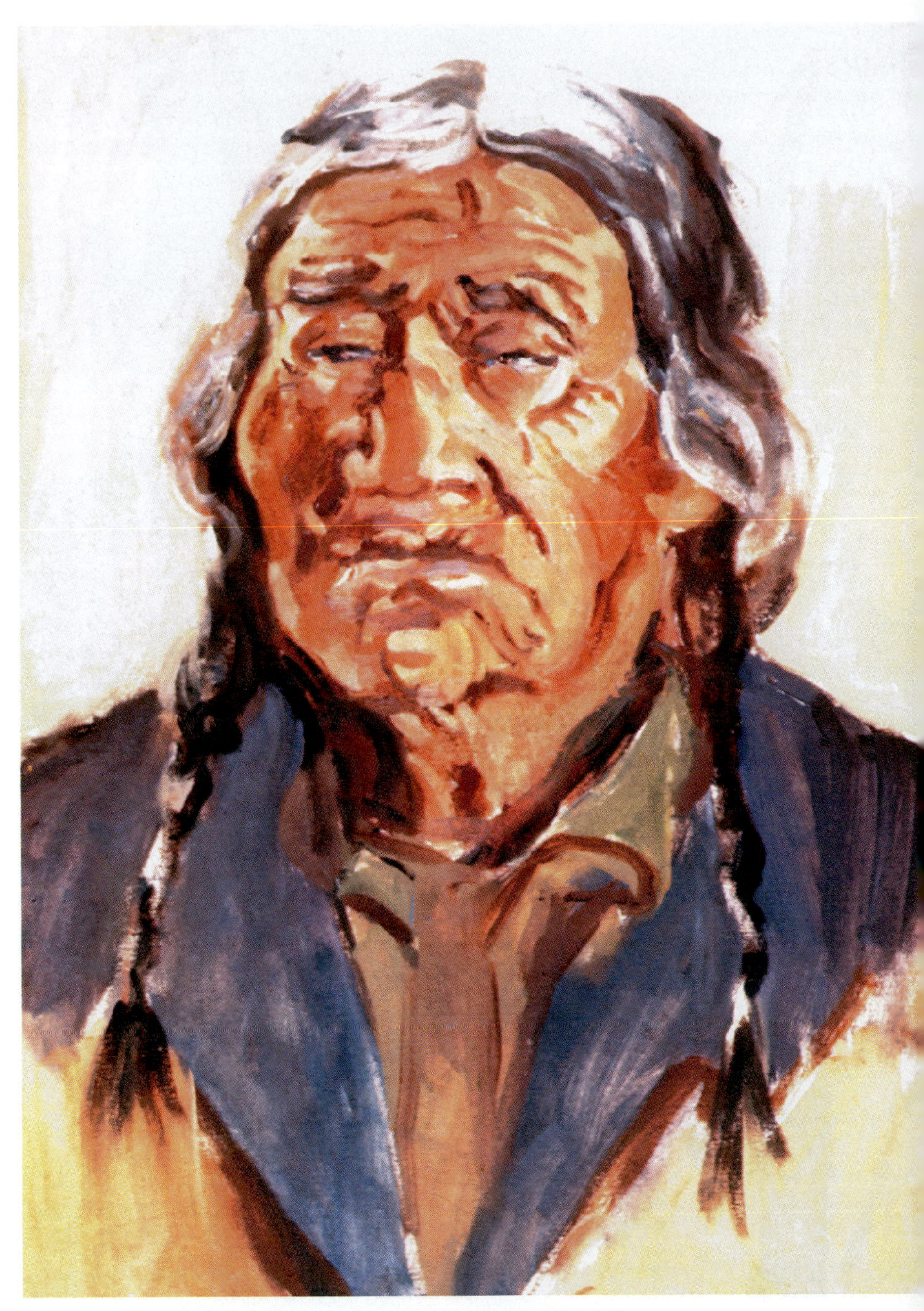

Joshua Hunter "Spotted Eagle"   ▸ *text page 70*

122

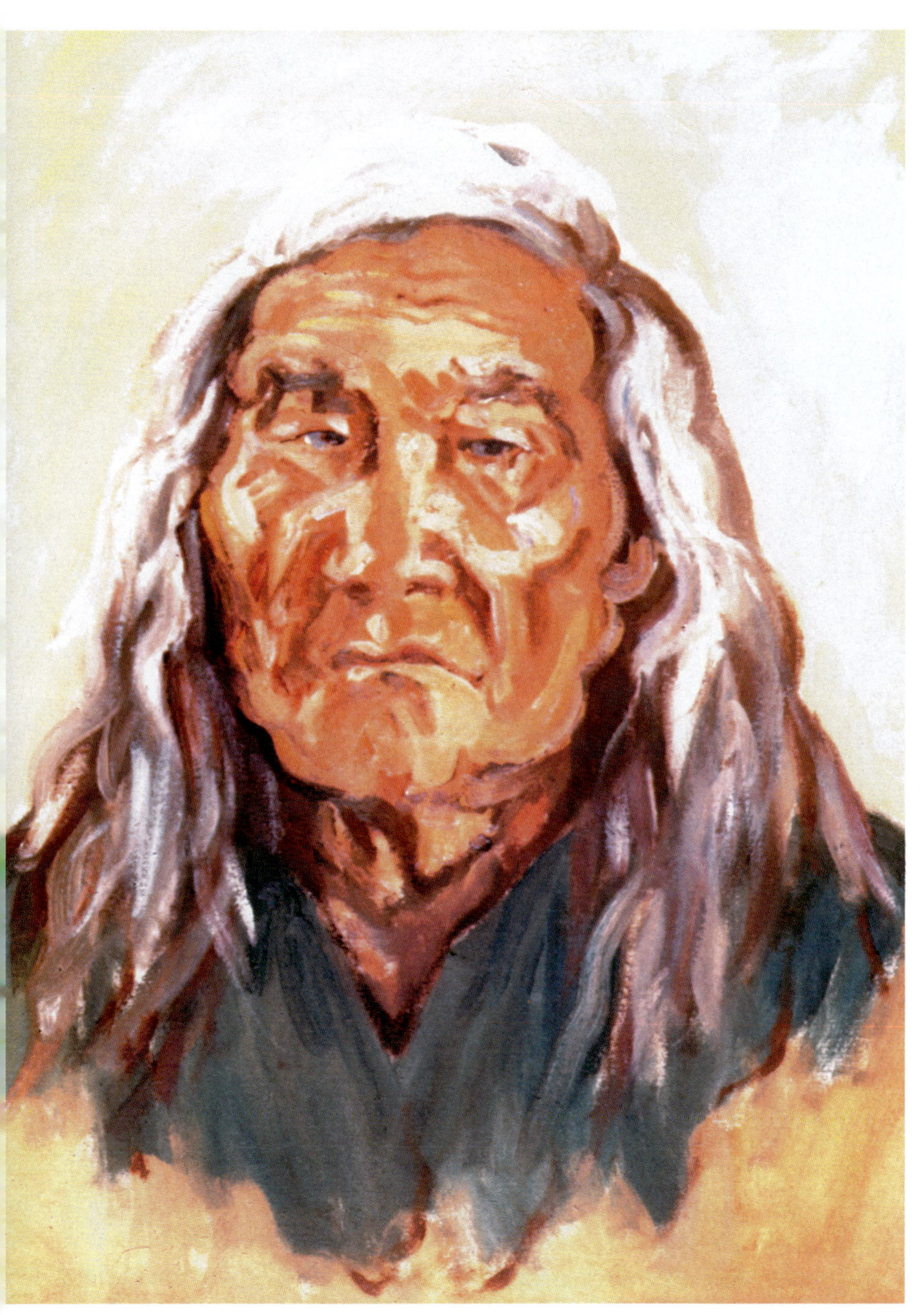

William Hunter *"Yellow Bear"* ▶ *text page 70*

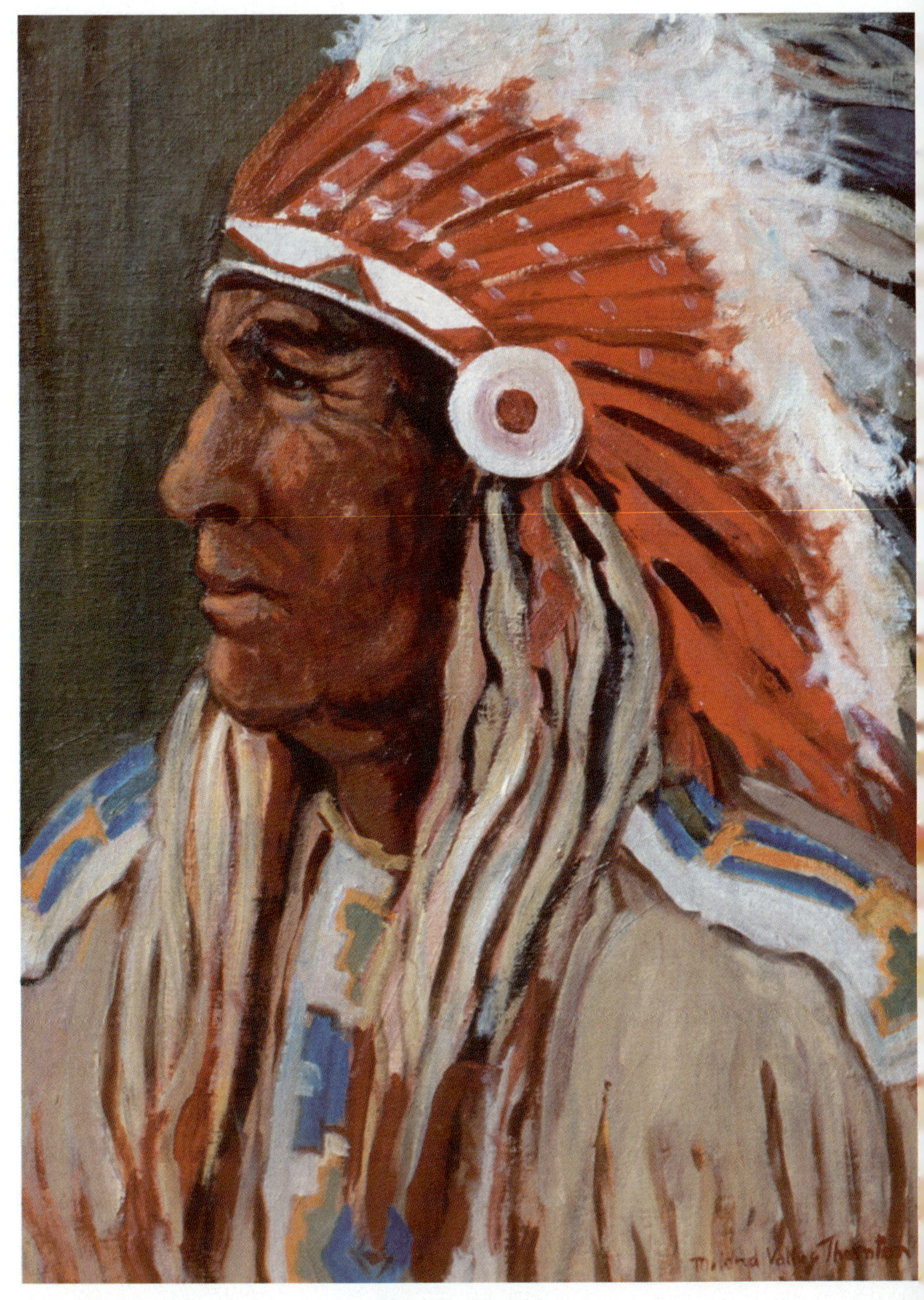

Chief Joe Big Plume   ▶ *text page 77*

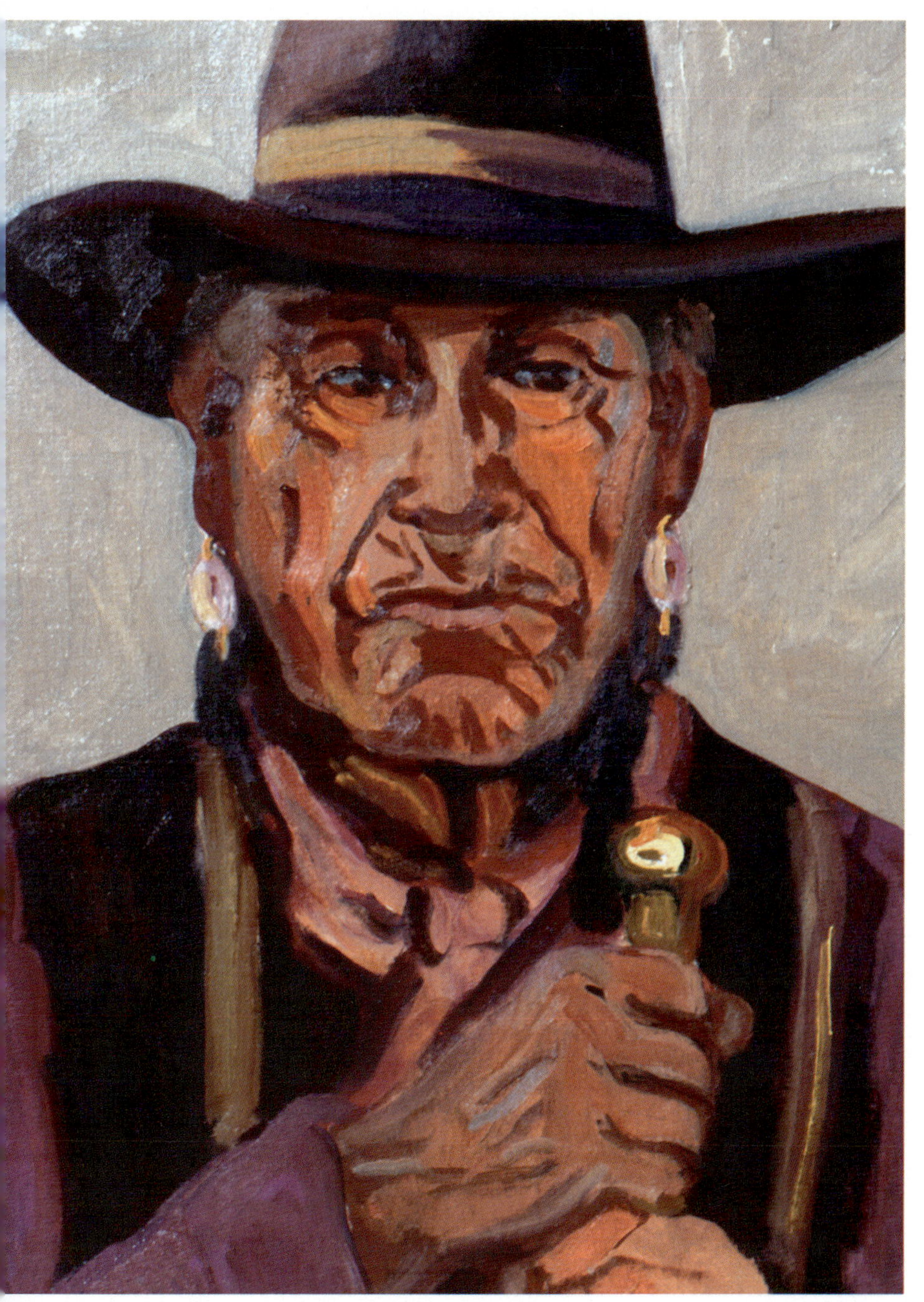

Pretty Young Man

▶ *text page 81*

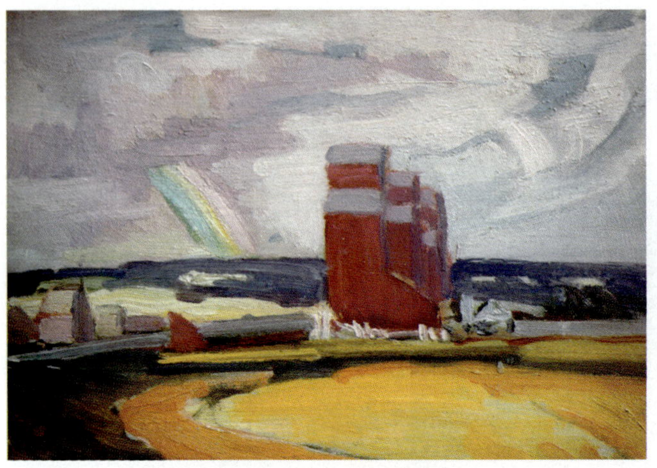

Prairie Grain Elevators (sketch)

Thornton has used artistic license when working up the finished canvas (below). She changed the curve of the road and the direction of the rainbow from the original sketch to make the composition flow better and be more pleasing to the eye.

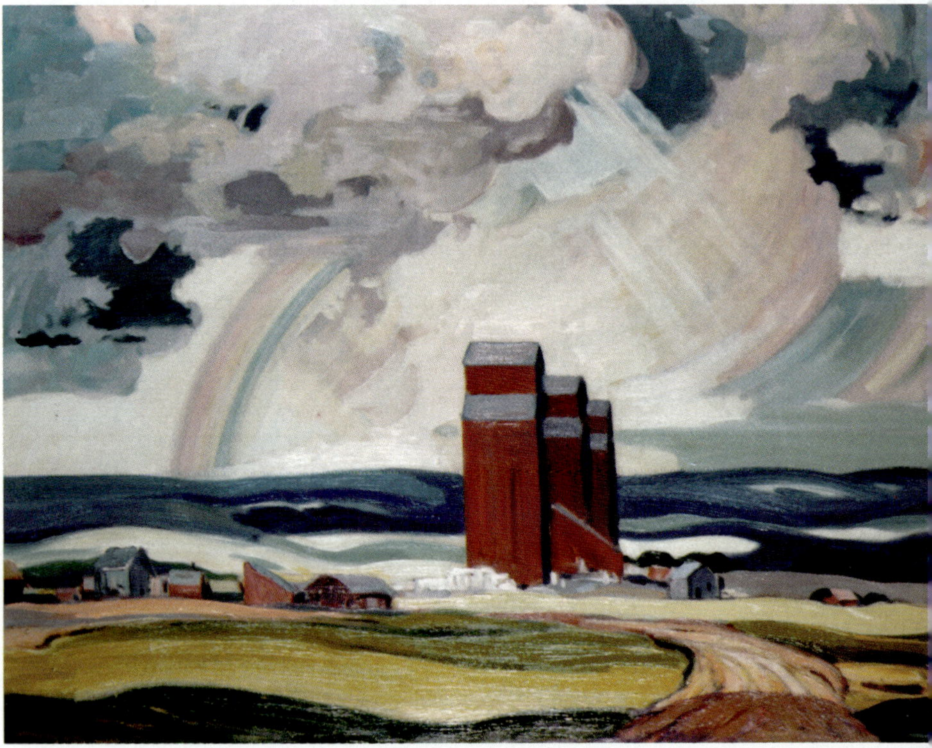

Prairie Grain Elevators

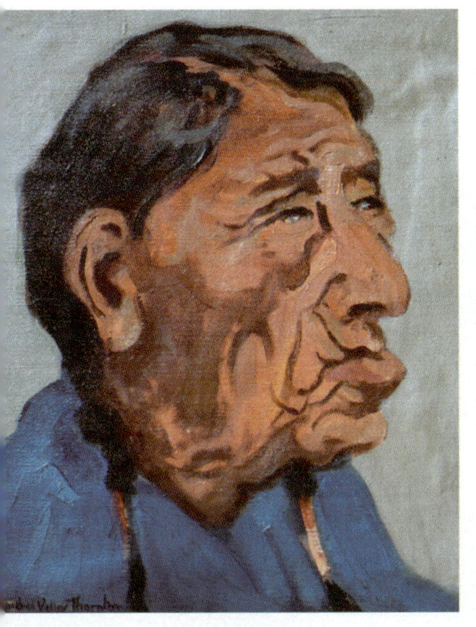

Turning Rope

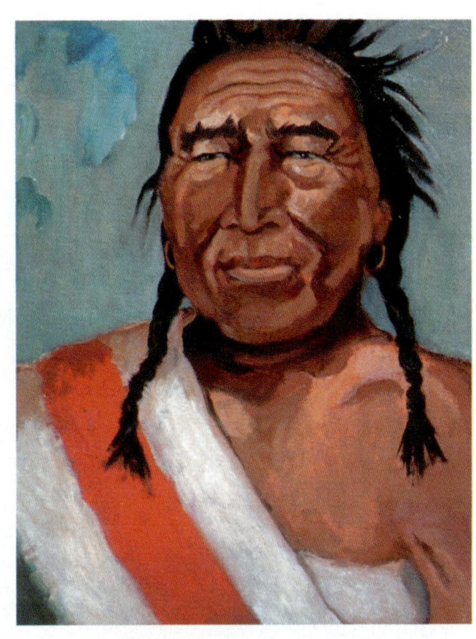

Crooked Guts/Bullet Head

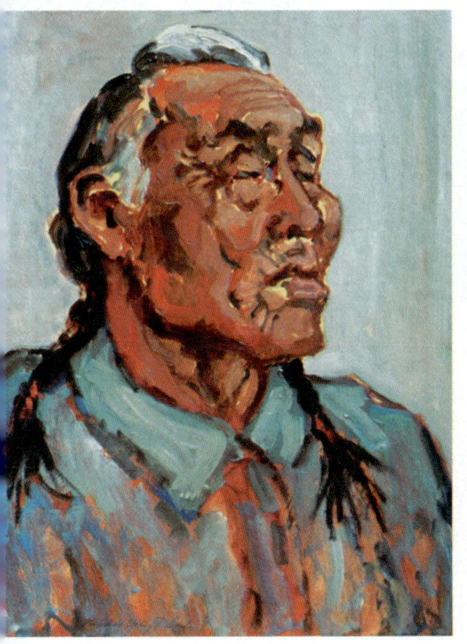

Heavy Head

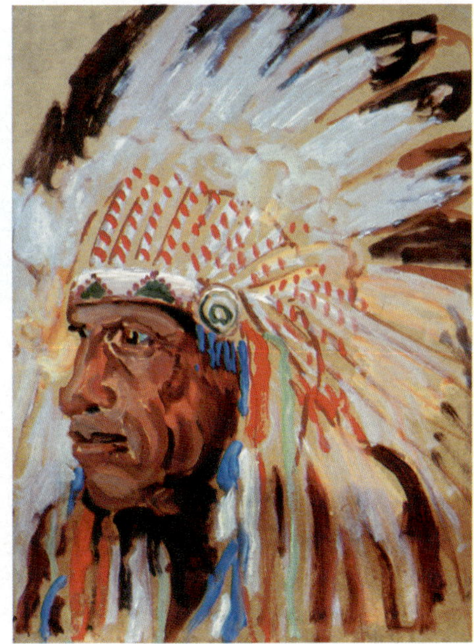

Tom Prairie Chicken

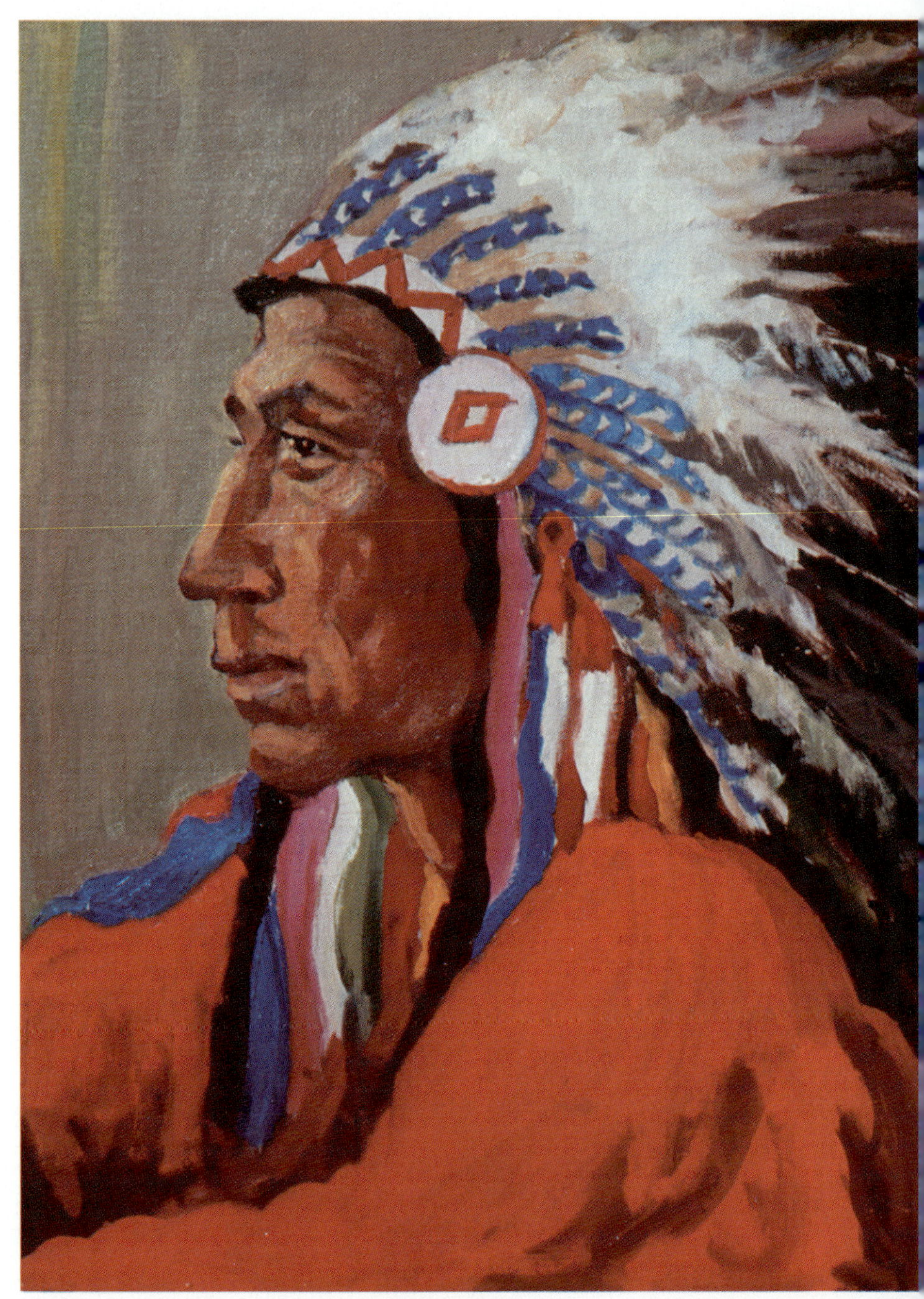

George Big Belly   ▸ *text page 82*

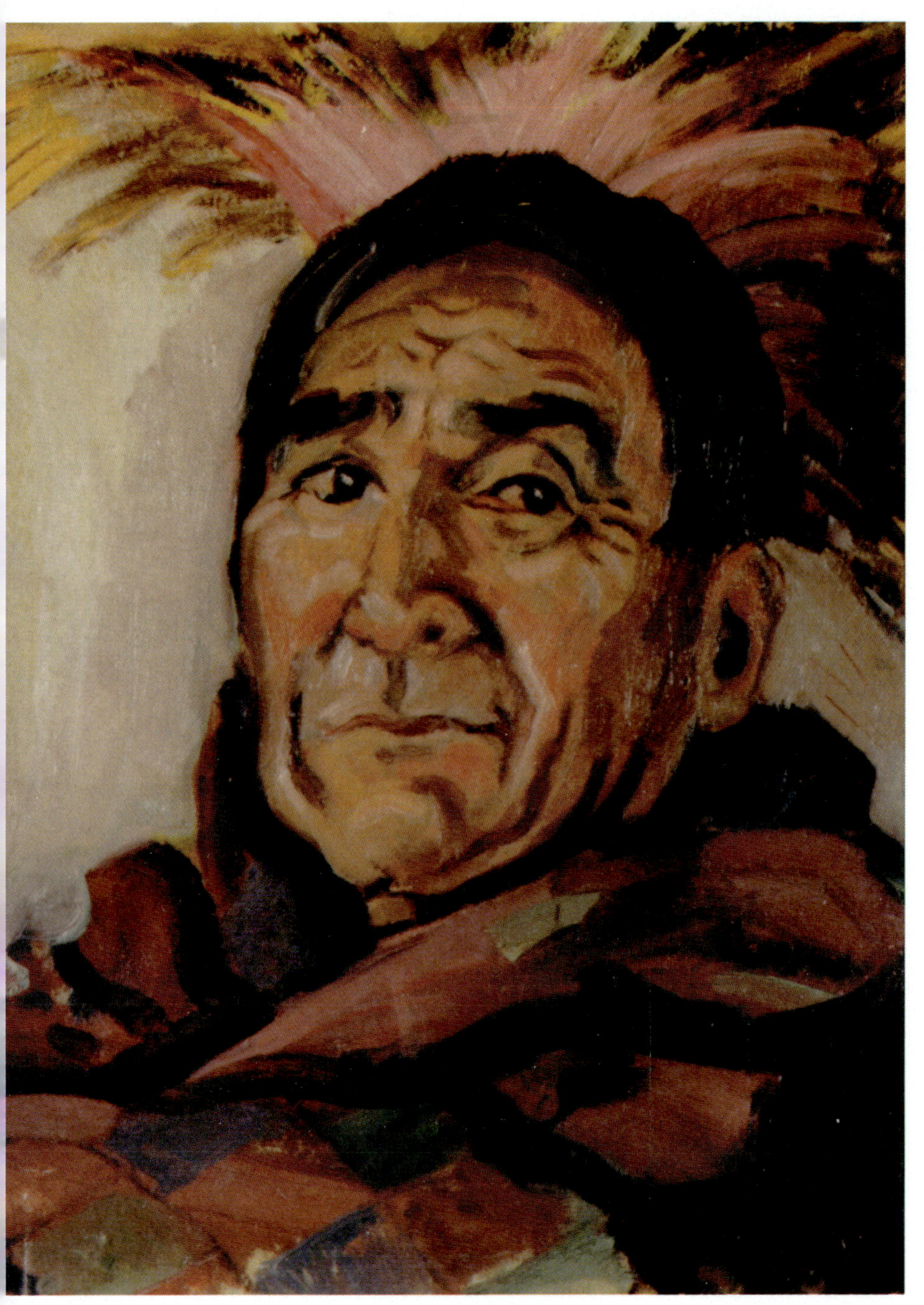

Chief Julius Buffalo	▸ *text page 85*

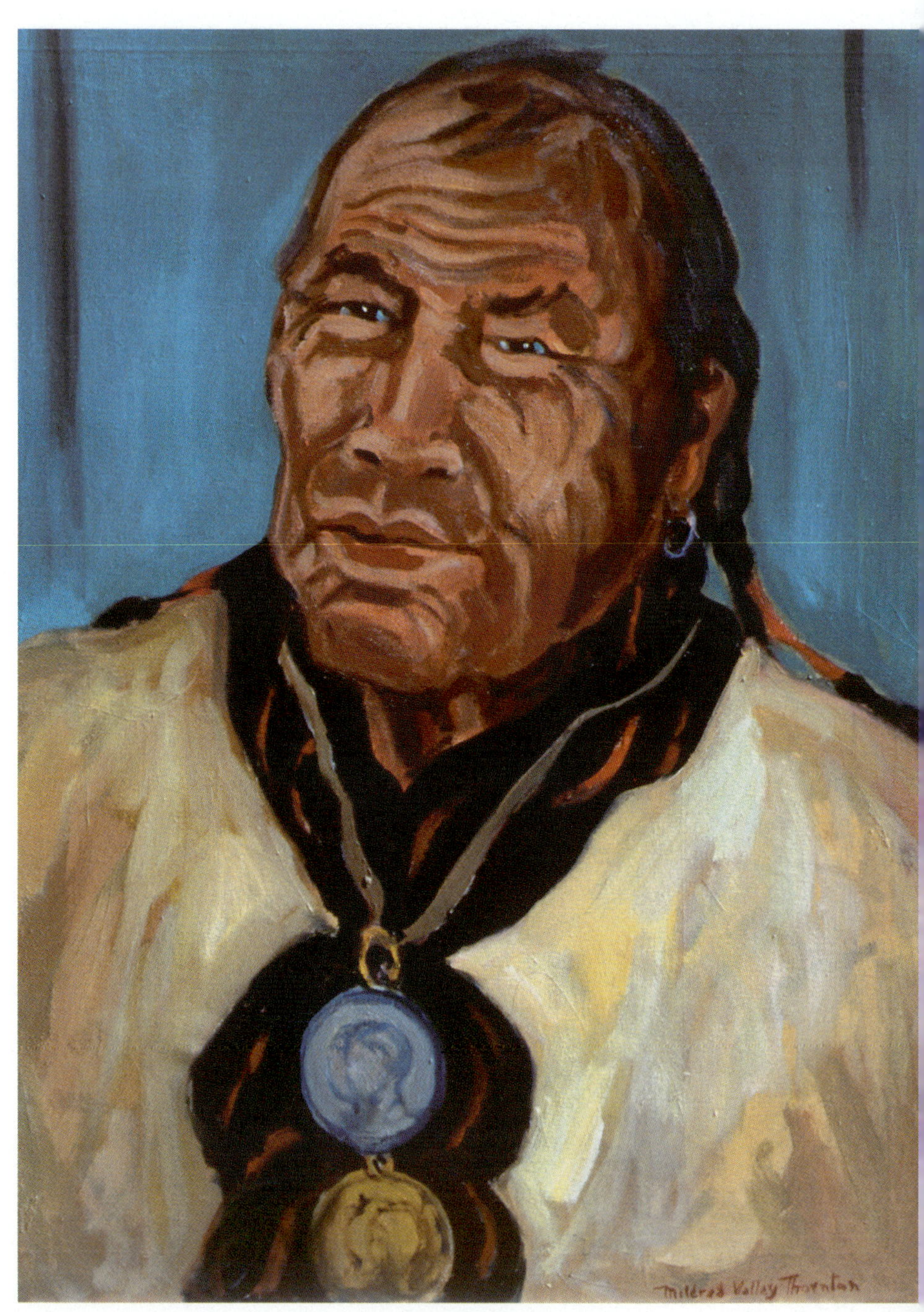

Duck Chief and His Medals   ▸ *text page 88*

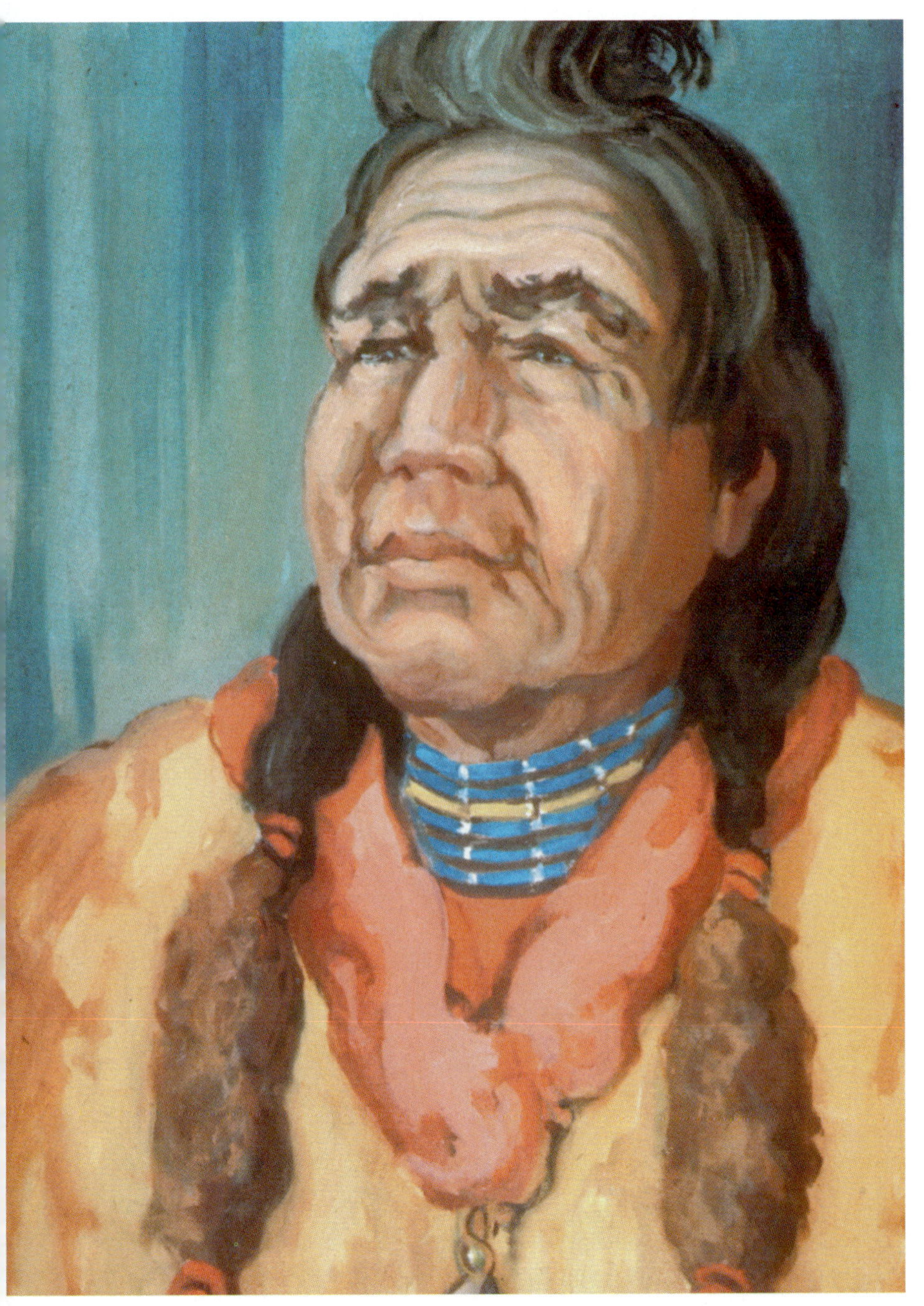

Chief Fish-Wolf-Ofe   ▶ *text page 93*

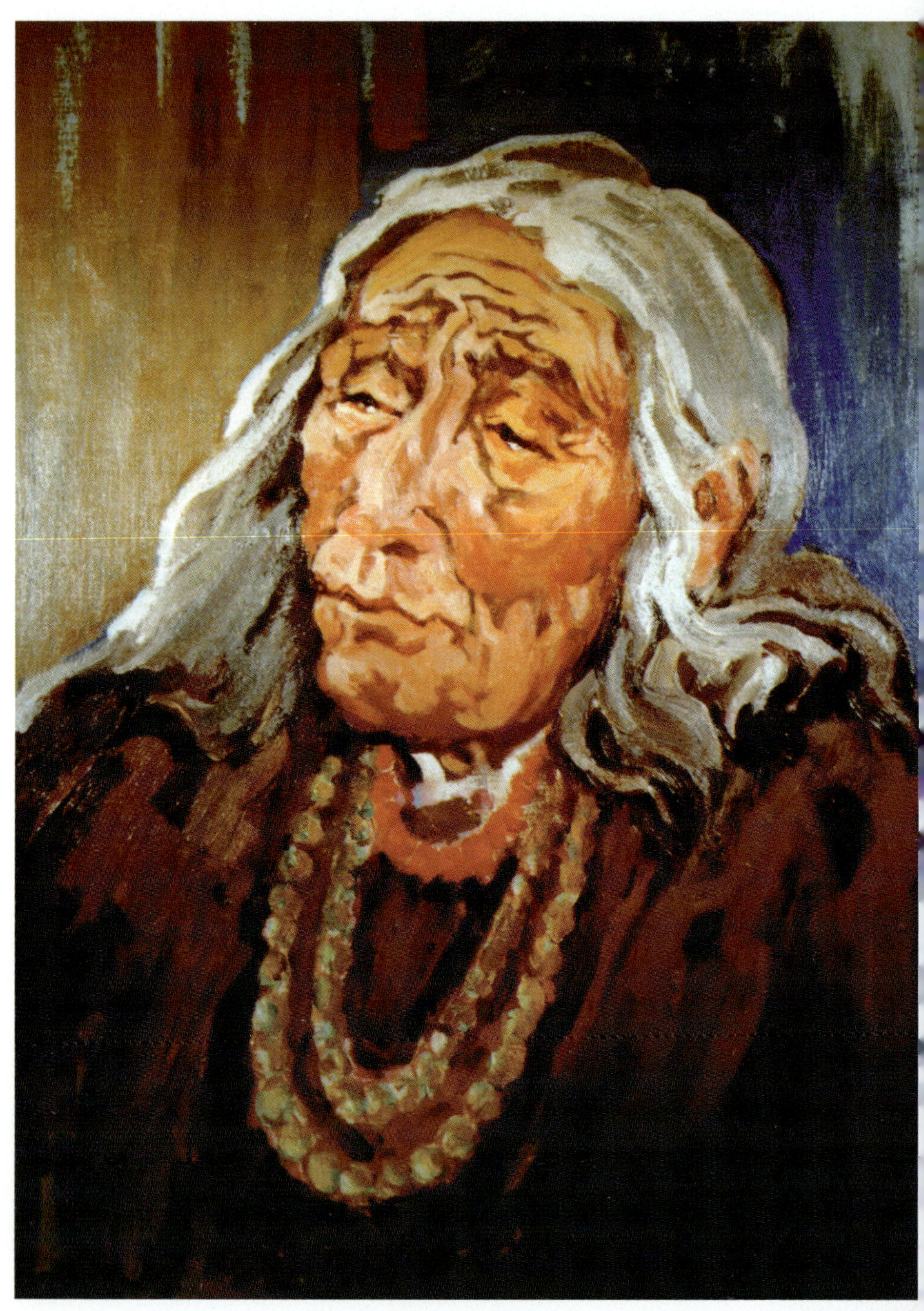

Crowfoot's Daughter

▸ *text page 145*

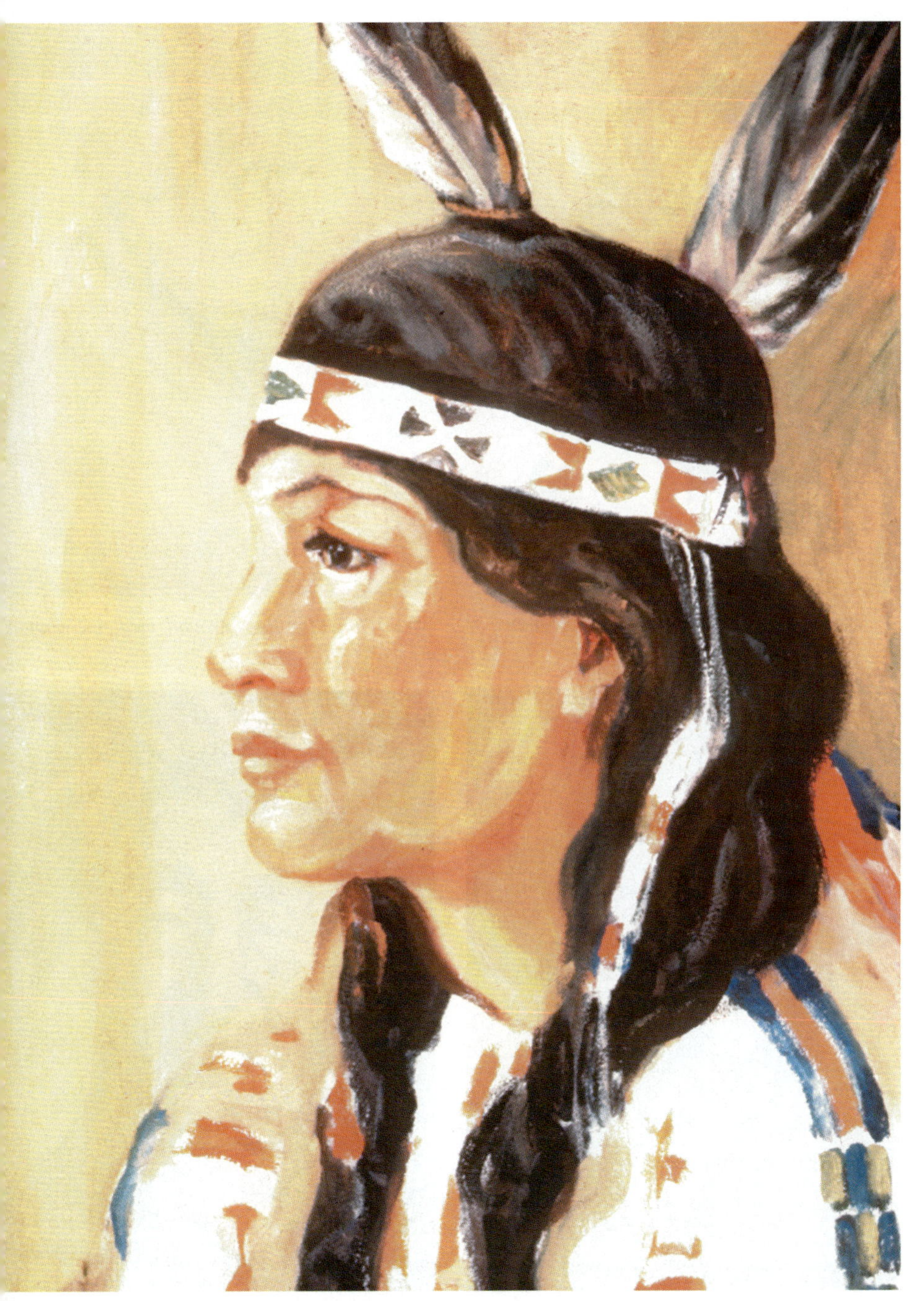

Margaret Crowfoot ▸ *text page 150*

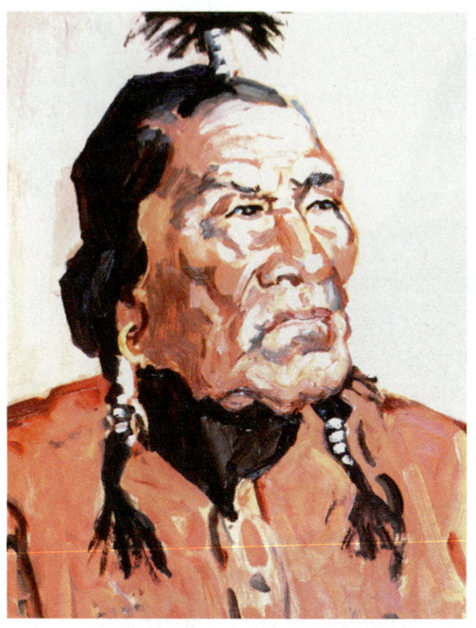

Big Face Chief, Piegan medicine man

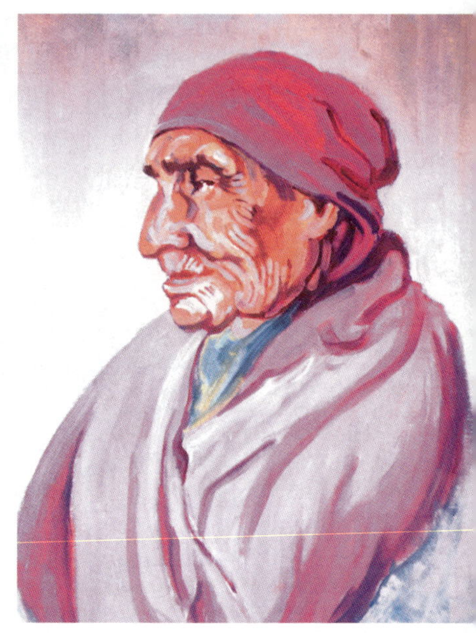

Mrs. White Man Runs Around, medicine woman

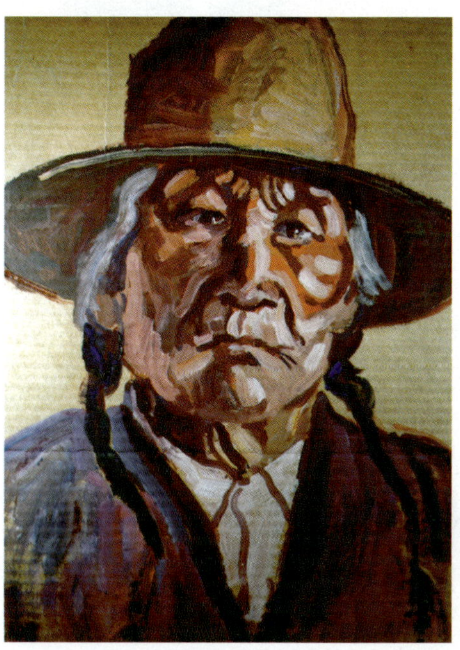

Dog Child, medicine man

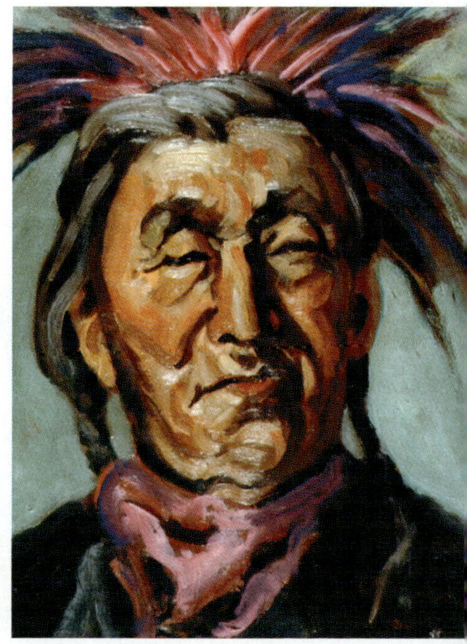

Piegan, medicine man

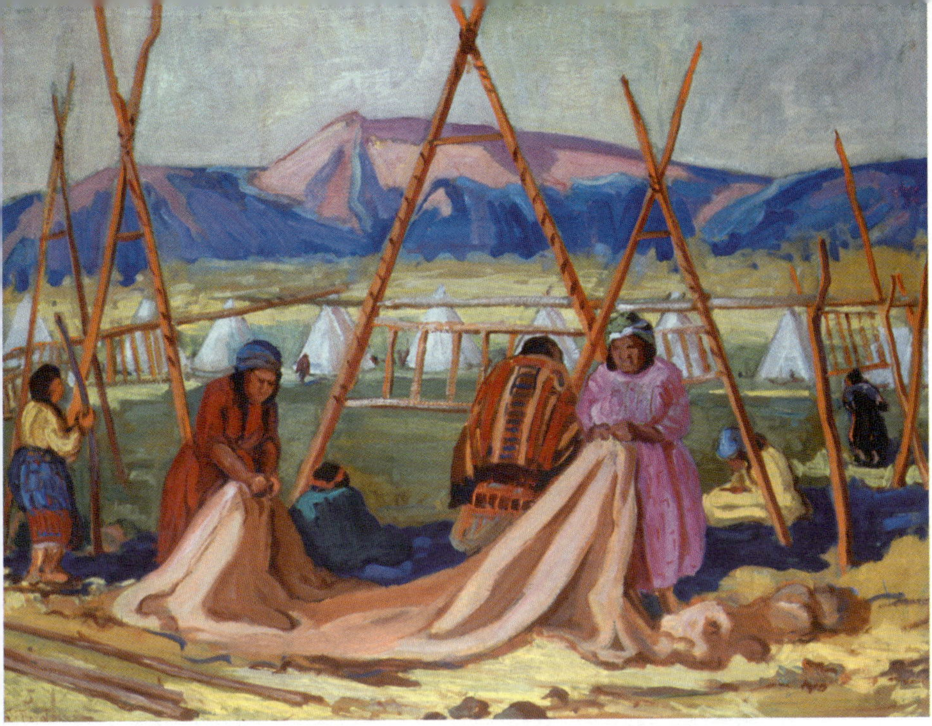

Indian Women Erecting Tepees

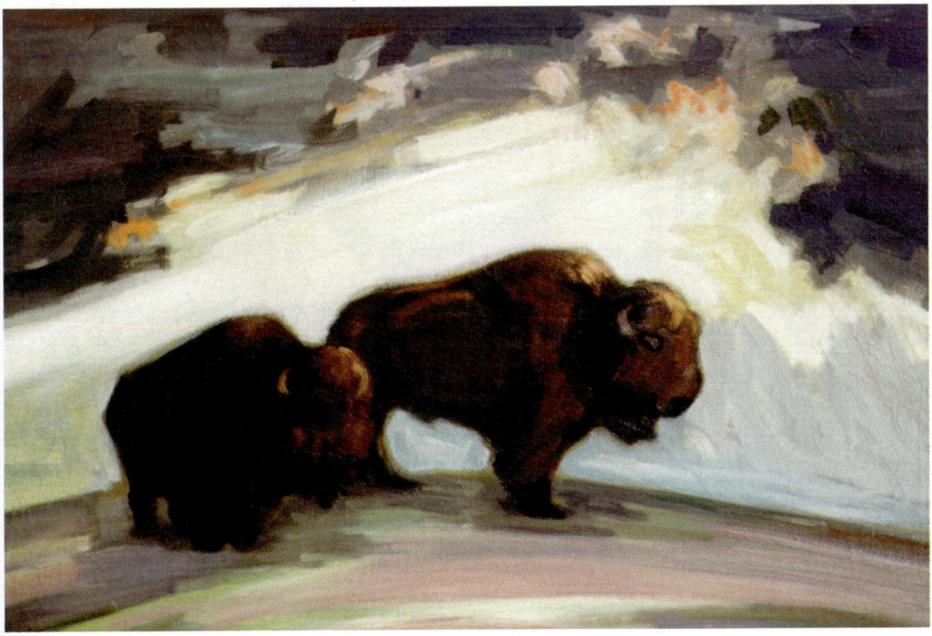

Buffalo on the Plains

135

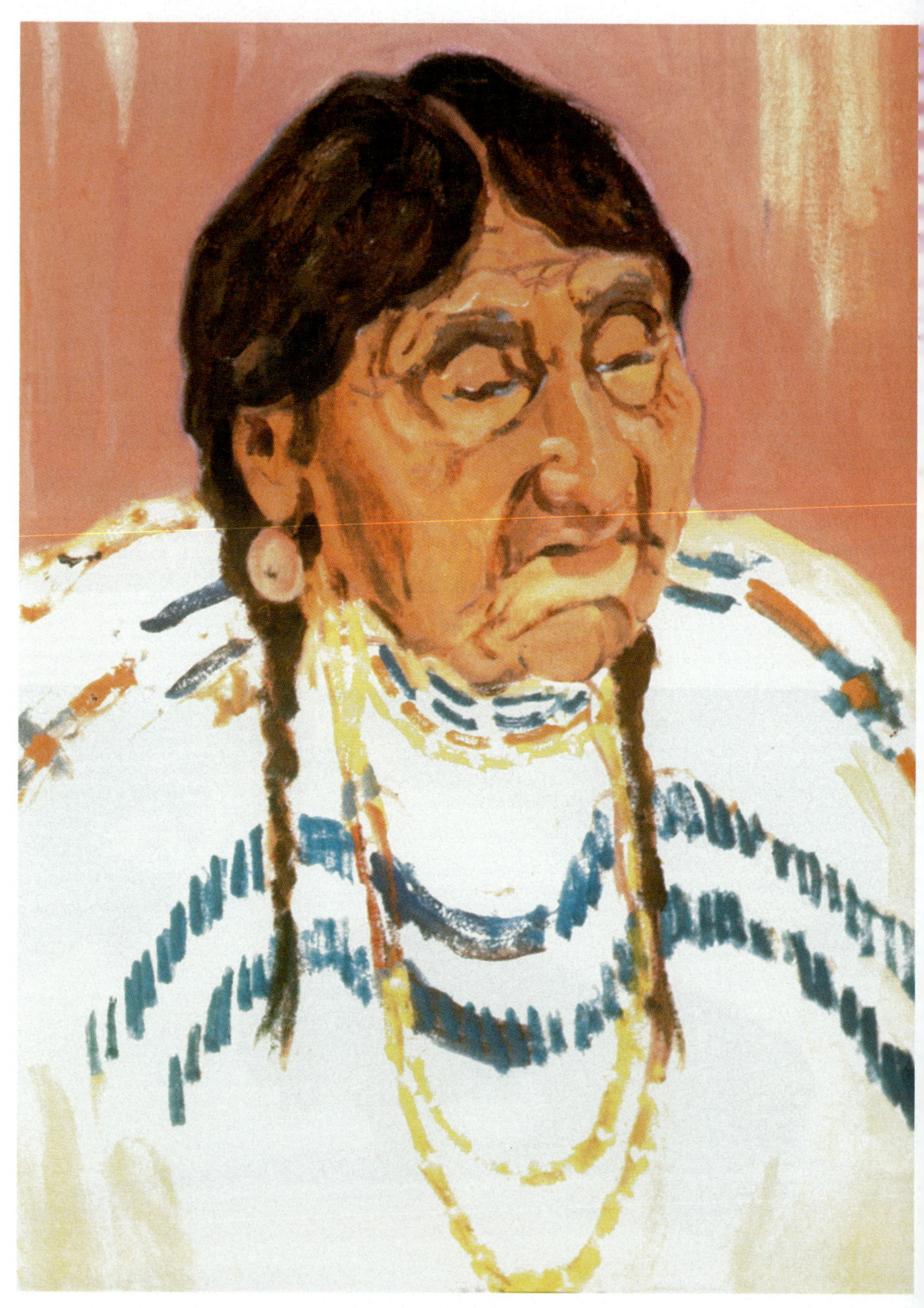

Under Badger

▶ *text page 151*

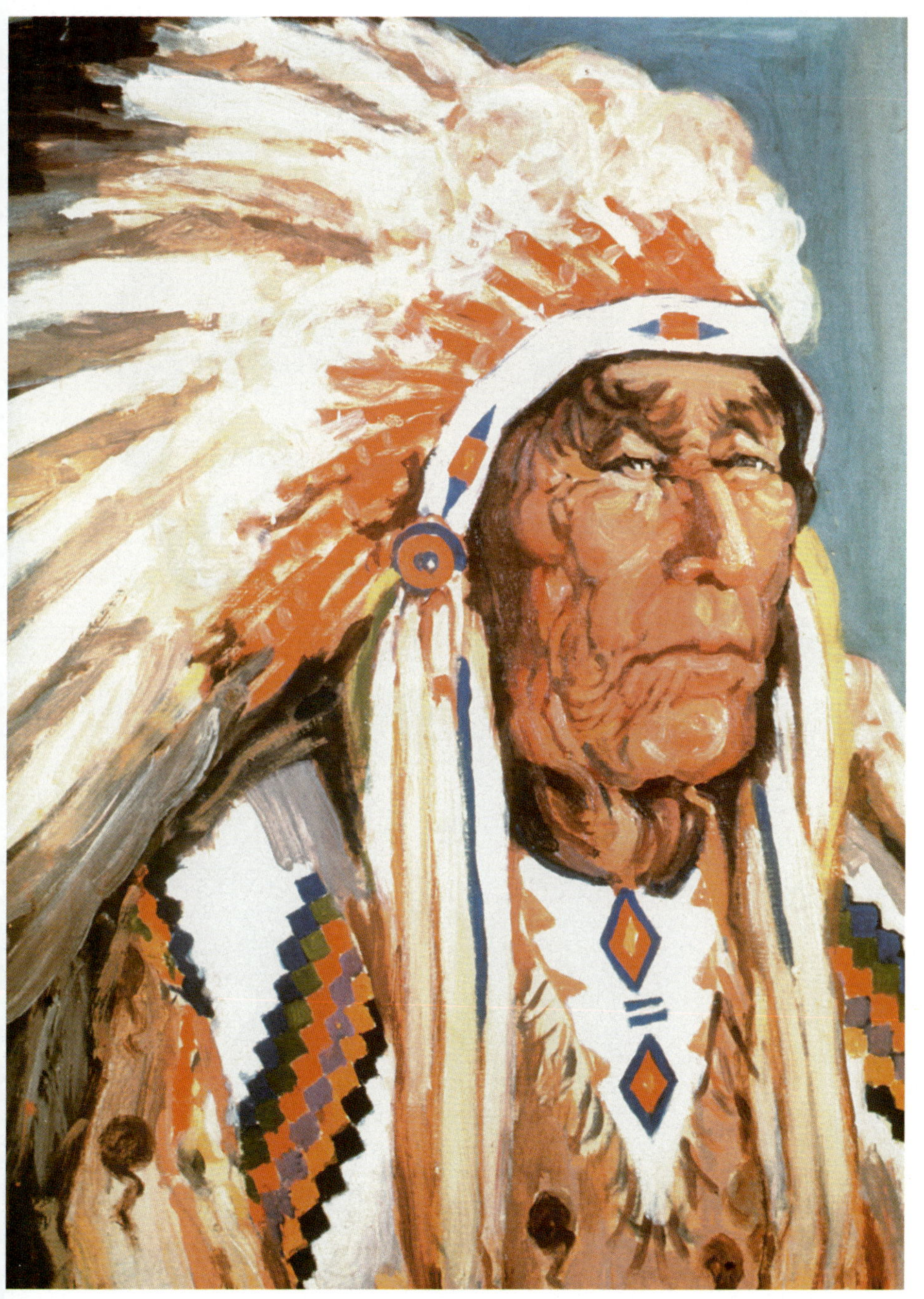

Chief Paul Little Walker   ▶ *text page 153*

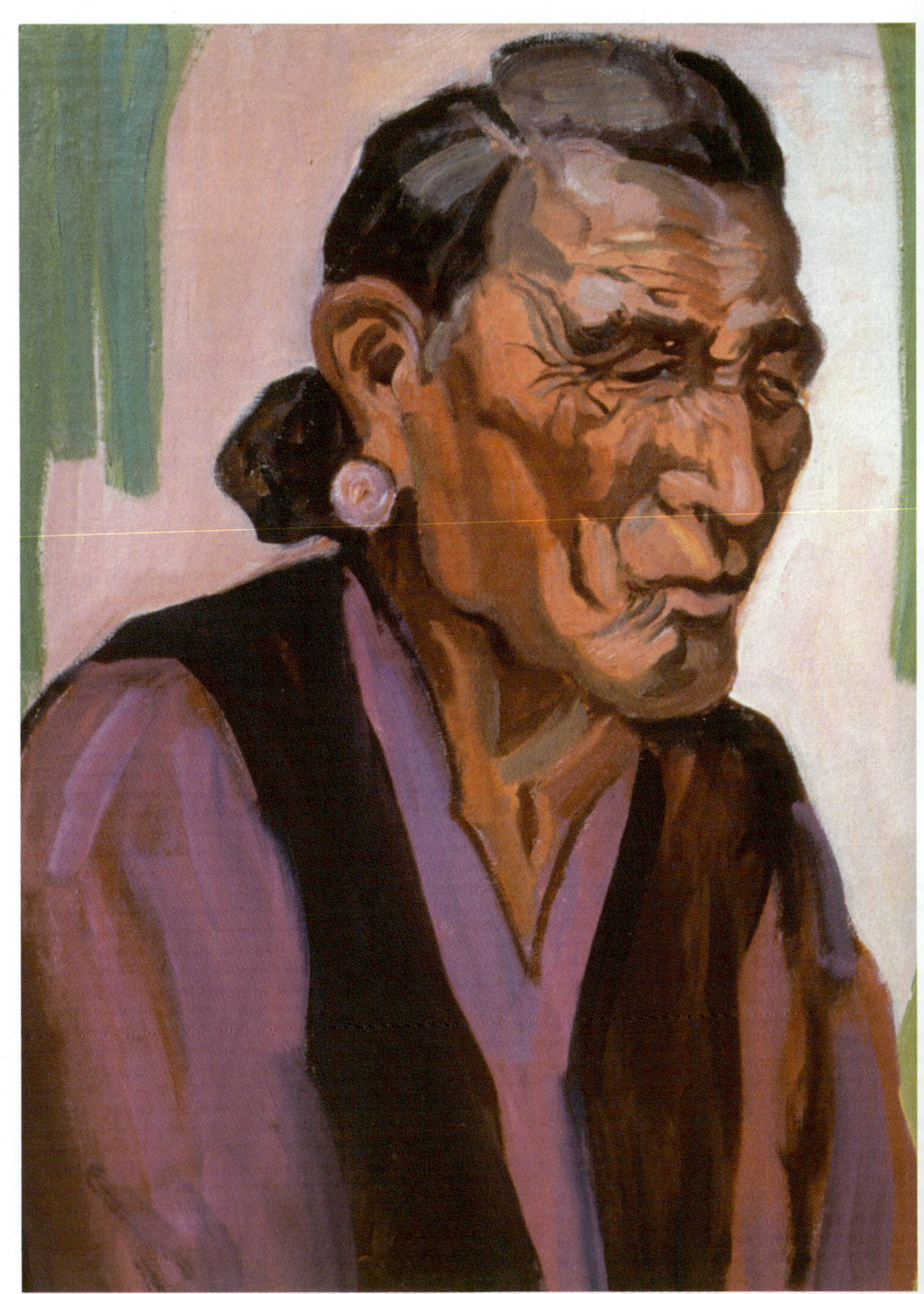

Charley Davis   ▸ *text page 156*

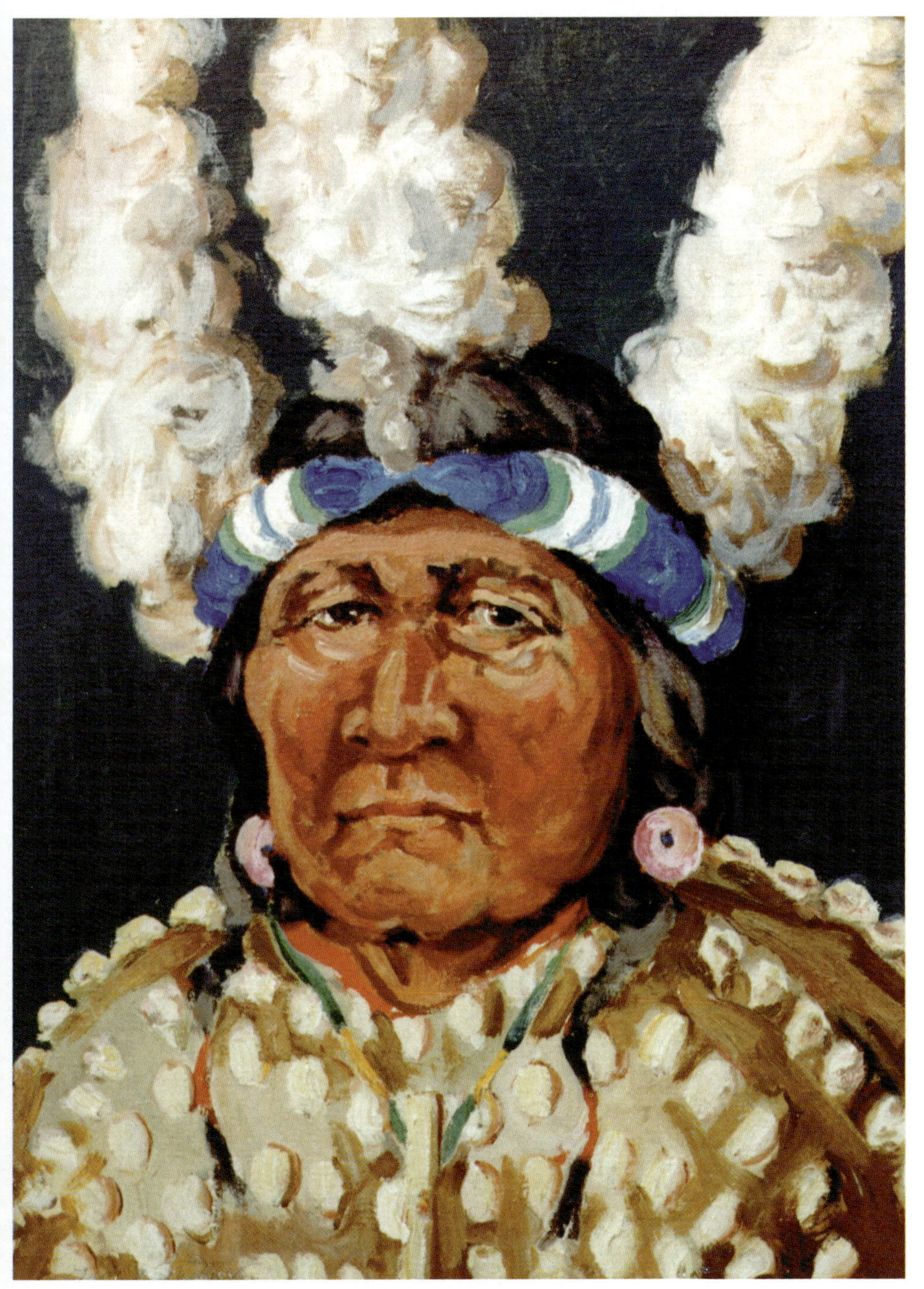

Pretty Kangaroo Woman ▸ *text page 158*

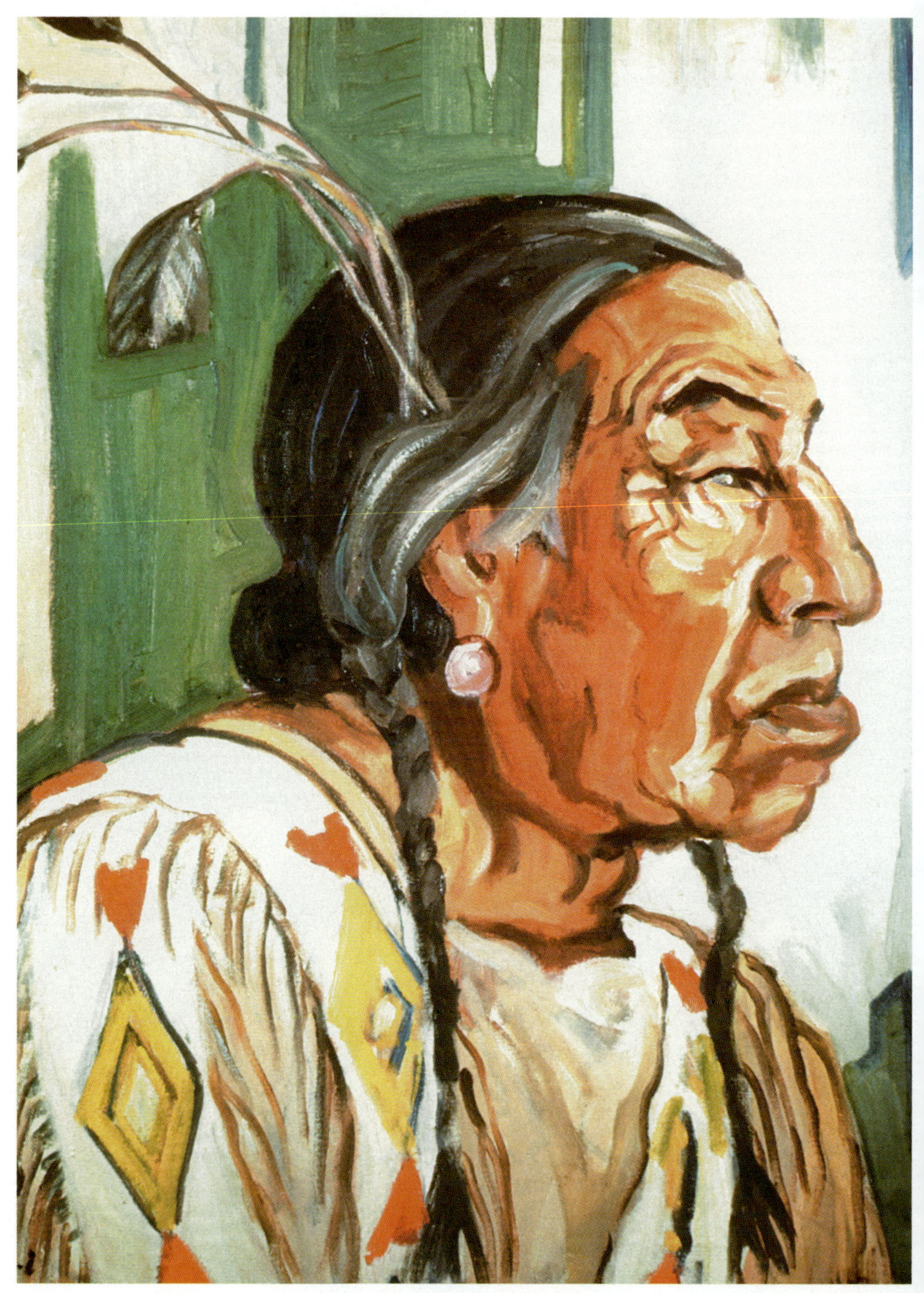

Chief Shot-On-Both-Sides

▶ *text page 164*

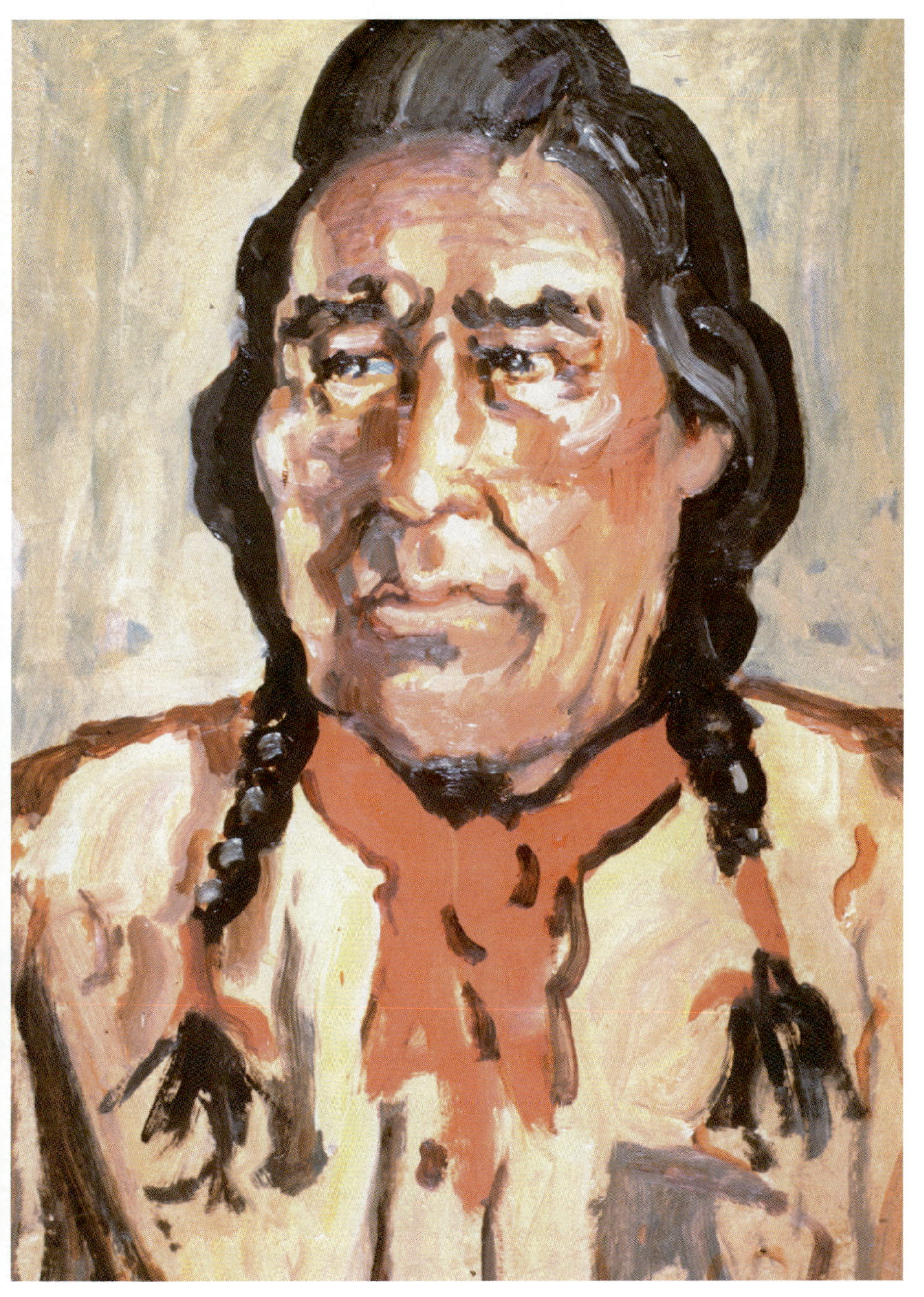

Chief Jim Crowflag   ▸ *text page 171*

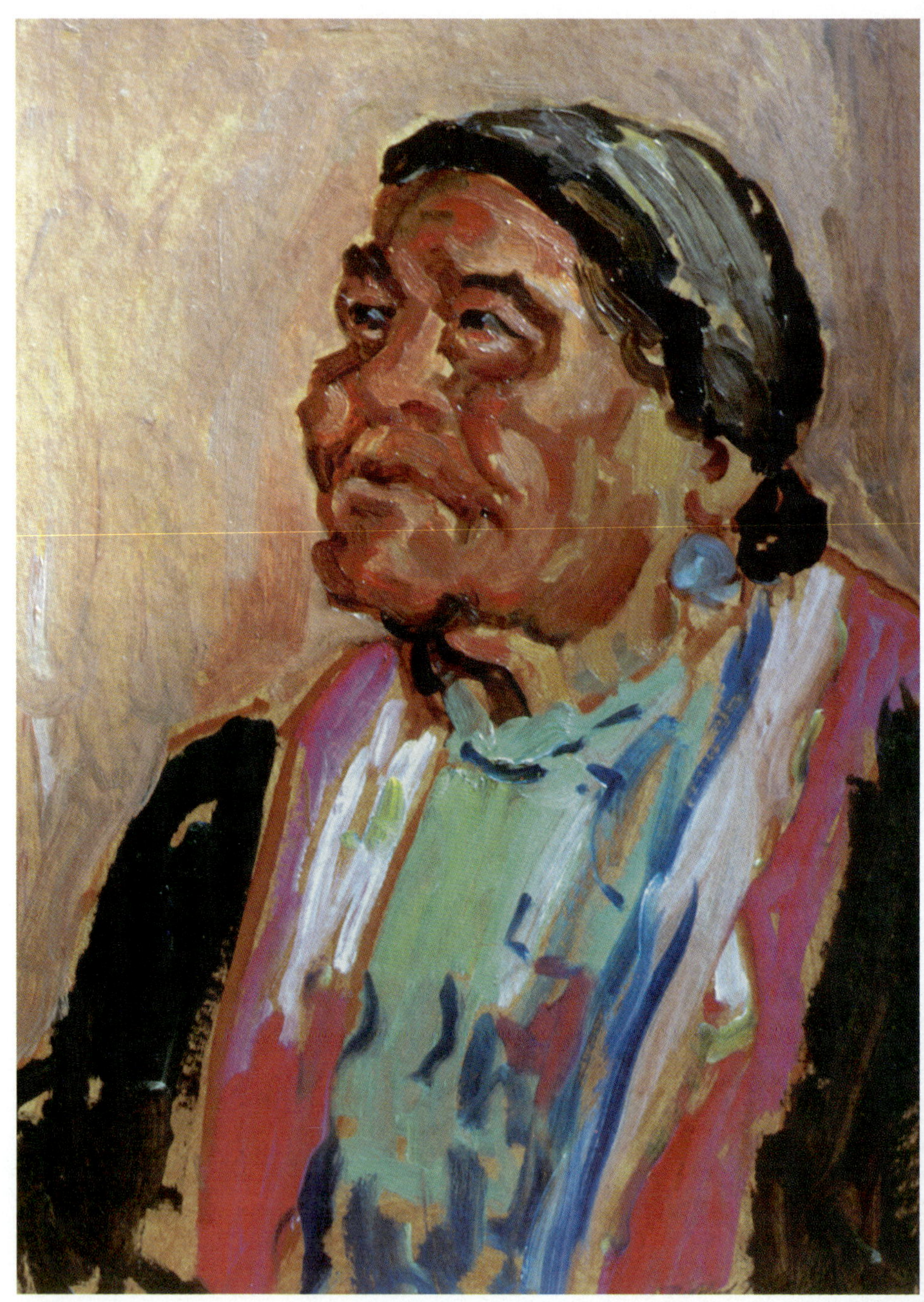

Rosie, Chief Jim Crowflag's Wife ▸ *text page 173*

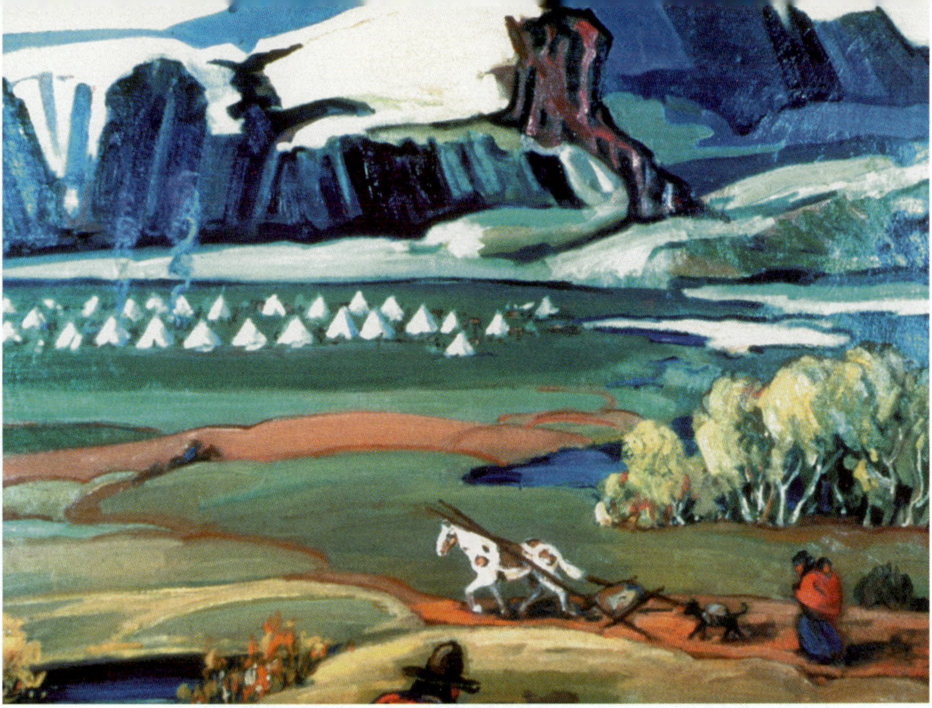

Circle of Tepees

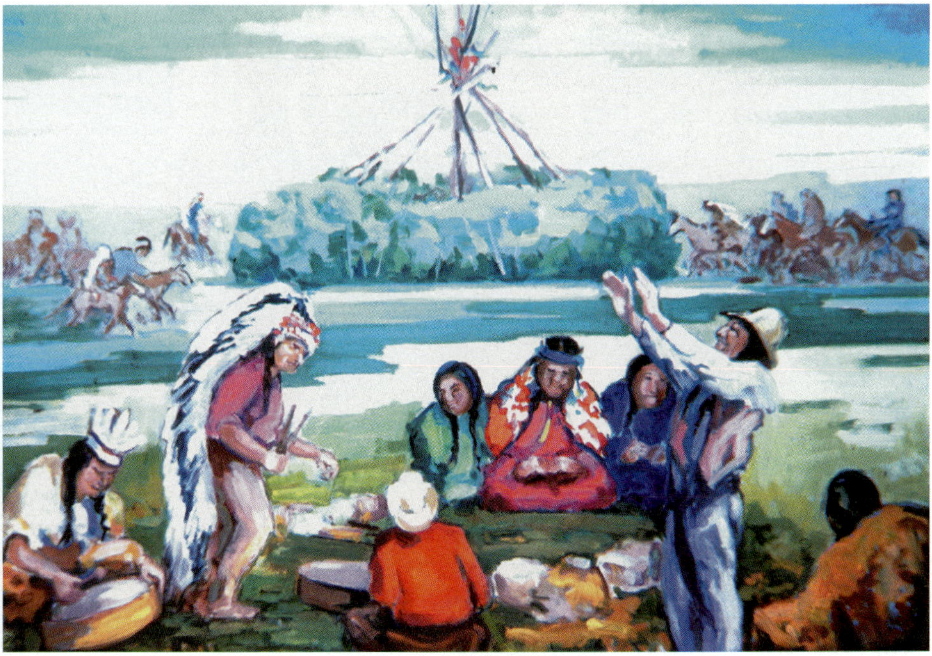

Preparation for Sun Dance

▸ *text page 175*

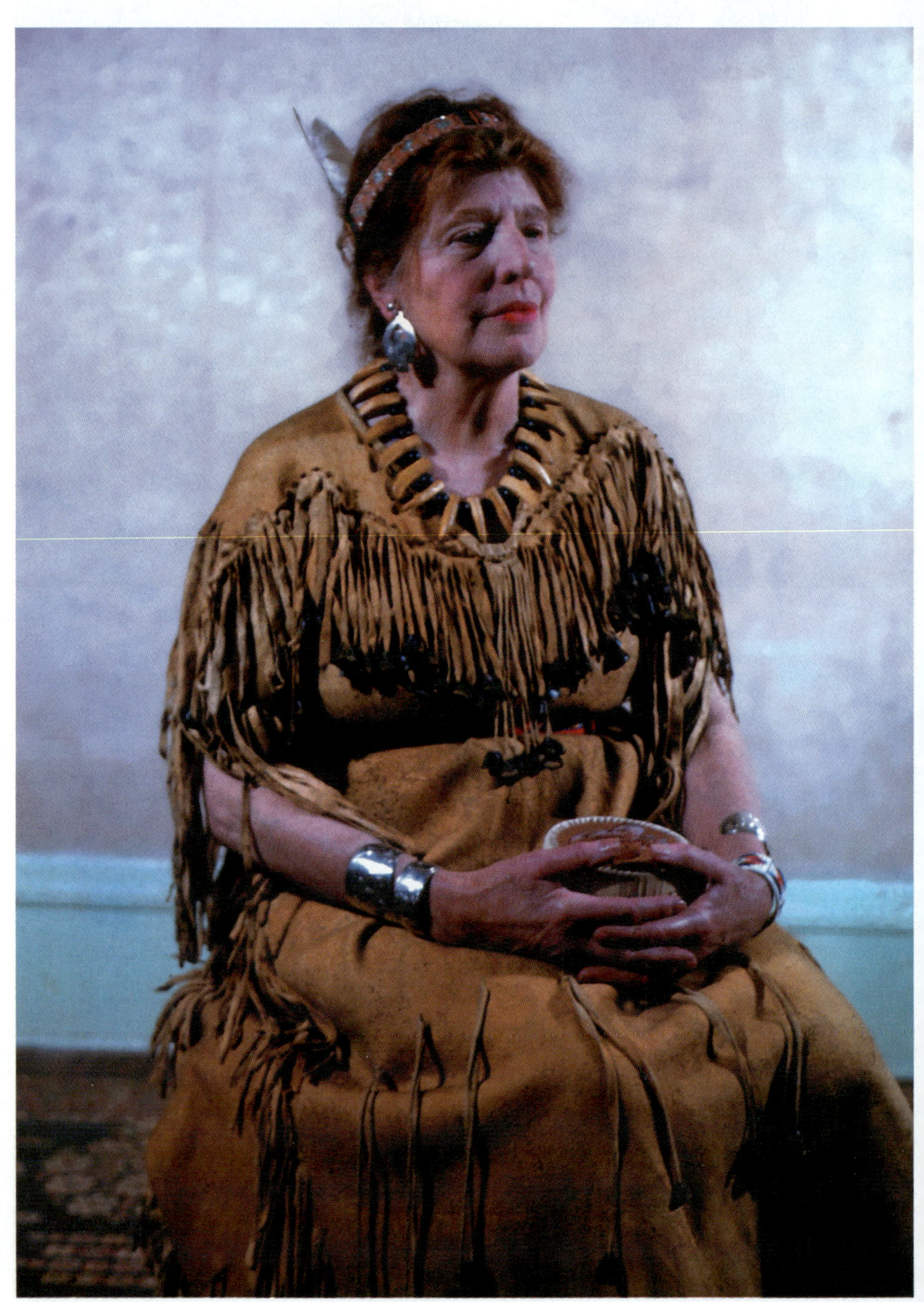

Mildred Valley Thornton

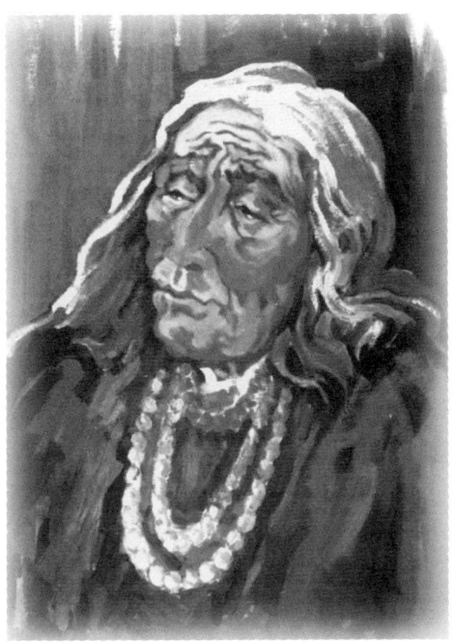

Crowfoot's Daughter

D o you know that Crowfoot's daughter is still alive?" asked a resident of Calgary who was interested in the Indians and their history. "No," I answered. "I never dreamed that he had one. I always thought that he had no children at all, no one to carry on the great traditions of the father."

Crowfoot had been a wonderful influence among all tribes during the difficult days before the extermination of the buffalo herds and in the efforts which culminated in the signing of the Indian treaties.

Suspicious and bewildered at the tumultuous onrush of events precipitated by the coming of the white men, Indians had turned instinctively to this great leader. He stands out as a man of infinite wisdom, tolerance and intellectual power, with a shrewd understanding of conditions and a superb gift of oratory.

I had been told by those who knew him that he was a keen-minded, highly-strung man, whose quick, flashing eyes were ever on the alert, leaping with incredible swiftness from one object to

▸ *colour plate page 132*

145

another. All the tribes on the plains recognized his ability and trusted him implicitly in his guidance. He was supreme chief over all and no one ever questioned his wisdom and authority.

That he was able to discern accurately the trend of the times, keep his undisciplined followers under control and, from the first, elect to work with the forces of law and order, was of the greatest possible importance to the Mounted Police. A high tribute indeed to the genius of this unlettered man who was so wise in the learning that no university could bestow.

I had often read accounts of the perplexity arising out of choosing a successor to the old Blackfoot chief, and perhaps this accounts for the prevailing notion that he had no children of his own.

Chieftainship is not hereditary among Prairie Indians. Their system is much too pragmatic and democratic for that. The chiefs are chosen because they have the necessary qualifications of bravery, wisdom, tact and leadership. In other words, this important position of honour and trust is bestowed because of a man's worth and for no other reason. So the word had been passed along that the great and wise Crowfoot had died without issue. Yet here was someone telling me that his very own daughter was still alive and, perhaps, available to be painted.

Immediately I made a vow that, if it were possible to secure the portrait, nothing would stop me. A year previously I had painted Margaret Crowfoot, a beautiful Blackfoot girl who had won a prize in the "best-dressed Indian woman contest" at the Calgary Stampede. She wore a stunning costume of beaded buckskin which had been embroidered by her grandmother. I had been told that she was the great-granddaughter of the famous old chief, but in view of popular belief, thought she was just someone having the same name which happens frequently among the Indians.

Now, however, I started out eagerly the next morning hoping I might find her again at the fair and so gain information of the woman I wanted to paint.

It was Stampede Week at Calgary and the Indians had come from miles around. I went from tepee to tepee in the Blackfoot encampment, and finally found Margaret's mother in the act of erecting her tent. She had arrived only that morning. I explained my quest to her and she said that if I went to the tepee of Chief Many Bears he would likely be able to assist me as he had married the woman's adopted daughter.

I had painted Many Bears the previous day and had much enjoyed the experience for he was a tall, handsome man, a joy both to look at and to talk to. He was standing in his tepee in full costume, painting his face in readiness for the daily parade, but stopped to tell me that he thought his mother-in-law was staying at Manchester Auto Camp and that her name was "Crow Caller."

Hastily I collected my equipment and in no time I was headed for my objective. A half-hour ride took me to the auto camp, but where were the Indians? I could see a tepee or two on the hill overlooking the auto camp so, laden with my painting kit, I started in that direction.

When I reached the heights a bewildering panorama met my eyes. Far and near there were tents, not tepees. Following the path of least resistance, I made for those which were nearest and began to inquire for Crow Caller who lived at Cluny.

The Indians, though courteous and friendly, had never heard of her and had no idea where the Cluny camp was, but thought that the people on the next hill might know. Undismayed, I picked up my paraphernalia, walked down the hill, through the wide coulee and up the heights beyond to the next cluster of tents. Again, blank looks, accompanied by a mystified shaking of heads met all my inquiries, so I trudged on in quest of my quarry.

In some mysterious manner the weight of my paint box seemed to be increasing steadily as I toiled along in the hot July sun. While this added to my momentum going down hill and even sustained me through the coulee it was a serious deterrent going up the next slope.

There were many horses grazing about me. I walked around and between some of them, but others snorted and galloped madly off at the sight of me as though I was an evil spirit.

I fared a little better on the next hill, for I was told that the Blackfoot camp was just over on the hill opposite and that there, no doubt, I would obtain news of the woman I was seeking. Full of hope I collected my gear again and started for the camp indicated.

A bright, cloudless sky looked down upon me and the prairie stretched to the horizon, mile upon mile, in bands of blue and gold, until it seemed that it must flow over the very rim of the world.

Leisurely I approached the next encampment, to be given a welcome by a number of dogs that seemed to disapprove of my presence. I have found that the Indians' dogs, though exceedingly noisy, are seldom vicious, so I did not deviate from my course and presently a couple of men came toward me, calling the beasts off. Though the men were kind and courteous and eager to be of assistance, they were unable to throw any light on my quest but pointed to where the Cluny camp was located.. I prolonged the conversation as long as I discreetly could, while I regained my breath and wiped my dripping brow.

Looking toward the distant tents on the farthest hill, my mind leaped back over the centuries and I felt a strange affinity with Moses when he first caught sight of the Promised Land. Though he had been longer on his trip, I felt, at that moment, that it could scarcely have been more exhausting. However, the mere sight of my objective was not enough for me. I wanted to BE there, so mustering my remaining strength, I "stormed the heights" which separated me and my paint box from the Cluny camp and Crow Caller.

Reaching the top, I made for the nearest tent, and a good-looking young woman came to meet me. "Yes," she said in perfect English. "Crow Caller is here with the Indians who came from Cluny. She is Crowfoot's daughter and she looks exactly like pictures of the old chief."

My heart gave a bound! At last I was nearing the end of my search. Pressing some money into the woman's hand, I said, "Lead me to her."

Meta White-Pup was my guide's name. When she found out that I came from British Columbia she immediately asked if I had ever met Canon Stocken, who was living in retirement in Esquimalt.

"If you ever see him, remember me to him," she said. "He was so good to me. My mother and my father died when I was very young and I was left all alone. Canon Stocken looked after me as though I was his own. He put me in a school and always watched over me. I wish I could see him."

The good Canon had been a missionary on the Blackfoot Reserve at Gleichen for more than fifty years, and here was evidence, not only of his solicitude for the Indians, but also of their great love for him.

Meta gave me a little snapshot of herself, and when I visited Esquimalt some time later, I saw Canon Stocken and passed it on to him. He remembered all about Meta and was interested to see the picture of the woman he had befriended as a child.

"There is the Cluny Camp," said Meta, pointing to tents some distance away and, thank goodness, no deep coulee or high hills lay between. She went straight to a tent in the centre of the group and spoke to several old women who were sitting on the ground within. One of them arose and came out to greet us. At long last I stood face to face with Crow Caller. Her strong old face broke into a faint smile as I shook her hand.

I was taking no chances at this stage. By a stroke of fortune I was wearing a string of bright red beads. Crow Caller was wearing beads too, but they were not as gay as mine. I removed them from my neck and placed them on the old woman.

This proved a fine piece of strategy, for she was now all smiles. Striking while the iron was hot I asked Meta to tell her what I wanted to do. She consented at once, and we walked around to the back of the tent where she could sit in the shade while I, alas, was forced to paint in the blazing sun, shading my canvas as best I could with my body. Since there was not enough shade for both of us, I had to stay in the sun and take my punishment, throwing a paintrag across the back of my neck to preserve me from sunstroke.

Crow Caller was a good sport and posed like a heroine with no fussing and no complaining. I worked as fast as I could for she soon grew weary and, upon finishing, I followed her into her tent. I wanted her to talk, if she would. There were so many things I wished to ask her, but I had to depend on the assistance of Meta, for not a word of English could Crow Caller speak.

Meta asked her a few questions, then laughed heartily at her reply. "She says she guesses you want her to tell you about all her boy friends!" I would have been glad to listen to Crowfoot's daughter talk about almost anything, but when she began to speak she coughed violently and explained to Meta that she was old and tired and that it always made her cough when she talked too much.

I could see that this was true and could understand, so did not press the matter. As I left the tent she followed me out to attend to some meat that was drying over a small fire. I had my camera and snapped her, busy at her task, and that was the last glimpse I had of Crowfoot's daughter.

I have taken considerable time to verify the authenticity of Crow Caller's background, as many will doubt her veracity. Canon Stocken, who translated the Blackfoot language into syllabics and was for so long a missionary to them, knew Crowfoot as well, and perhaps better, than any other white man. He told me that not only did Crowfoot have a daughter but that he also had a son, Bear Ghost, who was blind for many years which disability alone excluded him from chieftainhood. Bear Ghost's son became Headman Joe Crowfoot, father of the beautiful Margaret whom I had painted the previous year.

I had already been told that Joe Crowfoot was a very intelligent, industrious man who made the most of his opportunities and that his home was one of the best and most modern on the reserve with every comfort and convenience.

Mr. Gooderman, Indian agent at Gleichen, has verified all that Canon Stocken said. The only mistake I made was with the woman's name. Crow Caller was the name of her husband, hence she became Mrs. Crow Caller, and her Indian name was "Poh-Ka-Ki," meaning "small woman," but I like better to think of her simply as "Crowfoot's daughter."

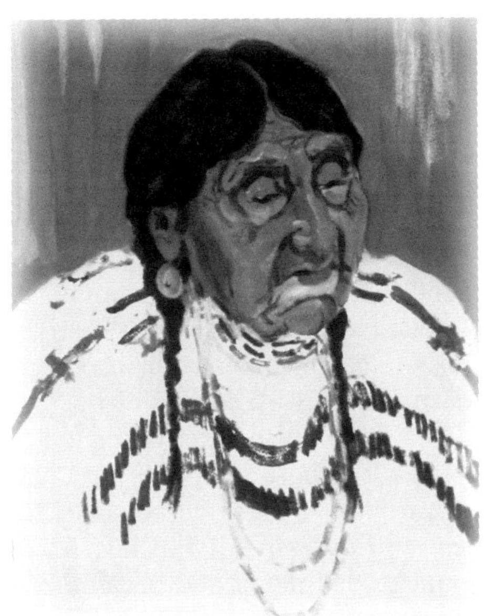

UNDER BADGER

As I walked through a Blackfoot encampment one day I noticed two very old women sitting on the grass outside their tepee. They seemed to be content to just sit and enjoy the passing scene. One had a ragged wisp of grey hair which straggled out from beneath a gay bandeau. Her face was dark and seamed and she sat with her head tilted slightly back as though peering down the long trail that she had travelled through the years.

The other woman, though she appeared old, had rich dark hair. I discovered that she could not speak English so I asked a young man to ask her if I could paint her. He explained carefully exactly what I wanted to do. At first she refused but I had learned never to take "no" for an answer. On a later occasion I mentioned the matter again, with the same negative result. Every time I passed her tepee I seemed to be drawn to her and wanted more and more to paint her. At last I showed her money and some beads, and finally won her consent.

Slowly and with great difficulty the dear old soul arose and hobbled into her tepee. After a long time she reappeared, clad in gleaming pure-white doeskin with many strings of heavy beads about her neck, a truly regal and beautiful figure. She sat on the grass before me and I began to paint, thrilled to have such a wonderful subject. Because of her great dignity I mentally christened her "The Duchess."

Other Indians walked back and forth and conversed in low tones. The old lady was quite oblivious of me and of what I was doing. Nor were the passersby of any concern to her. She wiggled and squirmed, looked east, looked west, and all the while I laboured frantically to catch some semblance of a likeness.

Finally, in desperation, I asked one of the young fellows to speak to her, as I could not finish the painting unless she kept reasonably still, if only for a short time. The "Old Lady," as they all called her, was quite deaf, so the young man knelt down and bellowed into her ear an impressive list of instructions. Ultimately she understood and settled down and became as immovable as the mountains and remained absolutely motionless to the end.

Perhaps she had never sat still that long before, though it was only half an hour, for she gave a great sigh of relief when I picked up my things and put the money and beads in her hand. I asked her name and her grandson told me that it was "Under Badger," but I will always think of her as "The Duchess," regal, calm and beautiful in her own way. She was eighty-nine years of age, one of the oldest Indians in attendance at the Stampede that year.

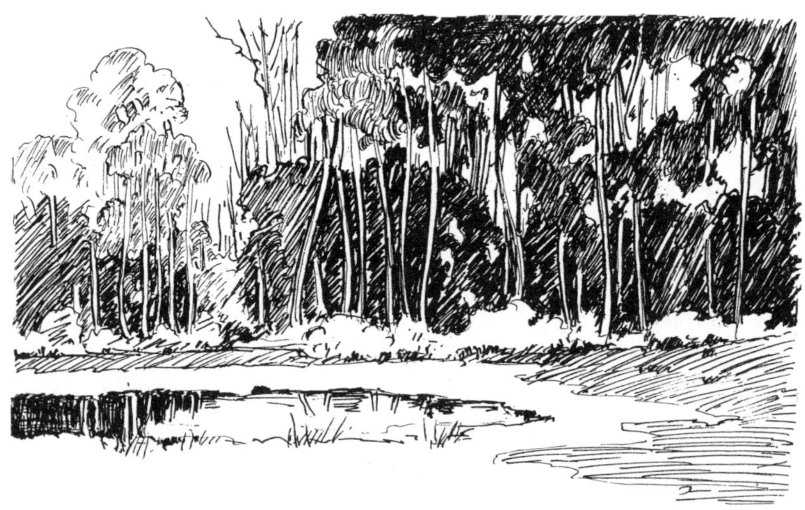

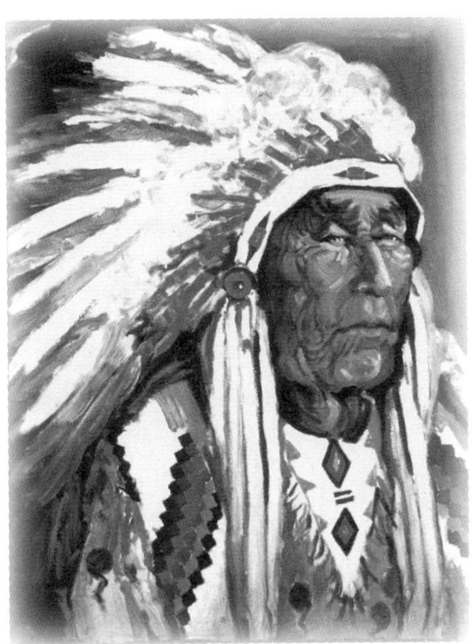

Chief Paul Little Walker

Chief Paul Little Walker was one of the few Indians of the older generation remaining on the Blackfoot Reserve when I was there. In his youth he had followed the buffalo herds and lived the hazardous, nomadic life of the Plains Indians. He had been a great horseman and hunter, trained in the ancient lore of his people.

With the passing of the years he witnessed the disappearance of the buffalo and saw, with mounting concern, white infiltration with its problems and complexities. He had welcomed the coming of the Mounted Police and the order and protection that they brought to his harassed people.

During the troubled days of transition, Little Walker, with keen observation, was quick to appreciate the good offices of the emissaries sent to his people by the various churches, and responded readily to the wise and kindly counsel of the missionaries who worked hard to help both the Indians and the white people during that period of strain and anxiety. With unexampled courage and heroic self-sacrifice, they endeavoured to be all things to all people.

It is said that Canon Stocken performed the first adult baptism on the Blackfoot Reserve in 1898. In the years that followed many more Indians were baptized into the Anglican faith by that saintly man. He translated the Blackfoot language into a syllabic system of writing which looked like shorthand. Once understood, it could be easily read. This was a great boon to an illiterate people who were desperately trying to adjust to a new way of life.

Canon Stocken's untiring efforts on behalf of the Indians won for him their whole-hearted affection and confidence. A strong attachment grew up between the Blackfoot chief and the Anglican clergyman which never faltered. As one of the leading men of his tribe, the influence of Paul Little Walker was very great. Little Walker was one of the first of the Plains Indians to cross the Rockies to visit Canon Stocken at his home in Esquimalt after the veteran churchman had retired.

Little Walker understood the Anglican church service thoroughly. Occasionally he would conduct the entire church service in the Blackfoot language, to the great satisfaction of his fellow tribesmen.

Paul Little Walker's Indian name was "Puke-Pin-Ni," meaning "Clear Eyes." It was an appropriate name for a man who was something of a mystic and who thought much of "other-worldly" things. All his life he remained a devoted Christian.

Once he had a remarkable vision. He clearly saw Canon Stocken ringing the church bell and he asked him what he was doing. The Canon replied that he was calling the people to God and asked Paul to go with him. He answered, "I will follow if you lead the way." Then he saw a ladder reaching from the earth to heaven, and with the Canon, he walked right up through the clouds to the most wonderful place. He never had dreamed there could be anything so beautiful as the scene which met his eyes. He heard a voice saying, "All that you have heard of the Christian religion is true. God wishes you to persevere." Then suddenly the vision vanished and he was wide awake in his own bed. Dream or vision?

As a Blackfoot chief, Paul Little Walker bore his honours with pride and dignity. He was born on the Blackfoot Reserve and had lived there all his life. He had known the famous Chief Crowfoot, one of the truly great men of his generation. According to Canon Stocken, Crowfoot's son was called "Bear Ghost." His daughter married a Scotsman who kept a small store at Cluny. MacDonald was his name and he drank heavily. Little Walker had been baptized and tried to convert MacDonald with indifferent success, yet MacDonald confessed to Canon Stocken that he thought a great deal of Little Walker. He said, "The way he talks is wonderful. I think a lot of that Indian of yours." Finally, he gave up drinking and became a justice of the peace at Fort MacLeod. It was a notable occasion of an Indian converting a white man.

When I visited Canon Stocken at his home in Esquimalt many years ago, he showed me the headdress of a priestess of the Sun Dance. She had given it to him on her death bed and told him never to let her own people have it again. She said she was depriving her husband and family of the value of four horses in giving it to him.

She said, "I am giving it to you. You can show it to the white people and say what we once believed in, but do not ever let my people have it." She said her mother had been a good woman and she believed in the Lord God who had made her mother so good. Somehow she felt that the headdress, if retained, would keep her apart from her mother and that was why she never wanted her people to have it again. It was a religious headdress, the Canon said, with the feathers standing straight up on it. A festival or ceremonial headdress would have the feathers slanting backward.

Speaking of Chief Crowfoot, the Canon said he was a most remarkable man, with an alert mind, quick-flashing eyes and a nervous twitch of the head, deep thinking, careful and deliberate in his speech, almost as though he knew he was making history.

He told me of a curious instance concerning Bull Bear who had extremely long finger nails. The Canon said, "Why on earth don't you cut those off? They collect dirt and the dirt gets into your food and makes you sick." Bull Bear refused because he said if he cut them off he would be cutting off some of his life.

The Blood Indians

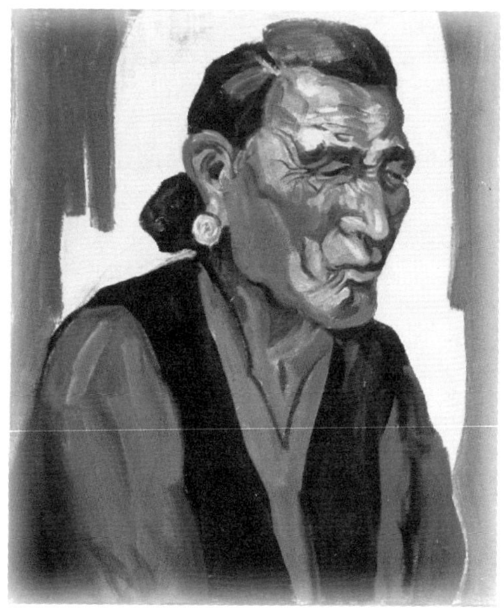

Charley Davis

At St. Paul's Residential School on the Blood Reserve, Archdeacon Middleton was kindness itself to me. Merely to be with him gave me the "open door" everywhere. Among many dedicated men of different faiths who gave the best years of their lives to work among the Indians, the selfless service of Archdeacon Middleton will long be remembered.

His inherent wisdom, tact and deep understanding won for him, not only the acceptance and co-operation of the Indians, but also their admiration and whole-hearted affection. "Chief Mountain," as he was dubbed by the Indians, was an appropriate name for one whose service to the Blood Indians of southern Alberta towers above many of his contemporaries as does the mountain from which was derived his Indian name.

The archdeacon and I went to see Charley and Rosie Davis one day. Charley was the son of an English army officer and a

Blood Indian woman. He was born near Fort MacLeod many years before our visit. When his father was transferred away from Alberta he wished to make arrangements for his son to be educated in a good school and could well afford to do so, but his Indian relatives refused to part with the child, so Charley grew up on the reserve.

When we inquired for him at his home we were told that he was "off" on the other side of his farm with his wife, shooting gophers. The archdeacon didn't bother driving on the road and, with sublime disregard for his car, or its occupants, drove straight across the prairie. The car jumped and bumped over gopher holes and ant hills. He never slackened speed and made straight for a team and wagon that we could see in the distance.

Rosie and Charley had sacks of wheat in the wagon. They had filled an old washtub with the wheat, then poured gopher poison over it and mixed it thoroughly. When we approached they were walking through the field scattering the poisoned wheat.

When the archdeacon explained our mission, Charley said I could paint him and promptly dumped the wheat out of the washtub and, with great gallantry, turned it upside down for me to sit on. I propped my canvas against a fencepost and he sat down on the ground a few feet away and we were in business. Rosie and the archdeacon had a quiet visit while I worked.

When the archdeacon came over to see how the work was progressing, he whispered, "Don't offer to pay these people. They are very proud and they wouldn't like it."

After I finished the painting I cast about in my mind for some means to recompense them. I had some photographs of several of my paintings with me of Saskatchewan Indians and showed these to Charley. He studied them with great interest and I said I would like to give them to him. He asked what tribe the subjects in the photographs belonged to. When I replied, "Cree," he handed them back and said, "No, I don't want them."

Old habits and old feuds die hard. The Cree had ever been sworn enemies of the Blackfoot and here, long years after the tomahawk and the hatchet had been buried forever, was a Blackfoot chief who wouldn't be caught dead, even with only the photograph of a Cree in his possession!

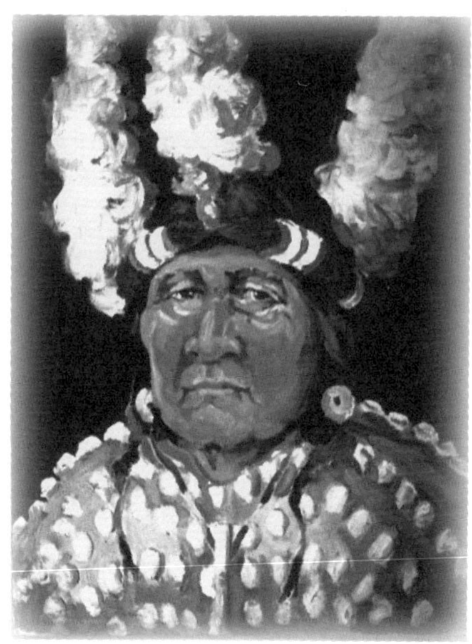

Pretty Kangaroo Woman

In answer to the Indian agent's questions there was a shuffling of feet in the next room accompanied by soft little chuckles and grunts. Then the door opened and in hobbled Wolverine, better known as "Pretty Kangaroo Woman," widow of the famous Indian outlaw Charcoal.

A couple of years previously she had suffered an injury to her hip which made walking difficult, but one look at her genial face, with its extensive smile and twinkling eyes, put all thoughts of her disabilities aside. Long years ago these same eyes had been the bedevilment of more than one amorous swain, including her illicit lover, Medicine Pipe Stem. They had, likewise, been the cause of sending her husband, poor Charcoal, to his doom.

Charcoal had two other names, "Dried Meat" was one of them, but he was known to the police as "Bad Young Man." Without punning, however, I do not think that Charcoal was as black as he was painted. Many a white man has taken the law into his own hands to justify his honour and to preserve the sanctity of his home, as did Charcoal, and got away with it.

Pretty Kangaroo Woman looked innocent enough today, and was instantly curious about me and my paraphernalia. The agent had sent for her to come to his office in order that I might paint her in the short time I had at my disposal. Anticipating important events and a little "ready cash," she had come prepared to look her best, dragging along a huge buckskin bag with a drawstring at the top.

She plunged her dark, knobby little hands into its cavernous depths and out "puffed" a white, powdery cloud before she extracted her deerskin costume. Many Indians sprinkle flour on their buckskin to keep it soft and white. She looked up, through the misty halo, with a childish grin, and groped in again for her beaded belt and headgear.

Pretty Kangaroo Woman's girth had become somewhat "extended" since she originally made the costume. It was a straight one-piece affair, quite long and very heavy. Alternate rows of dentalium shells and elk's teeth were its unusual decorations, with a long fringe around the sleeves and the bottom.

She lifted the heavy dress and slipped it over her head easily enough, but it stuck amidships and refused to go down over her plump tummy without a long and patient struggle. I went to her rescue and gave it a few little tugs all the way around, and, inch by inch, managed to pull it down. I think that the skin never fitted its original owner closer than it clung to Pretty Kangaroo Woman.

She fastened on her lovely beaded belt and then adjusted her incredible millinery. This, she assured me, was the snake headdress and was always worn when performing the traditional Snake Dance.

Her only other adornment was a long, slender whistle, made from the bone of an animal, which hung around her neck suspended from a string of rawhide and some ribbons. It was the emblem of the famous Buffalo Society. To possess it, I was told, was equivalent to a thirty-third degree in the Masonic Order.

When she was fully dressed, Pretty Kangaroo Woman underwent a strange transformation. Her affable, ready smile vanished and she adopted the reserved stolidity of her race. Never once did she relax until I was through painting her.

What was going on behind her brow and those inscrutable eyes? I would have given a good deal to know what were the memories stored behind her stolid countenance. Was she traversing, once again, with silent, stealthy tread, the hidden paths and trackless plains with her implacable husband by her side? Did she recall the gruelling, relentless search of the Mounted Police as she and Charcoal crept from bush to bush, from river bed to river bed, hungry and ill clad, stark terror in their hearts and the law always on their heels?

She had been a participant, nay, the cause of one of the most stirring chapters in Indian history. Police records tell the story briefly from the official point of view. However, behind the cold facts and figures lies an intense and moving human drama, punctuated with passion, severe hardship, whining bullets and sudden death.

Charcoal was a Blood Indian and a "wronged" man. In the tragedy that closed his career on a scaffold, I cannot think of him as a murderer in the commonly accepted meaning of the word. He was ignorant, blind with hatred and revenge, jealous of his honour among his own people and burning with a fierce pride.

Only a generation removed from the hereditary Indian code of justice that settled feuds and insults with the swift shedding of blood, Charcoal could not understand the white man's code. In his world, punishment, quick and certain, was meted out to those in conflict and the bravest man was the one who got his blow in first.

Small wonder then, when he found his home and his honour violated, that all the old instincts of his race rose up in fury within his turbulent heart and led him to avenge the wrongs according to the customs of his forefathers.

When his wife made an excuse not to help him with the haying one summer day he became consumed with suspicion, and, returning home, found the house empty. He followed horse tracks leading to the river where two horses were tethered to a tree. Hearing voices in an old stable nearby, he recognized one of them as that of Pretty Kangaroo Woman. The other was that of her lover, Medicine Pipe Stem.

Restraint, which the white man's law had imposed upon him, was brushed aside like a cobweb and the impulses bred of long centuries of native custom swept over his stormy soul with blinding fury.

Slowly he crept up to the old stable and, through a chink in the logs, deliberately aimed his gun at the heart of his rival. Swift and terrible was the price of treachery as Medicine Pipe Stem fell back dead in the arms of his beloved.

No one witnessed the deed, and for over a week no one missed Medicine Pipe Stem. Then a curious passerby discovered the gory corpse in the old stable. By this time, Charcoal had suddenly disappeared, taking Pretty Kangaroo Woman, another wife and two children with him. Suspicion was directed toward him, and soon the Mounted Police were on his trail.

What happened after that is an interesting speculation in psychology. Something seems to have snapped in Charcoal's tortured brain. Something irrevocably severed all respect and responsibility, not only for the law, but for anyone who happened to cross his path. All men were against him. All would destroy him. Therefore he would destroy all without mercy.

He was now not merely an outlaw Indian, he was a creature of the wild, with the stench of blood in his nostrils and black murder in his heart. Restraint was abandoned but not caution. Try as they could, the police could not waylay him.

Need of food led the fugitive to risk capture during many secret and daring visits to his own people. None dared refuse his requests or disclose his whereabouts.

One night, as the farm instructor was sitting quietly resting in his home, a bullet came crashing through the window, severely wounding him. On another occasion Charcoal visited the home of Little Pine, demanded food, confessed his guilt, and signified his intention of killing Red Crow, chief of the Bloods.

He was even audacious enough to steal up, one night, to the Mounted Police headquarters and take a pot shot at one of the constables who was going out to the stables with a lantern.

Though the police never slackened in their search, Charcoal always managed to elude them. He would stand on the brow of a hill and shout his battle song in wild defiance, then disappear as if by magic. Months went by. Indians and whites alike, were terrified at his depredations, not knowing when the killer would appear nor at whom his venom might be directed. Police said that Chief Red Crow was so much in fear of his life that he slept on the floor of his house rather than in his bed, the position of which was known to Charcoal.

White Calf, an Indian who assisted the police, slept in the loft of his house, drawing the ladder up after him when he ascended, lest he be killed during the night. This explains why so many of the Indians were willing to join in the search for one of their own. Meanwhile there were constant reports of Charcoal appearing in different places. First here, then there, but never within reach of the law. Many weeks lapsed and still he was free. It was rumoured that he was hiding in the Porcupine Hills, and Sergeant Wilde, with a small posse of Mounties and Indians, rode out to arrest him. He was spotted and a chase ensued. Pushing through the deep snow on fresh horses, they finally overtook Charcoal whose horse was exhausted.

Dismounting, the brave sergeant, knowing that he was risking his life, laid aside his gun and, unarmed, attempted to apprehend Charcoal who had also dismounted. Instantly a shot rang out and one more courageous man paid the price of his devotion to duty.

Quick as lightning Charcoal exchanged his tired horse for the sergeant's fresh one and swiftly disappeared. He was now a murderer twice over, but still, it seemed, he led a charmed life. One of the Indians bravely followed his trail all night long, but again, Charcoal evaded his pursuers, leaving them more frustrated, chagrined and bewildered than ever.

Many civilians now joined the police in their remorseless hunt for Charcoal. No one could sleep in peace while he was on the loose. No home and no life was safe.

Some accounts relate that Charcoal's wives deserted him as soon as they could get away safely, which is not at all unlikely, for he must have been bordering on insanity. Other accounts state that Pretty Kangaroo Woman, thrusting aside her infidelity, stayed with him, sharing all his privations to the end.

Be that as it may, he called one dark night on his brother, Left Hand, on the Blood Reserve, demanding food and shelter. Left Hand must have been a brother in name only, for by a ruse, he overpowered Charcoal, bound him and turned him over to the police.

In a short time Charcoal was in a cell, chained to the floor and under heavy guard. He was tried, found guilty of the murder of Sergeant Wilde, no mention having been made of his culpability in the little matter of killing Medicine Pipe Stem. He was hanged on 10 February, 1897.

Left Hand was rewarded for his part in the arrest by the Department of Indian Affairs by being made a chief. The Indians, however, never recognized him as such and regarded the betrayal of his brother as the treacherous and dishonourable act of a low-minded man. It is even said that, on one occasion, he was soundly trounced by them for his conduct.

The hanging of Charcoal was a sad and inglorious climax to one of the wildest man-hunts in the history of the Canadian West.

Many years have past since that fateful day, and now, here was Pretty Kangaroo Woman, plump, jovial and healthy, the cause and survivor of the whole dreadful business.

When she was through posing for me she assumed a roguish gleam in her eyes. Picking up my coat, she stroked it lovingly and pointed to the diamond ring on my finger as though to infer that I was wearing better clothes than she was wearing. Instantly I offered the garment to her, reaching for her buckskin dress in exchange, but she hastily retrieved her treasure. In no way would she trade it for my coat, much to my disappointment and amusement.

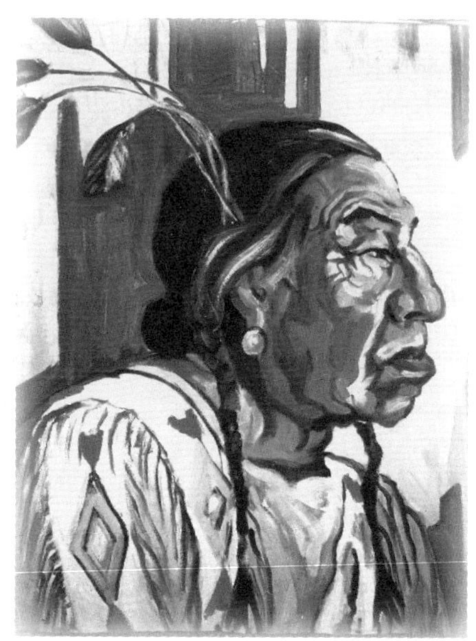

Chief Shot-On-Both-Sides

Chief Shot-on-Both-Sides was away. There was a lock on the door of his littlehouse and not a sign of life about the place.

Archdeacon Middleton, principal of St. Paul's Residential School, had driven me twenty miles across the vast Blood Reserve in order that I might paint the chief, so we turned away in disappointment. Oh well, we would go down the road a few miles and I would paint old Scraping White instead.

But Scraping White was not home either, so we went on to the home of Chief Cross Child as a last hope, and once more we were confronted by a padlocked door. It began to look as though my artistic aspirations were not to be gratified that afternoon.

Later, we discovered the reason for all the absentees. The big annual Medicine Pipe Dance was being held many miles away, near the Canada/USA border, and every Indian who was able had donned his regalia and galloped off to the dance. It would last for several days, so there was nothing for me to do but "cool my heels" and possess my soul in patience.

▸ colour plate page 140   164

A week later we ventured back again with better luck. A swarm of small brown children were tumbling about the chief's doorstep like so many playful puppies. The chief's wife, Wolf Woman, was at home with a daughter who had brought her numerous progeny for a visit with grandma. Wolf-Woman was aged and could speak no English.

The archdeacon, who could speak Blackfoot as though he had been born to the language, told her that I wanted to paint the chief. She replied that he had gone several miles down the valley immediately after breakfast, saying that he would not be back until evening.

It looked as though I would be disappointed again, but no, Wolf Woman had resources of which we knew nothing. She shuffled into the house, reached into the rafters and extracted a piece of mirror, then, standing on the back steps of her house, she turned the mirror to the sun and directed a long shaft of light far down the valley to where the chief was working.

She was signalling to him just as the Indian war parties had communicated with each other in the old days when a broken bottle or small mirror could give as much information as the Morse code.

And what was the chief doing in the valley the long day through? Why mending his fence, to be sure, in order to keep Long Time Squirrel's horses out of his wheat field!

For generations Indians had been practically born to the saddle. Horses were as the breath of life to them and upon horses their very existence depended. No horses, no buffalo and no buffalo meant no food, shelter or clothing.

The love of horses still lay warm and deep in the heart of the chief's elderly neighbour, Long Time Squirrel. Younger and more progressive Indians had long since replaced horses with tractors and automobiles, but not so with Long Time Squirrel. Yearly, his herd grew in numbers. He never sold any and never gave any away. Now, nearly two thousand head of horses galloped over the huge reserve, getting into crops and trampling grain underfoot, much to the annoyance of other Indians!

I thought that if I were head chief I would show my authority and call old Long Time Squirrel to account for the depreda-

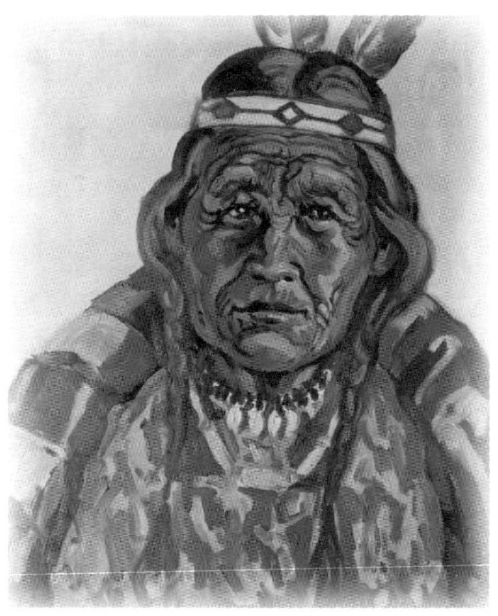

Wolf Woman

tions of his equine marauders, but Chief Shot-On-Both-Sides was merely mending his fences, a very tactful and peaceful way out of the difficulty.

Down the valley his keen eyes had caught the signal from Wolf Woman so he started for home. Meanwhile, I was making the most of the golden opportunity painting the chief's wife. She was seventy-six years old, she said, and there was a quality of sweetness and eternal peace etched upon her wrinkled face that bespoke of an untroubled mind within. She studied the painting when I had finished and said it was good, but she could see now that she was an old woman.

While many of the Indians on this reserve were very forward-thinking and prosperous with fine, modern homes, the hereditary head chief and his wife were content to live in a little one-room dwelling, furnished only with the bare necessities.

A kitchen stove occupied the middle of the room and in one corner was a table, a washstand and a bench. In another corner stood the bed and opposite that was a shakedown on the floor, presumably for guests.

The couple had wealth, though of a different kind. Under the bed in dilapidated suitcases and cardboard boxes were their treasures. Wolf Woman hauled them out, telling us as she did so that she was the only person left on the reserve who knew how to do the wonderful porcupine quill work.

Lovingly, she fingered the gorgeous buckskin costumes which she had embroidered with great care and talent. Blood Indian designs are geometric in character. Over and over again their most important symbol, the arrowhead, was repeated, interwoven with mountain peaks and other nature symbols.

The headdress of the chief was majestic beyond description. Because he was head chief, a long cascade of eagle feathers reached to the ground. When dressed in his full regalia, Chief Shot-on-Both-Sides must have presented a truly regal figure. As Wolf Woman displayed his costume there was a delicious tinkling like the sound of hundreds of tiny bells.

On examination I discovered the source of the tinkling to be hundreds of steel thimbles which hung thickly on the heavy fringe of the garment. A hole had been punched through the end of each thimble, the fringe drawn through and knotted. Who but an Indian would have thought of that? It was quite the best use of thimbles that I had ever seen.

A whip handle of elks' horn was so highly polished that it was satin-smooth to the touch. There was a peace pipe, too, with a long elaborately carved stem from which were suspended tufts of eagle feathers. Gay moccasins, blankets, head bands, fire bags and many other things of rare beauty were in the boxes under the chief's bed.

Most intriguing of all was a huge tepee lining that the chief had painted with many symbols telling the history of his people. It was "the history of the old men," so Wolf Woman said, and it was literally covered with small drawings, executed in natural dyes, depicting outstanding events in the story of the Blood Indians. A sort of "archive" of the tribe.

As I studied it the significance gradually became clear. Here was a group of mounted warriors, obviously counting the spoils of war over their fallen foes. I could recognize the figure of the famous Chief Red Crow in many of the graphic episodes. One such drawing showed him signing the Indian Treaty on behalf of his people. Another scene showed the victorious Bloods making off with many horses, stolen from their sworn enemies, the Cree Indians. There were drawings of important ceremonies in which I could recognize figures of the Mounted Police. "The police were always our friends," said Wolf Woman, "so we were the friends of the police."

As I scrutinized the tepee covering some one said, "The chief is coming!" And, sure enough, there was the wagon and team in the distance bearing the head chief home. Joyfully we welcomed his return. He countered my exuberance with a quiet smile of true cordiality and a warm handclasp.

There was immense dignity about the man. Power, intelligence and gentleness were mingled in a face that was almost sad in repose but which was instantly transformed into friendship when he smiled. Though he was tired and it was late in the day, the chief courteously acceded to my request to paint his portrait, and he proceeded to don his gorgeous costume, choosing to wear a cluster of partially stripped eagle feathers in his hair in preference to his war bonnet. Like the thimbles, this was new to me, and gave added character.

Chief Shot-on-Both-Sides seemed the incarnate being of the best that his people had stood for throughout the years. In his own way he was every inch a king and no monarch on his throne ever displayed more grandeur than he when arrayed in his ceremonial robes.

Never did I see these qualities better illustrated than a few days later at the unveiling of a cairn in memory of the late Chief Red Crow. The Indians had raised money for the project, prepared the site and made all necessary arrangements for the ceremony, selecting a spot not far from Standoff which had been the geographical divide between Alberta and Montana in the old days. This was beside the Alaska Highway, looking toward Belly Buttes where the annual Sun Dance of the Bloods was always held.

Red Crow had been a true representative of his noble race, and knew what he was doing when he signed the Treaty. And he kept his pledge to the government of Canada. Forty-six summers had passed since Red Crow passed away. Crop-Eared Wolf had succeeded him as chief, and he too, had been sleeping these many years, close to the place where Red Crow lay.

On this occasion their successor, Chief Shot-on-Both-Sides, had gathered together six minor chiefs of the tribe, Cross Child, Little Dog, Owns Many Horses, Frank Red Crow, John Cotton and Wades in the Water, to officially dedicate the cairn to their predecessor's memory.

They looked very impressive as they stood in their splendid apparel, a proud people, jealous of their rights and their honour. Though they occupy the biggest reserve in Canada, 547 square miles, not one inch will they surrender. This is the territory that Red Crow claimed for his people when the Blackfoot Treaty was signed. The tribe was camped there at the time. They are there today, and there they intend to remain.

When Mr. J.Y. Card, the founder of the Mormon town of Cardston, came to the country in the early 1880s, he cast longing eyes toward the vast, rich and fertile areas of the Indians and tried hard to bargain with Red Crow to purchase some of their land.

Red Crow plucked a handful of grass from the ground and held it to him saying, "This grows every year, we will rent you the grass. This is our land. It was given to us by the Great White Mother and we are going to keep it as long as the sun shines and the waters flow." They would not even rent a portion of the land for a race track, but they would rent it for pasture and pasture it has remained to this day.

When Mr. Card and his party camped just south of the reserve, Red Crow politely invited them to leave the vicinity, then departed to return with ten braves, in full war paint, to give point to his suggestion.

The matter was left to the Indian agent for decision. The Mormon party was permitted to remain so long as they did not encroach upon the Indian's rights. Then a banquet was held at which Mr. Card and Chief Red Crow smoked the pipe of peace together.

Just before the ceremony at the cairn, Red Crow's grandson and Mr. Card's grandson met in the great Mormon Temple at Cardston, one of the finest in the world, to repeat the historic ceremony, smoking the peace pipe together, even as their grandfathers had done half a century before.

Hundreds of Indians and other Canadians were on the scene at the cairn. The dedication included speeches and choral music. Aloysius Crop-Eared Wolf, son of Chief Shot-on-Both-Sides, acted as interpreter.

Principals of both Indian residential schools spoke. Archdeacon Middleton, associated with the Blood Indians for over forty years, gave his address in fluent Blackfoot.

Mr. Card spoke for the Mormons and a few old timers also made brief speeches. Then Chief Shot-on-Both-Sides rose to speak for his people. It was mid-July and a hot prairie wind tugged at the feathers of his magnificent headdress. Notwithstanding, the chief looked the embodiment of dignity, holding his headdress with one hand and his richly beaded tobacco pouch with the other.

He spoke in short, forceful sentences, punctuated by eloquent pauses. He declared that he was following in the footsteps of Red Crow and obeying the laws of the dominion of Canada. He called on the "fates" to witness his devotion to the highest ideals of his tribe.

He had a tremendous voice for oratory, louder than any I have ever heard. Red Crow must have stirred in his slumbers in response to that thunderous sound. Non-Indians did not understand his words but caught the serious import of his message. Then Crop-Eared Wolf rose, to interpret in perfect English, all that the chief had said. As a climax, he quoted him as stating that he was very happy indeed to see so many of his Anglican friends present. He was also pleased to welcome his Roman Catholic friends, and with a magnificent gesture of non-partisanship, said that if there was anybody present who belonged to the Salvation Army, he extended a cordial greeting to them also.

Chief Shot-on-Both-Sides was not without a sense of humour!

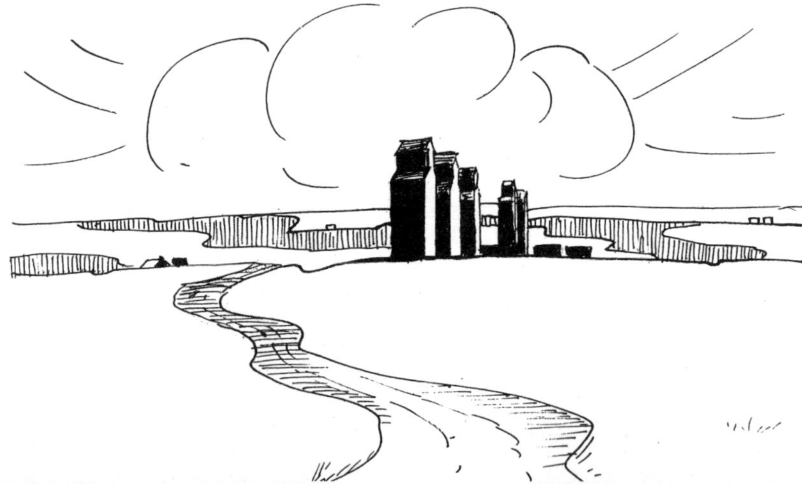

The Piegan Indians

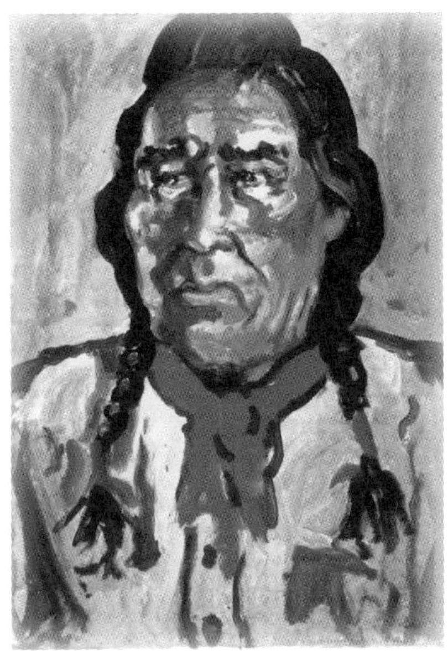

Chief Jim Crowflag

B rocket is a small village in southern Alberta. In my eyes, its only claim to fame lay in the fact that it happened to be the headquarters of the Piegan Indian Agency. Not far from Pincher Creek and the Rocky Mountains, it is in wide rolling country with big coulees which break the monotony of the landscape.

I was in the agency office when Chief Jim Crowflag chanced along on business, so I "corralled" him and painted his portrait on the spot just as he was. Fortunately for me, his wife Rosie was with him, so I painted her also.

All in all it was a lively and profitable morning in the little room where I worked with the blessing of the Indian agent. Typewriters were tapping away on the other side of the wall and the busy routine of the office went steadily on with people coming and going continually. I caught glimpses of them through the door and fragments of their conversations came drifting in like waves from a distant shore, but they did not distract me from my work.

Piegan Indians are a part of the great Blackfoot Confederacy and Jim Crowflag had the splendid physique common to all Blackfoot. At sixty-three he was a product of the age of transition, somewhat divorced from the old regime, yet not quite integrated into the changing world about him.

He had been born near Brocket and had lived there ever since. He could remember when his brother, Sarcee by name, had undergone the Sun Dance initiation torture. He was only a child then, but the event left a vivid impression in his mind. He could see it all again as he told me about it.

The medicine man had used fresh willow sticks to pierce his brother's flesh to make holes for thongs of buffalo hide and had not cut into the flesh as was customary in other tribes.

The youth had a bone whistle which he blew as he leaped and danced around the Sun Dance pole until he tore himself free. If he could not have broken free by his own efforts some one else would have rushed to help him, thus ending his agony.

Chief Crowflag never saw the buffalo roaming the plains in countless thousands but he had often heard the elders tell of the excitement and danger of the buffalo hunt. He thought the old ways were the good ways. He also knew the old songs, the old legends and the old dances.

"No swearing, no cheating, no doing wrong. Those were the ways of the old days," he said. "They should let us do things the old way now. It was a good way always to tell our children they must not do anything bad."

With great earnestness he told me about the Sun Dance and how his Rosie had given it several times, and because of this she was greatly respected.

The Sun Dance was still being held at that time, 1948, just as it had always been held except for the torture initiation ritual which had been forbidden by the government long ago.

On the Piegan Reserve that year the festivities came to an abrupt end just before my arrival. Everything had been going along normally, with many people in attendance, when suddenly a furious thunderstorm struck the encampment and cyclonic winds flattened the huge Sun Dance lodge and most of the tepees. Inasmuch as the ceremony was nearing its end, there was no attempt to rebuild the camp so the people all packed up and went home. "We will hold it again next year just the same," the chief said.

Crowflag had been a chief for fifteen years. He had three sons and two daughters. Only one daughter was still living on the reserve where he could enjoy the company of his grandchildren.

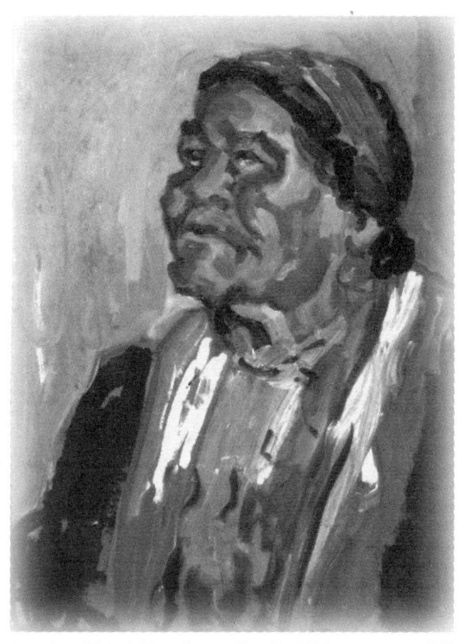

Rosie, Chief Jim Crowflag's Wife ▸ *page 142*

Another aspect of life on the reserve remains engraved in my mind. I shall always remember the valiant little priest who was slowly and labouriously remodelling the Indian church with great devotion and industry.

He was a zealous man with dreams of providing many recreations for the junior members of his flock, if only his parish premises could be improved. The church was literally falling to pieces with no prospect of restoration. His situation would have daunted most men, but not Father Ruax. Since no benevolent patron had appeared to provide the financial support he so sorely needed to do the necessary work, he had decided to do it himself.

There he was, sleeves rolled up, sawing logs, hauling timber, pouring cement and turning his dreams into tangible reality. Of such stuff were the pioneers of our country made!

Many years have passed since William Duncan, Father Lacombe and the gallant MacDougall gave their lifeblood to the Indian cause, yet here in a more gentle age, was another of their breed, doing his evangelistic work with the same burning zeal that burned in the hearts of his predecessors. The contributions of these missionaries, of all faiths, should never be forgotten.

Father Ruax explained that the Indians had great faith and mortal courage. "No matter how they live, they have no fear of death and hardly ever go into a terminal coma. They remain conscious to the end and believe that they will go straight to heaven."

As an instance of this he told of old Goose Chief who told him that he was "going to die a week from today." This said the old man: "I want you to baptize me and prepare me for that day so I will go straight to heaven, and I want you to bring me an apple pie, and that will be my last meal, and that is all I want."

Goose Chief made the priest promise that he would do this. A week later Father Ruax was attending a children's picnic when one of the sisters reminded him, "Isn't this the day when you were supposed to take an apple pie to Goose Chief and baptize him?"

"My goodness, yes!" exclaimed the good father, so, taking an apple pie, he promptly set off to see Goose Chief.

When he arrived at the house he baptized the old man, talked to him seriously about the meaning of baptism and asked, "Do you believe all this?"

"Yes," answered Goose Chief. "I believe it all."

They talked for a long time when suddenly Goose Chief asked, "Did you bring the apple pie?"

"Yes," the priest replied, "It is right here.' He gave the pie to Goose Chief who asked his wife to cut him a good big slice. Father Ruax then went home, and in two hours time he received a message that Goose Chief was dead.

"They know when they are going and are never afraid," he explained simply.

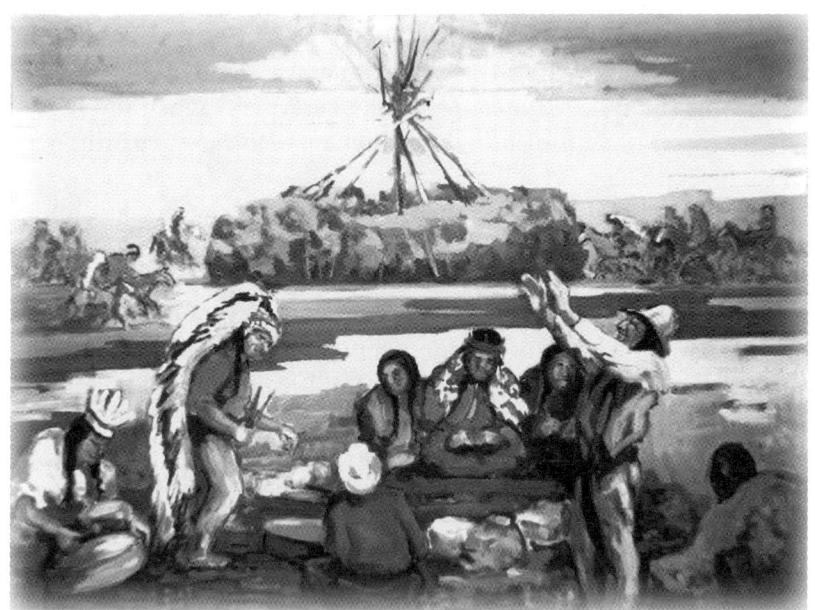

The Sun Dance

In Alberta where "the heavens declare the glory of God" on every summer's evening, the country is not lacking in sun worshippers.

To the Blood Indians the sun is the symbol of life, light, warmth, fruition and omnipotence. It represents the Great Spirit, the ruler of the universe, who is all, over all and everpresent. Small wonder that the Sun Dance was the big event of the year.

In July, when the hot prairie sun shines high and bright and the long winds run rippling waves over the ripening grain fields, all trails lead to the Sun Dance.

For generations past this great annual festival has been held at the foot of the Belly Buttes whose high, craggy cliffs cut a jagged pattern into the periwinkle blue of the wide sky above them. Here the Indians gather at the call of the head chief, to pitch their tepees in a huge circle for the ceremonies which may last from a week to ten days or longer.

▶ *colour plate page 143*   175

The Indians have a very direct and effective system of nomenclature. It was no accident that the great cliffs became known as the Belly Buttes, for in the early days when the buffalo was the very staff of life, the Buttes were the scene of frequent and gory carnage.

On the open plains the Indians stampeded the buffalo into a "pound" where they skilfully herded the mighty bison before dispatching them.

Here, on the Blood Reserve, nature had provided an enormous abattoir. The tribe stampeded the great herds over the steep cliffs where the beasts fell in a struggling mass to their doom below. Then the wounded animals were quickly dispatched and every part put to use. Because of the entrails lying all about, the cliffs were called the Belly Buttes and the nearby stream is called Belly River.

No longer do the buffalo, in countless thousands, make the earth tremble beneath their maddened hooves. Never again shall the great animals be slaughtered at the foot of Belly Buttes. But the memory of those days has not died in the hearts of the old men.

"Give us back the buffalo," they say, "and you can have your reserve and all that goes with it."

Yet the Indians know the irrevocable past cannot be retrieved. Many of them are prosperous farmers today, up-to-date in every way. Others are successful stockmen and some get a good return from lands leased to non-Indians. They own tractors, cars and all the comforts of modern life.

Nevertheless, once a year all normal activity is foresworn and the accoutrements of modern life shed, as they gather to celebrate the historic Sun Dance.

Much has been written about this event. A general idea of its purpose has been gained and a favoured few outsiders have been permitted to witness some of its rituals. It is doubtful, however, if the secret inner meaning of the Sun Dance has ever been revealed to non-Indians.

The Blood Indians are a part of the Blackfoot Confederacy which consists of the Blackfoot proper, the Bloods and the Peigans. Closely allied to them are the Sarcees and, according to ancient custom, none of these tribes hold the Sun Dance except upon the fulfilment of a woman's vow.

The woman, whose goodness and purity makes this possible, is the recipient of much esteem during the remainder of her life. None but a woman of irreproachable character and fidelity may make such a vow.

The first time that I visited the Sun Dance, Carrying Something Woman had made the vow. A few years later, when I was on the reserve again, the Sun Dance was sponsored by Mrs. Crow Spreads Its Wings.

All women who "vow" the Sun Dance automatically belong to the Holy Women's Society. They erect their own lodge at the Sun Dance site, the framework of which is made of travois poles.

That year, just after Christmas, the son of Mrs. Bear Shin Bone was lying at death's door from poisoning. His mother ascended to the highest point of ground in the vicinity and gravely turned to the east, the south, the west and the north and vowed to the Great Spirit that if her son was restored to health and strength she would give the Sun Dance that year. The boy got well and, accordingly, the Sun Dance was held in fulfilment of his mother's vow.

The Blood Indians are highly organized into many secret fraternities, from the powerful Horn Society to the Children's Association.

In some instances membership demanded considerable stoicism. Long ago, when men were men, and braves were braves, it was at the Sun Dance that aspiring youths were initiated as warriors into the tribe. Brave indeed must any man be who could withstand the agony of that gruelling test without flinching or showing the slightest sign of pain or emotion.

Wearing only a breechcloth and a crown of wild sage with more of it entwined around his wrists and ankles, the youth knelt before the medicine man who cut gashes into his breast, through which thongs of buffalo hide were securely passed. These, in turn, were tied to a long rope of buffalo hide, the other end of which was firmly attached to the top of the Sun Dance pole.

Similar gashes were cut through the flesh of the shoulders of the initiate, from which a shield or, perhaps the skull of a buffalo, was suspended. A variation of this procedure was to punch holes through the flesh with a sharpened willow stick in preference to the medicine man's knife. Which method was the more unpleasant is a matter of conjecture.

The youth must then run and leap around the Sun Dance pole, pulling and lunging until his tortured flesh gave way and he was released.

Should he fall or faint in his sufferings, friends and relatives would rush to lift him to his feet and urge him on. Sometimes he would be placed on horseback and the horse would gallop away, tearing him loose from his bonds.

Those who could endure this ordeal without murmur or wincing were considered worthy of being accepted as braves into the war parties. Those who could not were scorned as weaklings, unfit for society.

From earliest childhood the boys were trained to grow up to be patient, enduring and fearless. No wonder that some non-Indians thought of them as reserved, aloof and taciturn.

Indian women did most of the work around the camp, preparing food, fuel and clothing. Indian men procured the food and the hides for clothing and they must be prepared, at all times, to stand to the defence of the tribe.

Bravery was the supreme virtue. Next in importance was skill at hunting and then, the gift of oratory.

Long ago the government of Canada outlawed the Sun Dance because of the torture ceremony, but the Indians continued to hold it, substituting symbols of offerings and sacrifices for the initiation torture and the government, wisely and indulgently, did not interfere. Ceremonies that are so rooted in antiquity as to be part of the very fibre of a peoples' soul cannot be legislated out of existence. The Sun Dance had a deep, religious significance, mystical, sacred and profound.

I was on the Sun Dance grounds one morning, the only non-native present. The Indians had been up at the crack of dawn and were going about their business in a world of their own. For miles around I could see their painted tepees gleaming in the early Alberta sunshine. They were pitched in a huge circle and behind them were dozens of ordinary tents with a jumble of horses, dogs, wagons and people.

Beside the tepee of the head chief two tall saplings had been driven into the ground. That was the official entrance through which young men would later enter, singing and rejoicing, bearing cedar boughs from which the Sun Dance lodge must be constructed

In the centre of the circle was the tepee of the Horn Society, the most important of the men's brotherhoods. Near it was the lodge of Mrs. Bear Shin Bone, the woman who was giving the Sun Dance that year. Her abode was a sacred place which no one else could enter. Green poplar boughs had been placed around the outside.

The encircling tepees were painted in symbols and colours peculiar to the tribe, all emphasizing the Indian's instinctive affinity with the forces of nature. Stripes painted around a tepee indicated the Milky Way. Large round spots at the bottom were the stars. Seven stars on the side depicted the Great Dipper.

On some of the tepees were paintings of horses and buffalo. There was a stag and a cow elk tepee, a snake tepee, a bear tepee and an otter tepee, each having some special significance for the occupant.

The interiors of these "lodges" were inviting and comfortable. A really smart one would have a lining of canvas about five feet high, tied to the poles all around the inside. This would have Blackfoot designs on it, painted in bold and gay colours. The designs were wonderfully balanced and symmetrical.

The Indian backrest is a fascinating device. Some of the tepees had many of them, made of small willow sticks fastened together like slats. They were about thirty inches wide at the bottom, tapered to about twelve inches at the top where they were fastened into gaily beaded shields and tied securely to the tent poles. One sat on the lower end of this ingenious seat, stretched out one's legs, and leaned back to talk, smoke or nap as fancy willed. When not in use they were rolled up for travelling.

Though the Sun Dance is actually a tribute to womanhood, it is only a woman of means who is able to give it. She must bear all expenses in connection with it and these are quite considerable. Offerings are tied to the Sun Dance pole and may be calico, fur, ribbons, jewelry or anything else of value.

When the Sun Dance pole is erected the tribes people bring their offerings to the sun, and the woman who made the vow prays that each of them be blessed. She puts an offering on the pole herself and pays for the cost of all the offerings. Another expense that she must cover is the hiring of young men who have to travel a long distance to obtain the pole and cedar boughs to decorate the Sun Dance lodge.

When the ceremony commences the people are called together and a ritual akin to Holy Communion takes place. The Sun Dance woman takes the tongue of a cow, which has been thoroughly dried in the sun, in former years the tongue of a buffalo, and breaks it into small pieces. These, she gives to the people, trying to serve everyone, it is considered a delicacy. Then she addresses them.

In the words of Mrs. Bear Shin Bone, "I am going to do all the praying for you. You are welcome here. I appreciate your coming. I am an honest woman. I am giving up the best prayers of my life for the people. I am making a great blessing for you. I have had only one husband and have always been true to him. I am giving my blessings to everyone: to men and women and children. I am praying to the sun for all of you."

The people crowded around to hear what she was saying. Then she retreated into her lodge for a period of fasting and prayer, which continued for several days.

Great rejoicing attends the raising of the Sun Dance pole. It is a sacred object which no one may touch with bare hands, save the Sun Dance woman. The men must use sticks or leather or small poles to carry it to the place prepared for it in the centre of the lodge. This is an anxious moment as it must be handled with great care.

Should the pole fall, it is considered a sign of ill luck, and it is thought that the Sun Dance woman has "vowed" falsely. Thenceforth she would be disgraced for the rest of her life. So great care is exerted and I have never heard of a pole falling. Naturally, everyone breathes a sigh of relief when the pole is finally in place not the least being the Sun Dance woman!

When the pole is firmly fixed to the ground the cedar boughs
are arranged in a wall around it, partially screened on the inside
like a sanctuary. Into this secluded place the Sun Dance woman
and her husband then go to pray. The husband must previously
have taken a sweat bath for the purification of mind, body and
soul. The sweat bath is accompanied by prayers and ritual incantations of a spiritual nature.

The next day a man, who has also made a vow, will sing and
dance around the Sun Dance pole. He will be completely naked
except for a breechcloth. Like the Sun Dance woman, he would
have made his vow many months before.

He sings his own song and no one else may sing it. It is his
song of praise to the sun, a song of devotion and consecration. As
he sings he never takes his eyes from the pole, keeping his undi-
vided attention fixed upon it.

At this point the Sun Dance woman and her husband feast,
sing and dance for several hours. The people know what is going
on and they are happy about it. When the Sun Dance couple
emerge there is much jubilation as everyone joins in singing and
dancing. Indians from adjacent reserves, both Canadian and
American, join in the ceremonies.

Big Face Chief of the Piegans always prayed long and
devoutly at the Sun Dance. He was a noted mystic and medicine
man who often healed people of their ills. The Indians told me
that he "is kindhearted to everybody," that he has the power of
the Great Spirit. The whole concept of the Sun Dance is based
upon prayer.

What could be more impressive than the Indian manner of
consecration? While I was on the Blood Reserve I was asked to
act as godmother to a beautiful little baby in the Anglican chapel.
Just four months old, she was as sweet and lovely as could be
with long silky black hair. Caroline Gwen Soup was the name her
proud parents had chosen for her.On similar occasions not so
long ago, one of the elders would have taken the infant outside in
his arms and held it up reverently to the sun, praying to the Great
Spirit that blessings might attend her all the days of her life.

When I visited the Sun Dance for the purpose of painting
some of the old people who still remained, I worked within sight

and sound of all that was going on. I loved to hear the familiar "Hi, hi, hi, hi," of an old man calling his people together. I could never forget that call or mistake it for any other.

Sometimes the little boys would go into a huddle. They would be sitting on old boxes, or maybe a wagon tongue, and some of them had small sticks which they tapped on a board to keep time as they, too, called out "Hi, hi, hi, hi." It was amusing to see them wearing ten-gallon hats around their little ears and practicing songs their elders sang with exactly the same intonation.

While at the Sun Dance I was welcomed to the tepee of Heavy Head as my temporary abode, and his daughter greatly assisted me when I needed an interpreter.

The fire was, of course, in the centre of the tepee. I was very careful to walk around the fire according to custom. It would have been considered unforgivably bad manners if one were to step over even the cold ashes.

About the tepee were many rugs, quilts and pillows. After I had painted steadily for two hours I was glad to eat my hastily-prepared lunch and stretch out, as the others were doing, for a quiet siesta in the comfortable surroundings.

My main objective was to paint Heavy Head, who was the last Indian living to have gone through the Sun Dance torture before the practice was forbidden by the government. A hale old man of eighty-nine, he could look back over a long vista of years when history was being made in the West. He and two other youths, Red Large Crow and Spotted Buffalo, went through the ordeal.

Heavy Head said that the shield suspended from his shoulders had been made of buffalo hide and was exceedingly heavy. He still bore the scars of the torture on his chest and shoulders.

People who have not participated in the intimate life of the Indians have no idea what a refreshing experience it is to relax with nothing but the white canvas of the tepee between you and the weather. With good companions around you and that indefinable detachment in the air which is the Indian's very special heritage.

Though the day was hot outside, it was very comfortable in Heavy Head's tepee. There was plenty of light but no glare. The scurrilous wind, that irrepressible prankster of the prairies, rattled and tugged at the tent poles but the canvas gave us all the protection we needed. The wind can blow tepees down, however, but I suppose that it may have been different in earlier times when the tepees were covered by buffalo hides. It was difficult, even for Alberta winds, to push them over.

The Indian encampment was very remote here. For miles and miles around, this land was their own, with no one else to hinder, no one to criticize and no one to scorn. How they must have loved this spacious land with its tremendous skies and its interminable distances. How they must love it still—and love it the more as they see the alien avalanche gaining momentum all around them!

Soon, alas, they will become immersed in that avalanche, but always, through the years, they will carry with them the memories of the wide, free life when their ancestors walked in the footsteps of nature and listened to its heart beat.

Here in the tepee I liked to harken to their quiet voices speaking in the musical accents of their race. The conversation, soft and restrained, was punctuated at intervals by the indescribable sound of the old men giving approval. Their "Um, m, m, m, m," was long and throaty. It came from deep down in their diaphragms; from the very centres of their being. It would be a great pity if future generations loose this articulate approbation

Life was very simple in the tepee. Happiness was something that you could hold in your hands. Meals were of no particular concern. Food was always available and you ate when you felt like it. In short, there was a sense of complete freedom.

I have painted over two hundred Indians during the years and I have done the work in many unusual places and under many strange circumstances, but the only work that I ever did, literally "on the run," was my sketch of Mrs. Long Time Squirrel.

I knew a lot of strange stories about the old woman and they were all good ones, which is why I sought her out at the Sun Dance.

She was sitting on the ground trying to fasten the seams of several new stove pipes together. Over and over again she tried but the sections would fly apart under her dark little hands. Her frustration was evident but she uttered not a sound. There are no words of profanity in the Indian language.

Hoping to cultivate her good graces, I took hold of two of the stove pipes and attempted to join them together. I could see how they were intended to fit and, sure enough, I got the ends into the opposite grooves and snapped them together whilst Mrs. Long Time Squirrel was still struggling unsuccessfully with the other pieces. To prove my prowess further, I affixed the others also, but when we tried to fit them both to the stove in her little tent we found that they were all too small.

This made the old woman so mad that she would not let me paint her. She was far too busy, so she said. From long experience I knew better than to argue, so went off to do other work but returned later to see what the prospects were. She was still too busy.

The day wore on and it was nearly time to leave when I went to look for Mrs. Long Time Squirrel one last time. I felt that I simply must get her portrait. It was now or never.

A number of women were driving tentpegs into the ground by this time and there was great activity everywhere. They were getting ready to erect the Holy Woman's lodge. Mrs. Long Time Squirrel was participating and she was not going to be bothered by any white artist—however ardent.

Humped over nearly double, the wrinkled old woman scurried back and forth, dragging the long travois poles behind her.

Determined not to be beaten at this stage, I ran back and forth also, beside her and in front of her, sketching like fury, exerting every ounce of energy and skill of which I was capable whilst I clung to my equipment.

By some miracle, for which I shall always be grateful, I was able to get a recognizable likeness of the agile old lady which I shall always treasure. My most "mobile" painting!

Shot-on-Both-Sides, head chief of the Bloods, said that it would only be a few years—four or five at most—until the famous Sun Dance was no more.

Each year the head chief makes the decision when the Sun Dance will be held. Each year he is the first to pitch his tepee on the grounds.

In the old days people waited eagerly for this signal and other tepees went up like magic. Never, in all the years that they can remember, have they failed to have the Sun Dance.

Now the chief waits sadly, for days at a time, while his tribe comes straggling to the site on foot, on horseback, on wagons and in automobiles. The older people, to whom it is of supreme importance, are heavy at heart as they brood of the past and peer with apprehensive eyes into the future.

The younger generations know little of the true meaning of the Sun Dance—and care less. They are willing and eager for progress. They seek to loosen their traditional bonds in adapting to modern society. Remorselessly the years go by and relentlessly time is erasing the imprints of centuries foregone.

Here and there in the vicinity of the Belly Buttes are remnants of Sun Dance lodges. Like the Indians of the coastal tribes, who prefer to leave their old totems and long houses to the ravishes of nature rather than to demolish them, the Blackfoot never tear down the Sun Dance lodges. Tattered offerings flutter from the center poles for many months after the ceremonies are over until wind and weather work their will.

Sometimes the remains of three or four Sun Dance lodges may be seen near the Buttes. But soon, too soon, the lonely winds will come searching and calling and there will be no returning echoes from the great cliffs, no prayers ascending to the impartial sun. No song. No dance.

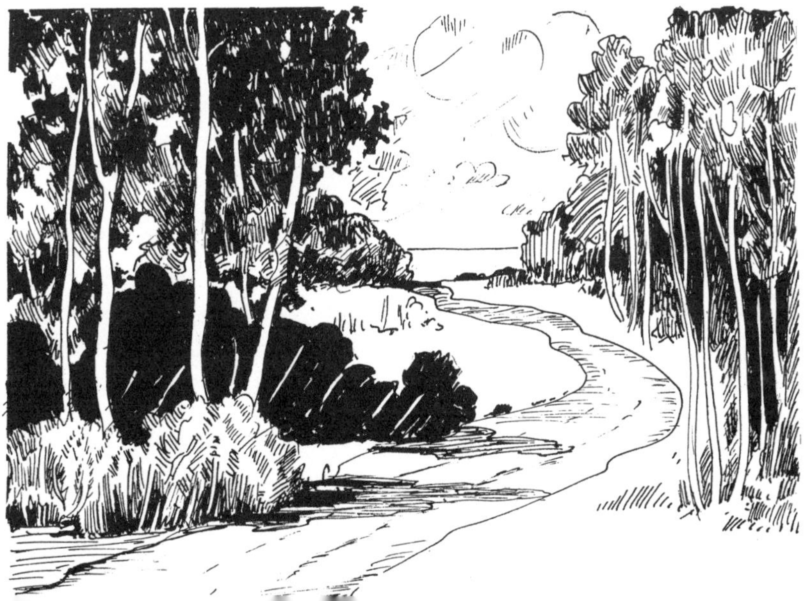

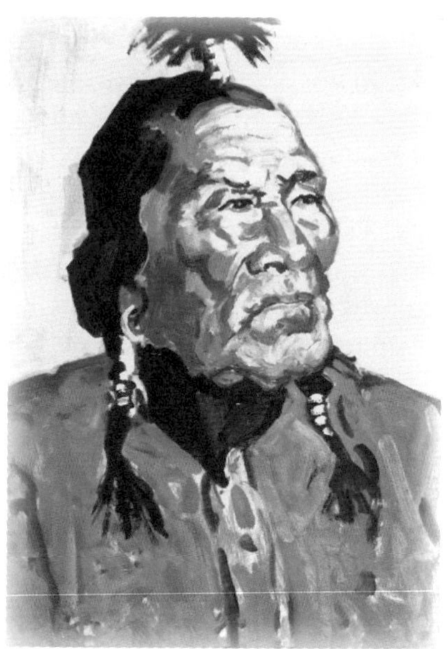

Big Face Chief, Piegan Medicine Man

Medicine Men and Women

In past generations medicine men were easily the most powerful people in all Indian tribes. They were surrounded by an aura of mystery and awe as beings who could obtain special favour from the spirit world. They professed to have supernatural powers denied to ordinary men and women. It was generally believed that when a person became ill, an evil spirit had taken possession of him, or her. Only when this was driven out by magic and incantations would the sufferer be restored to health.

Very few people attained the power to dispel evil spirits. Only those chosen in their youth and trained by the medicine men themselves achieved such status. This limited their numbers and hence, competition.

Some medicine men were greatly feared by wrong-doers. It was thought that they could invoke spells which could cause death. Death did, indeed, sometimes occur through sheer terror, increasing even more the power of the medicine men over the credulous tribesmen.

▶ colour plate page 134

A chief would consult the medicine man to inquire if the signs were favourable for war or hunting. No great venture was undertaken without his advice. They seldom made predictions which were unlikely to materialize and, if perchance they should fail, there was always some adroit excuse to be found.

In most cases medicine men and medicine women hotly resented white doctors and nurses coming onto the reserves. They did not want anyone interfering with what they considered to be their legitimate business. Old traditions die hard among all people, so even after the Indian hospitals were established many old people preferred the ministrations of the medicine man.

In actuality, their methods had some basis in fact because most of the medicine men had a vast knowledge of the medicinal value of native roots and herbs in addition to having a deep understanding of human psychology which they applied with much skill and resourcefulness.

Some years ago on the Blackfoot Reserve an old medicine man called He Will Be Back was very influential in the tribe. He gathered roots, herbs and berries of various kinds and used them to good purpose. Many medicines used today were first discovered by Indian "doctors."

When a fine new modern hospital was built on the Blackfoot Reserve He Will Be Back could see his powers waning and that was not at all to his liking. It so happened that one of his grandchildren became very ill with pneumonia and he was called to heal the child. With mysterious charms and incantations the old man worked his magic but the child grew steadily worse. Younger members of the family, in great alarm, sent to the hospital for help.

The matron, who had just taken up her position, was totally unfamiliar with Indian customs and beliefs. Full of rectitude and good intentions, she went immediately to the little house where the child lay, prepared to take charge of the case. She had not reckoned with He Will Be Back. He was not going to allow this presumptuous white person to take over his prerogative and forcefully let the matron know how he felt. Though she could not understand a word of the volley of abuse which he heaped upon her, his meaning was clear, particularly when he grabbed a butcher knife and made a lunge at her. She did not stop to argue, and made the return trip to the hospital in record time with He Will Be Back in hot pursuit. The sick child subsequently recovered.

There were medicine women as well as medicine men, and they held equal power and influence. Old Mrs. White Man Runs Around was one of them. She had a mind of her own and entertained a low opinion of well-meaning white people. She had several grandchildren at the residential school at Cardston in whom she took a deep pride and interest. One of them was a very obstreperous youngster who continually misbehaved. Finally, when every other means of discipline had failed his teacher gave him a strapping.

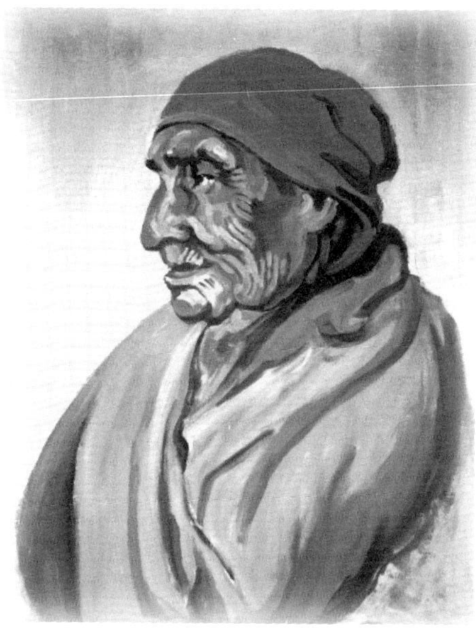

Mrs. White Man Runs Around ▶ *page 134*

When Mrs. White Man Runs Around heard of this she didn't ask any questions or waste any time. She just picked up a big stick from the woodpile and made straight for the residential school. She stormed into the quiet well-ordered lobby of the school and prepared to battle all comers.

It so happened that the teacher who had administered the strapping was busy in a classroom but the school nurse, who had nothing to do with the matter, happened innocently along the corridor to the lobby. Mrs. White Man Runs Around did not stop to quibble who was the guilty party—any white person would do. Without warning she charged at the nurse and flailed her unmercifully until the nurse made good her escape in complete ignorance of why she had been attacked.

The feisty medicine woman continued to heartily despise all hospitals, doctors and nurses, yet when she grew infirm and none of her family wished to care for her, she packed her meagre belongings, went to the hospital at Cardston and calmly took residence without so much as a "by your leave."

She had a comfortable bed and good food and, doubtlessly felt it was all due to her from the people who had usurped her vocation.

The sisters at the hospital accepted her presence with kindly toleration. She performed light duties around the place, but occasionally took offense at some fancied insult. Then she would go into a tantrum again and gather her belongings in her big red kerchief, tie it to a pole, sling it over her shoulder and storm out the door. She was off to the Indian agency to lodge a complaint that would put them all in their place.

The agency was a long distance from the hospital and, in the summer, it was very warm. The old woman would trudge along in the hot sun, mile after mile, with the little bundle on her back becoming evermore wearisome. When she finally reached the agency she usually found the staff very busy with their official duties and would sink down on the floor to rest. She did not trouble anybody and nobody troubled her. After an hour or so she would cool off both mentally and physically. Her mind would go back to the cool corridors of the hospital and the appetizing odours that would be coming from the kitchen about then. She would begin to feel the need of food of which there was no evidence of that commodity at the agency.

Pretty soon she would pick up her little bundle and start off down the road again. In due course she would arrive back at the hospital and walk in as though she had just been out to inspect the garden. No one would appear to notice her and no one would make any comment about her absence. Everything went on as before until she became annoyed again and the little comedy would be repeated.

Many stories are told of medicine men and medicine women and the amazing feats that they performed. One of the chiefs of the Blood Reserve had a stroke and became so paralysed that no one could understand a word that he tried to say. He was taken to the Indian hospital and, after all treatments had failed, the doctor said that nothing more could be done for him. On hearing this, the chief wanted to go home. He did so and sent for the medicine man who performed an old-fashioned job of bloodletting. He opened the flesh under the chief's chin to relieve the swollen tongue and also at the back of the head and at the elbows. The chief felt better immediately and, in a short time, was so well that he built himself a new barn!

A doctor north of Edmonton vouches for the truth of the following story. A white man, who had been working in the mines, cut his thumb very badly and started off on horseback to the city to have it treated. He could not stop the wound bleeding; he was becoming very weak and the sun was setting. His horse was also weakening from its exertions so he made for an Indian camp, which the miner could see in the distance, with the objective of seeking sanctuary until the next day.

One of the Indians looked at the blood-soaked thumb and said he would soon "fix him." He road off bareback on his pony and returned with a very dirty-looking mushroom which he clapped over the open wound and tied it up.

Next morning the man continued on his way and about three in the afternoon, arrived at the doctor's office The doctor was reluctant to touch the thumb, as by this time it was a gory-looking mess with blood, dirt and mushroom clotted over it. However, he got water, antiseptics and other essentials together, cleaned the dirt off the thumb and, to his utter amazement found the cut perfectly healed.

A woman in Moose Jaw had a rash on her arms which the doctors could not cure. An old Indian woman saw the rash and said she would "fix" it. She went off to the river and returned with an herb. This she gave to the woman and told her to boil it and use the liquid to bathe the affected parts. She did this and the rash disappeared completely within a few hours.

According to Alice Wolf Child, when her husband was sick, five or six medicine men tried to help him. One used a rattlesnake skin and when he started to pray the skin came to life and wriggled away. One used a dead crow, and when he began to pray the crow came to life, flapped its wings and "cawed" loudly. Another used a weasel skin for his power. He put a stick on the chief's body where the pain was and laid the weasel skin upon it. Then he prayed and made wishes over the skin four times. The weasel came to life and ran along the stick. Another man used a winter weasel skin, a white one. He prayed four times also and the white weasel came alive and jumped onto the place where the pain was. "They have the power to do this. They never sing or dance. They just pray," said Alice. Her husband had cancer of the liver and, unfortunately, died despite the ministrations. She then unbraided her long, black hair and let it hang loose for a long time as a sign of mourning.

Not all medicine men were magic makers. Some of them were men of great wisdom, prophets and seers, who spent much time in meditation and seldom revealed their thoughts to any but the chosen ones who would succeed them.

Big Face Chief was such a medicine man. One who had unusual powers of healing. He did much praying at the Sun Dance and understood the "laying on of hands," and was always kind to everybody. Alice recalled that he had healed many sick people with the application of heat.

He would pick up a hot stone with his bare hands and put it on the affected part. The stone did not burn him or his patient and the sick person got well. One look at the strong, calm face of that remarkable man, whom it had been my privilege to paint, was sufficient to assure anyone that he was no charlatan, but one possessed of great inner power.

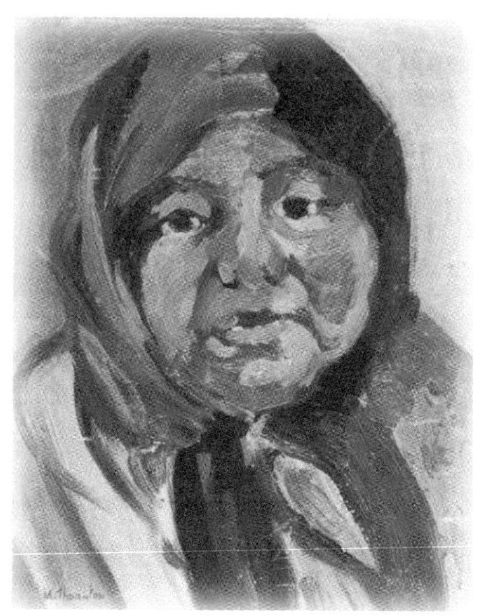

Just by the Way

She was sitting on the cold floor of the railway station at Calgary, just inside the door, when I first saw her. The hurried crowd of travellers rushed past the bowed, shawled Buddha-like figure. She never raised her head or spoke a word. Her world of vision was a kaleidoscope of feet in rapid motion. She was a silent oasis in the swirl of activity around her.

The Indian woman was old, how old, I dared not guess. Many suns of many seasons had gouged deep seams into her drawn cheeks. Her features, however, were strong and her deep-set eyes glowed like live coals beneath her broad brow. An orange-coloured scarf was tied securely under her resolute chin and one bony little hand clasped a bright plaid shawl over her breast. Her feet, clad in well-worn moccasins, stuck straight out in front of her. Why no one tripped over them remained a mystery.

Younger members of her race dressed like white people and tried to behave like them too, but this was not for her. She was changeless in her unmoving solitude. Under this stoic exterior her mind, no doubt, weighed and measured the scene around her, and finding it wanting in many ways that had been important to her and her people.

Long past was the freedom, the wild exhilaration, the hard bright paths she had trodden in her youth. Suffering and privation she had known and sorrow, too. She had conquered them all. Grinding toil and bitter weather had not broken her spirit. Much had changed in her life and made her heart sick with fear. She was "in it" but not "of it" present in body, but absent in spirit. All this was written in her inscrutable features.

She was a stranger in her own land. Nothing belonged to her now. She belonged to no one. She was the forsaken remnant of a day that was past, the pathetic symbol of departed glory, a mere whisper of the vanished past. I wanted to speak to her, but hesitated to do so. Perhaps she would not understand English. I might embarrass her. Maybe she was waiting for someone of her own kin. I would never know.

I left the station to look around the town and when I returned an hour later to catch my train, she was still there, as quiet and immobile as the grey pillars around her. Once more I longed to speak to the lady. Something drew me to her, yet something held me back. I studied the calm, dark face. It was as though time stood still in her world as though it could never harm her more. She had no part in the ways of today. She belonged to a generation that had gone, though there were still signs of its passing. She was oblivious alike to joy and sorrow.

She sat on the hard, comfortless marble floor just as she had sat before the fire in her tepee in years long gone. The toil-worn hands that had scraped and cured countless deerskins and carved the carcasses of many buffalo were idle now. Surely her mind moved in calm retrospect back over the years,

All the way to Lethbridge I thought of the old Indian woman and reproached myself for not sitting down beside her and clasping her rough little hands in mine. Though she may not have understood a word of what I wanted to say, she would have sensed the language of sympathy and kindness.

Why I did not speak to her I shall never know.

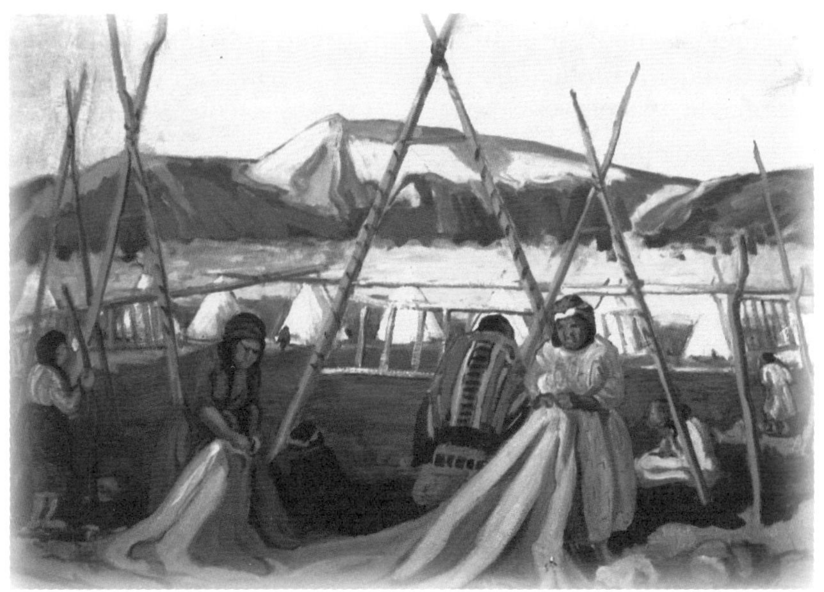

Legends and Interludes

The Blackfoot had various names for the Great Spirit. They said the Ancient Being had other names such as "Napir" and "Old Man." He made Indians after His own likeness. Nor was the place of creation left in doubt. Some of the legends are as follows.

It was in the West, where the shadows of the Mis-tak-ist touch the tepees. There was the beginning. Old Man talk to everybody, to all trees, to stones, to all nature, to His own body. He never would be angry. When he talks everybody listen.

Napir made the first man and woman out of clay. He breathed upon them and they became alive. Then He picked up a buffalo chip and threw it into the river, saying, "If this floats people will rise again four days after they die and return to life."

Now the woman doubted Napir in her heart, though she dared not say so openly.

Thinking she had greater wisdom than He, she picked up a stone and threw it into the river saying, if this sinks so will all people remain dead for all time when they die. Otherwise there would be no mourning and people would not care for each other.

Napir did not scold the woman but he caused her to bear a child which took sick and died. The woman wanted Napir to make the commandments all over again, but Old Man said, "No, it's finished, commandments made once, not twice."

The mother cried for her child and wanted to take back her words, but Napir said, "No, you have decided for yourself. As the stone sinks, so will the child not rise again."

Thus did Napir teach the people to be careful about the words they speak.

It appears that mortals were slow to learn. On another occasion Napir said to the woman, "One stick of wood shall burn continually from the time that it is lit until the camp is moved."

But the woman said, "No, we are strong and willing to bring more wood, so let it burn away."

Napir said, "Have it your own way." So the women have had to cut and carry wood to this day. That is the significance of fire. If you have a fire, you have a home.

Another legend states, "When a person prays he can ask the sun to pray for us. A tree, an animal or a person all believe in the morning star. If an Indian worries about something he asks the sun to help him out of his trouble."

Indians have their own medicine. There is no poison in it. Indians each know their own medicine and will not steal another man's roots or herbs because that would bring bad luck. They pay the medicine man and always make a gift if he helps them.

Another story related by Duck Chief goes, "I saw a medicine man make tea at the Tea Dance. There was a big pot of water boiling over the coals but there was no tea. Indian man takes a handful of dirt and throws it into the boiling water and it turned into tea. I saw it with my own eyes. That's the power of the medicine man. I saw it when I was young. I stirred it and tasted it. It was tea! All Indians know this is true. White people do not believe, but Duck Chief know, all Indians know."

❖

Here is another story which I was assured was true.

A few hundred years ago Old Man gets up very early and talks. He says the white people will come, we will get sickness. We will eat things we should not eat. Eat candy and bad stuff, have stomach trouble, loose teeth, loose hair.

❖

The following story was told me by a Blood Indian.

Once there was an old man and old lady. They had a son-in-law who had married all four of their daughters. At first, old man owns all, but son-in-law is greedy and takes everything. Leaves nothing for old people and was very unkind to them.

The youngest daughter is very sorry for her parents. She does not like to see them go hungry, so she steals a little meat and bones to feed them.

They heard that there was a place where buffalo used to come out of ground. The old man looks for the place and finds some congealed buffalo blood. He put it in a skin bag and took it home—no meat, just blood. He told old lady, "Now we got something to eat. Put kettle on fire."

Old lady thinks son-in-law gave them the blood, puts on the fire and puts blood in kettle. In a little while they hear a baby cry and suddenly the blood was transformed into a baby!

Amazed, they took the baby out of the kettle. Old man tells old lady to look after it "good." It is a boy baby. That night the baby talk, tell old lady, "Put me by tepee pole near door." She did this and then the baby went to each pole of the tepee growing as he went, and at the last pole he had become a big man.

He tell old man, "You fix your arrows, we go fishing in morning before son-in-law gets up." So they went fishing in the morning before the others awoke. They kill buffalo and the boy-

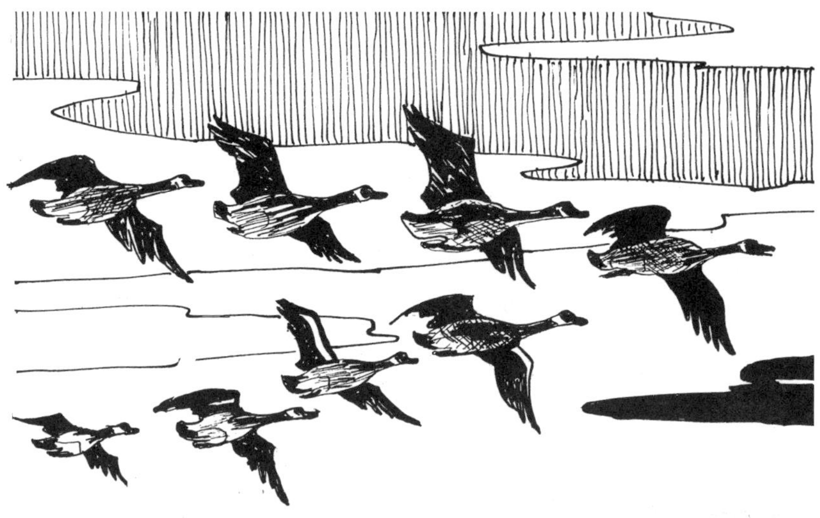

man tell old man, "You take the meat home." The boy-man then hide himself.

Son-in-law come home and said, "You should not kill buffalo before I get up. Old man say, "I kill anyway."

Son-in-law very angry and tried to kill the old man with arrows. Suddenly the boy-man came in and said, "All the time you have been very cruel to old people, so now I kill you."

After that he told old lady, "You move into your son-in-law's house. You own everything now."

Then the boy-man asked which daughter had been good to them. They said, "The youngest one." So he kill other three daughters.

He kill all the people who were cruel and unkind. Only the good people, the good animals, the good birds and other good creatures were left.

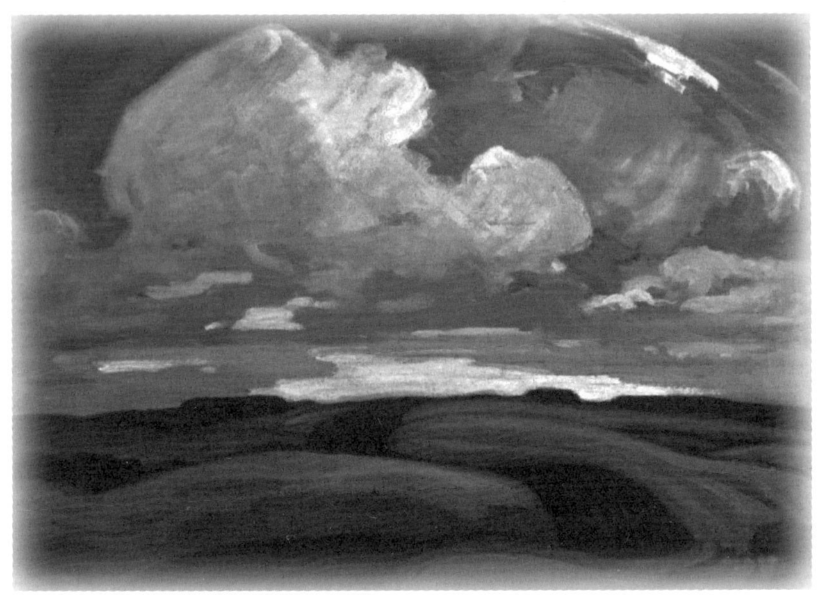

Raising the Wind

When moving camp toward a herd of buffalo the Indians would not want the wind to move from their position to the direction of the herd. In order to "make" the wind blow in the desired direction, the women and children would take buffalo chips and roll them back on their approach trail, that is, in the opposite direction to the direction they were heading, and it had the desired effect. The buffalo would not get their scent. The wind always came the way the Indians wanted it to come.

On moonlit nights, if there were no clouds, and the people wanted rain, the men produced their medicine bags, take water from them and squirt it through their teeth, and the rain would come.

If they wanted clear weather, the medicine man and others, would sing and beat their drums, and call upon the elements to improve and that would cause fine weather.

▶ *colour plate page 103*   198

The following explanation of how the Chinook winds began was told by an old Blood Indian. Chinook means melting winds.

Napir made the buffalo, the wild game, everything that exists. Even stones and trees and flowers. All are His creation. He made the seasons, giving seven moons to each.

It was during the seventh moon of the first winter that a woman went to see Him to complain about the cold moons. "It is very cold," she said, "and the buffalo are hard to get. We are cold and hungry."

"You are right," said Napir. "The weather should be changed. I will go to the mountains and talk to the spirits. I shall seek the melting winds."

While Napir was away the Indians on the prairies had a hard time. Snow was deepening and hunting was not easy. At last He came back to them and with Him was the melting wind. The nearer He came the warmer the wind became. Snow melted and water ran where only ice had been before.

The Ancient Being had kept his promise on the seventh moon even though He was not quite all-powerful and had to consult the spirits. After that the melting winds always came on the seventh moon!

When a chief dies, a circle of stones is placed around his lodge and from the circle are placed extending arms of stones to the four points of the compass. The chief's comrades paint his exploits on the lodge, and a horse is shot to take the dead man to the Sacred Hills.

In early days the Indians believed that a certain root found in the mountains, if eaten, would cause their hair to turn grey. In later years they attributed the cause of this phenomena to eating the white man's flour.

The famous Chief Red Crow said that his people never smoked when going on the war path because they thought that smoking caused shortness of breath and would make them unfit for battle. For the same reason, they never drank tea or coffee at such a time.

A child was named at birth, then again when he went on the war path. He might earn any number of names during his lifetime according to his conduct. When Chief Red Crow first took to the war path he was called Lately Gone. When he distinguished himself in battle he earned the name of Red Crow. Many years after this he returned home from a visit to Eastern Canada following the signing of the treaty and acquired the name of Sitting White Buffalo. Since the white buffalo was a very rare animal and the object of much veneration, it was a very high honour, indeed, when the name was conferred on the chief.

I was told that Bob Tail Chief of the Blood Reserve was jailed long ago for horse stealing. He wanted to get out so he chewed his soap and pretended he was frothing at the mouth. The attendants thought he had really gone mad, so they let him go. Surely this was a most ingenious solution to his problem!

The oral traditions of the Indian seem to have provided them with an unending fountain of marvellous stories, each enriched so colourfully that I could have lived with these noble people for many lifetimes. As I hope these preceding stories show, I could not have succeeded in my self-imposed task of painting and recording their lives but for the goodwill of so many friends and well wishers who gave voluntarily of their time and influences to help me. And finally, let me say that no matter what the hazards were, or how high the hurdles I loved every moment of my privileged experiences and if it were possible, I should like to do it all over again.

What's in a Name?

The traditional names of the Plains Indians are fascinating, colourful and full of meaning. Listed below are names of other Indians that I have painted, each one as exciting as the name and each experience something to be treasured in my memory.

Assiniboine

Chief Ochankughe
Running Wolf

Blackfoot

Chief Turn Up Nose
Heavy Shield
Many Bears
Low Horn *and*
Mrs. Low Horn
Mrs. Boy Chief
Mrs. Little Walker
Mrs. Good Rider
Prairie Chicken Man
Minnie Little Light

Blood

Yellow Squirrel
Bruised Head *and*
Mrs. Bruised Head
Ruth Standing Alone
Charlie Pantherbone
Michael Pantherbone
Mrs. Night Gun
Dog Child

Weasel Tail
Mrs. Crazy Crow
Tom Prairie Chicken
Rough Hair
Iron
Chief Cross Child
Mrs. Calf Robe
Black White Man
Alice Wolf Child

Cree

Pemotat
Money Bird
Catasso
Adelard Star
Kanouse
David Gordon
Harriet Yellow Mud Blanket
Com-e-you-com-qua

Stoney

George Crawler
Enos Hunter
Eagle Hunter

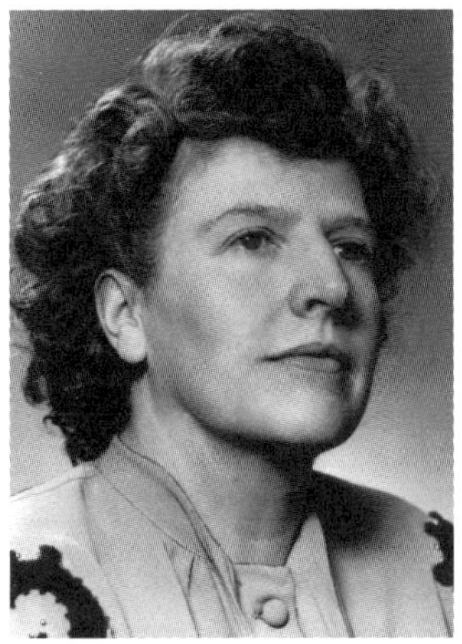

Mildred Valley Thornton

Index to Colour Plates

- *Page 105*
  Mrs. Rock Thunder
  Cree, c. 1940
  Oil on canvas, 20 x 16 in.
  Collection: J. M. Thornton

- *Page 106*
  No Name
  Cree, 1942
  Oil on board, 16 x 12 in.
  Collection: private collection

- *Page 107*
  Mistatatim "Horsechild", Cree
  Oil on canvasboard, 24 x 18 in.
  Collection: Westbridge Fine Art Ltd.

- *Page 107 #2 image*
  Mistatatim "Horsechild"
  Cree, 1948
  Oil on canvasboard, 24 x 20 in.
  Collection: Westbridge Fine Art Ltd.

- *Page 108*
  Cree Mother and Child
  1932
  Oil on board, 20 x 16 in.
  Collection: private collection

- *Page 109*
  Stanislaus Almighty Voice
  Cree, 1942
  Oil on canvasboard, 24 x 18 in.
  Collection: Westbridge Fine Art Ltd.

- *Page 110*
  Saskatchewan Landscape
  c. 1930 (sketch)
  Oil on panel, 9.75 x 13.75 in.
  Collection: Westbridge Fine Art Ltd.

- *Page 110*
  Saskatchewan Landscape, c.1930
  Oil on canvas, 24 x 30 in.
  Collection: private collection

- *Page 111*
  Mrs. Goodrider
  Blackfoot, c. 1941
  Oil on canvasboard, 20 x 16 in.
  Collection: private collection

- *Page 111*
  Eagle Hunter, Stoney, 1941
  Oil on canvasboard, 16.5 x 14 in.
  Collection: Westbridge Fine Art Ltd.

- *Page 111*
  Blue Wings, Piegan, 1942
  Oil on canvasboard, 20 x 16 in.
  Collection: Westbridge Fine Art Ltd.

- *Page 111*
  Prairie Chicken Man
  Blackfoot, 1942
  Oil on canvasboard, 24 x 18 in.
  Collection: private collection

- *Page 112*
  Old Blind Helen
  Cree, 1942
  Oil on canvasboard, 23 x 18 in.
  Collection: Westbridge Fine Art Ltd.

- *Page 112 #2 image*
  Old Blind Helen
  Cree, 1942
  Oil on canvasboard, 24 x 18 in.
  Collection: Westbridge Fine Art Ltd.

- *Page 113*
  Nanepowiskh
  Cree, 1932
  Oil on board, 20 x 16 in.
  Collection: private collection

- *Page 114*
  Pat Cappo's Wife
  Saulteaux, 1929
  Oil on board, 20 x 16 in.
  Collection: W. M. Thornton

- *Page 115*
  Pat Cappo
  Saulteaux, 1929
  Oil on canvas, 24 x 18 in.
  Collection: J. M. Thornton

- *Page 116*
  Chief Ben Pasqua's Fifth Wife
  Saulteaux, 1930
  Oil on board, 20 x 16 in.
  Collection: W. M. Thornton

- *Page 117*
  Chief Ben Pasqua
  Saulteaux, 1930
  Oil on board, 20 x 16 in.
  Collection: W. M. Thornton

- *Page 118*
  Lowland Landscape
  Qu'Appelle Valley, c. 1930
  Oil on panel, 10.5 x 13.5 in.
  Collection: Westbridge Fine Art Ltd.

- *Page 118*
  Qu'Appelle Valley, c.1930
  Oil on board, 16 x 20 in.
  Collection: private collection

- *Page 119*
  Achim, Cree, 1930
  Oil on panel, 20 x 16 in.
  Collection: Westbridge Fine Art Ltd.

- *Page 119*
  Mrs. Little Walker
  Blackfoot, 1941
  Oil on canvasboard, 20 x 16 in.
  Collection: Westbridge Fine Art Ltd.

- *Page 119*
  Mrs. Bruised Head/Yellow Squirrel
  Blood, 1949
  Oil on canvasboard, 24 x 20 in.
  Collection: private collection

- *Page 119*
  Cree Chief
  Saskatchewan, c. 1940
  Oil on canvasboard, 30 x 22 in.
  Collection: Westbridge Fine Art Ltd.

- *Page 120*
  Chief David Bear's Paw, Stoney
  Oil on canvas, 24 x 20 in.
  Collection: J. M. Thornton

- *Page 121*
  Chief Walking Buffalo
  Stoney, 1941
  Oil on board, 30 x 22 in.
  Collection: private collection

- *Page 122*
  Joshua Hunter "Spotted Eagle"
  Stoney, 1942
  Oil on canvas, 24 x 20 in.
  Collection: Westbridge Fine Art Ltd.

- *Page 123*
  William Hunter "Yellow Bear"
  Stoney, 1942
  Oil on canvas, 24 x 20 in.
  Collection: private collection

- *Page 124*
  Chief Joe Big Plume
  Sarcee, 1941
  Oil on canvasboard, 23 x 18 in.
  Collection: Westbridge Fine Art Ltd.

- *Page 125*
  Pretty Young Man, Sarcee, 1941
  Oil on canvasboard, 20 x 16 in.
  Collection: Westbridge Fine Art Ltd.

- *Page 126*
  Prairie Grain Elevators
  c.1931 (sketch)
  Oil on panel, 9.5 x 13.5 in.
  Collection: Westbridge Fine Art Ltd.

- *Page 126*
Prairie Grain Elevators, c. 1931
Oil on canvas, 32 x 39 in.
Collection: private collection

- *Page 127*
Turning Rope
Sarcee, c.1941
Oil on canvas, 14 x 12 in.
Collection: Westbridge Fine Art Ltd.

- *Page 127*
Heavy Head, Blood, c.1949
Oil on board, 22.5 x 16 in.
Collection: Westbridge Fine Art Ltd.

- *Page 127*
Tom Prairie Chicken
Blood, 1943
Oil on board, 22 x 16 in.
Collection: Westbridge Fine Art Ltd.

- *Page 127*
Crooked Guts/Bullet Head
Piegan, 1949
Oil on canvasboard, 24 x 18 in.
Collection: Westbridge Fine Art Ltd.

- *Page 128*
George Big Belly
Sarcee, 1942
Oil on canvasboard, 24 x 18 in.
Collection: Westbridge Fine Art Ltd.

- *Page 129*
Chief Julius Buffalo
Sioux, c.1930
Oil on board, 14 x 12.75 in.
Collection: private collection

- *Page 130*
Duck Chief and His Medals
Blackfoot, 1941
Oil on canvas, 24 x 20 in.
Collection: Westbridge Fine Art Ltd.

- *Page 131*
Chief Fish-Wolf-Ofe, Blackfoot
Oil on canvas, 30 x 20 in.
Collection: private collection

- *Page 132*
Crowfoot's Daughter
Blackfoot, 1942
Oil on board, 24 x 18 in.
Collection: private collection

- *Page 133*
Margaret Crowfoot
Blackfoot, 1941
Oil on board, 24 x 18 in.
Collection: private collection

- *Page 134*
Big Face Chief
Piegan, 1949
Oil on board, 22 x 16 in.
Collection: private collection

- *Page 134*
Mrs. White Man Runs Around
Blood, 1943
Oil on board, 24 x 20 in.
Collection: Westbridge Fine Art Ltd.

- *Page 134*
Dog Child
Blood, 1943
Oil on cardboard, 22 x 16 in.
Collection: Westbridge Fine Art Ltd.

- *Page 134*
Piegan, Cree, c.1930
Oil on artboard, 14 x 10.75 in.
Collection: private collection

- *Page 135*
Indian Women Erecting Tepees
c.1940
Oil on canvas, 36 x 48 in.
Collection: private collection

The line drawings featured throughout the text are by Mildred Valley Thornton. Many are preliminary sketches for later art canvases and panels.

The Estate Collection of paintings and watercolours by Mildred Valley Thornton, FRSA, CPA (1890-1967) is represented by Westbridge Fine Art Ltd., 1737 Fir Street, Vancouver, British Columbia V6J 5J9.

Additional paintings by Mildred Valley Thornton are available from Westbridge Fine Art Ltd. These include portraits of both the Plains and West Coast First Nations peoples, painted in the 1940s and 1950s, together with a selection of paintings dealing with native culture, mythology and lifestyle, as well as many fine Canadian landscapes in both oil and watercolour. Many of these pieces can be viewed online at www.artstats.com.